HOT CARS

A Collector's Ultimate Source for Hot Wheels, Matchbox and Johnny Lightning

Presented by Beckett Publications

Hot Cars: A Collector's Ultimate Source for Hot Wheels, Matchbox and Johnny Lightning
Copyright©1999 by Dr. James Beckett
All rights reserved under International and Pan-American Copyright Conventions.

Published by: Beckett Publications
15850 Dallas Parkway
Dallas, TX 75248

ISBN: 1-887432-69-8

First Edition: May 1999
Beckett Corporate Sales and Information (972) 991-6657

YOUR VALUE GUIDE

When it comes to reporting on values for secondary market collectibles, Beckett Publications is recognized and respected worldwide as the most trusted authority. Founded in 1984 by Dr. James Beckett, the company has sold millions of price guide books and magazines to collectors of sports cards, sports memorabilia, toys and other licensed collectible products.

Presently, Beckett Publications publishes eight popular monthly magazines on collectibles. They are *Beckett Baseball Card Monthly, Beckett Basketball Card Monthly, Beckett Football Card Monthly, Beckett Hockey Collector, Beckett Sports Collectibles and Autographs, Beckett Racing & Motorsports Marketplace, Beckett Hot Toys* and *Beckett Sci-Fi Collector.*

This reference book is intended to provide an objective and unbiased representation of values for the subject collectibles on the secondary market. The independent pricing contained in this guide reflects current retail rates determined just prior to printing. They do not reflect for-sale prices by the author, distributors or any retailers of collectibles or memorabilia who've contributed their skills and knowledge to the production of this guide. All values are in U.S. dollars and are for informational purposes only.

The values published in this guide were compiled in a joint effort by a staff of full-time expert Beckett Publications analysts and independent contributors knowledgeable in this field of collecting. The information was gathered from actual buy/sell transactions at collectibles conventions, hobby shops and on-line sites, and, to a lesser extent, from buy/sell advertisements in hobby publications, for-sale prices from collectibles dealers' catalogs and price lists, as well as discussions with leading hobbyists in the U.S. and Canada.

Great care and diligence were taken in determining the prices reported within this book. Our desire to supply independent pricing that is more accurate and reliable than that which may be supplied by any other source is paramount to our efforts. It is also a prime reason why the Beckett name is synonymous with collecting and memorabilia. Collectors have come to know Beckett as "the hobby's most reliable and relied upon source.™"

Contents

HOT WHEELS '69 BEACH BOMB

MATCHBOX '69 ISO GRIFO

JOHNNY LIGHTNING '69 WHISTLER

Collecting Hot Cars

There's fun for everyone as die-cast cars come in all shapes, sizes and designs.

Why You Should Collect Hot Cars

The thrill of the hunt or profitable gains are reasons to collect hot cars, but don't forget the fun

Rev up those engines.

If you're already a die-cast car collector, you're probably supercharged about the miniature replicas and the needle on the speedometer is already off the chart. If you've just starting to get interested in die-cast cars, buckle up. It doesn't take much exposure before beginning collectors find themselves shifting into high gear.

Die-cast cars hold an inherent attraction. Give one to a young child, and soon the cars will be flying across tile floors, sidewalks and tables. Give one to an adult, and soon the cars will be rolling across desks and perched on top of computer terminals.

People collect die-cast cars for a variety of reasons. Some people collect because they love cars and can't afford a 200-car garage. For many of us, these little vehicles are actually time machines. Many collectors enjoy collecting toy cars because it reminds them of the fun times and carefree joy of their youth. If you spent entire days of your childhood putting together Hot Wheels tracks, re-arranging the order of your cars, putting together a village with Matchbox toys and testing the speeds of your cars against those of your best friend – you are a likely candidate to be a die-cast car collector.

Matchbox '58 Bentley

Many collectors get supercharged over die-cast cars because the replicas are like time machines, sending them back to their youth.

If cool cars keep popping up in your dreams, you're ready to collect.

Hot Wheels Gran Torino Torpedo Dragster

Collections don't have to be full of vintage classics. Hobbyists should collect whatever they want and have fun.

But many collectors have a more serious motive than nostalgia: they hope to profit from buying low and selling high. The idea is that a collection will rise in value over a period of time and then be sold for a profit. Sometimes just the act of assembling a collection will add value to the sum. A complete run of the 16 original Hot Wheels, for example, might fetch more on the open market if sold together rather than individually.

Many collectors have profited from their hobby, but almost all veteran hobbyists will tell you to collect what you like, even if passion isn't your main motive. Then no matter what happens, you'll be able to enjoy your collection.

Mark Winkelman is one such veteran collector. He has built such a reputation that when Mattel wanted to put together a traveling display to celebrate the 30th anniversary of Hot Wheels in 1998, the company put him in charge of building their collection.

"Collect what you like because you never know what is going to happen to the market, but you always know what you like," Winkelman says. "You just have to collect what you enjoy. If you do that, you will always be able to feel good about your collection."

Where to Collect Hot Cars

Hot Cars can be found at convenience stores, hobby shops, estate sales and the Internet

Finding die-cast cars to collect can be as easy as checking out the toy box and attic in your own home. Collectors never know when or where they are going to discover the next great find for their collection.

New cars and the latest releases of almost any brand are as close as your corner 7-Eleven. Yes, your favorite department store, drug store, grocery store and even convenience store routinely stocks toy cars. As do toy stores. At the very least, you can buy your cars at retail prices from these kind of outlets before scalpers can boost prices on the secondary market for rare pieces.

But sometimes, you can even find cars that have been stored away in a warehouse for two or three years at these type stores. These aged cars are almost always sold at discount, and often are great bargains for collectors. Special toy liquidation issues help businesses get rid of those products that have been sitting in inventory long beyond their shelf life. These liquidations can often add great value to your collection.

Hot Wheels Gran Torino Tarantula Dragster

Collectors will have to dig a little deeper for vintage vehicles.

Hobby shops are a great source. They're usually operated by a collector who has a love and great knowledge for collecting. Many hobby shops will carry both new and vintage cars, but some may handle just new stock. Many dealers will also run a mail-order business offering value for collectors who live in rural areas.

Other collectors can be your best source for die-cast cars. You can meet these brother and sister hobbyists by joining a club or collectors group, attending toy or die-cast shows or searching the Internet for discussion groups or on-line auctions.

Matchbox '57 4 Ton Leyland Van

Collectors can find die-cast replicas just about anywhere, from toy shops to flea markets.

Collector club meetings often turn into mini-shows. These meetings or major local shows – held in venues such as local recreation centers, hotel ballrooms or VFW Halls – usually offer a decent mix of both old and new cars. Because the crowds at these shows are primarily knowledgeable collectors, prices remain reasonable.

However, the best bargains can usually be found at places where selling die-cast cars is not the primary focus. Garage sales, swap meets, flea markets, thrift stores, antique dealers, estate sales and rummage sales offer great opportunities. One of the major drawbacks to this approach is that you can stop at dozens and dozens of garage sales without even seeing a die-cast car.

Of course, the more knowledgeable a collector is, the better position they are in to make a bargain. Beginning car collectors, on the other hand, should be wary. Just because a car looks old and the guy at the flea market says he has never seen one like it before, that doesn't ensure that the car is of any significant value. While buyers can benefit from a seller's unfamiliarity with the die-cast collectible market, they can also be hurt by it. A good strategy is to take a collector's guide to help you determine prices and identify models.

Entire collections often will go up for sale in auctions or estates sales. Many veteran collectors buy entire collections this way.

This can be a great way to significantly boost your collection at a low cost. With transactions such as these, you will often get duplicates of cars you already own.

Matchbox '57 Bedford Car Transport

Collectors can turn this into a plus by then using these duplicates as trade bait at the next club meeting or die-cast show. Or perhaps collectors can sell these duplicates to other hobbyists, then use the cash to fill in holes in their collection.

How to Collect Hot Cars

Car collectors have many categories of scale, model and budget to focus on

Even if a collector has just hit it big in the lottery, there's simply no way to collect every die-cast car ever produced. All beginning collectors come to the point where they realize that their collection needs to a focus point, a particular direction.

With the diversity of both new and vintage die-cast cars available, the decision of what to collect is a difficult one. Scale can be a consideration, though many Hot Wheels and Matchbox collectors tend to stick with the popular 1:64 size. For some, staying with just one scale is enough. Other may stick with a particular brand, but even then most collectors need to narrow down their focus to levels of price or availability.

A beginning collector's best option is to start out with a particular criteria, then expand based on time, space and budget. Nobody can choose your game plan for you because it should be based on what makes you happy. You can even mix and match as most collectors do. They'll collect Johnny Lightnings from Topper, for instance, but pick up every Mustang they can find from every die-cast companies.

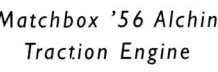

Matchbox '56 Alchin Traction Engine

Here are some of the most common ways that car collectors approach the hobby:

Special Items – Manufacturers frequently release limited editions and promotional items. Matchbox and Hot Wheels issue special cars for their national conventions each year, while Johnny Lightning joins them in annually producing a car for the New York Toy Fair. But these just scratch the surface. Die-cast car makers celebrate an anniversary or special relationship just about every month.

Year – Many collectors will simply get one version of a car released from a certain year, then move to another year. Most often these collectors will limit themselves to one manufacturer.

Many beginning collectors will only chase current releases. A Hot Wheels collector, for example, will chance First Editions, Treasure Hunts and the Series and non-series cars for 1999. Then, before the 2000 cars come out, they'll shift into reverse and go after the 1998 and 1997 releases. Or perhaps they'll make the current year their goal while also going about picking up reasonably priced pieces from Hot Wheels' 1968 debut.

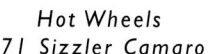

Another fun way to collect is to chase cars from the year you were born.

Street Model – Some collectors base their chase on the car they drive to work every day. If you like Camaros, you can pick up die-cast versions in a variety of model years, colors, scales and die-cast makers. Some collectors will seek a broader scope, seeking out all of the pick-ups or recreation vehicles they can find.

Hot Wheels
'71 Sizzler Camaro

Replica Model – Alright, so you really like the 1968 Beatnik Bandit from Hot Wheels. Well, that car doesn't exist anywhere except in the world of die-cast cars. Fortunately for collectors, at least a dozen versions of the Bandit are known to exist. Some of these are just different colors, but others are variations caused by a mistake at the plant or a change in wheel styles right during the middle of a run.

Variations – Many collectors love these variations, created by changes in a die-cast car during its production run. Often times, the reasons for these changes have been long forgotten. Sometimes the plant will just run out of paint or a certain kind of wheel and switch to something they do have to keep from shutting the factory down for the day. Other times a major change in the system, such as the latest innovation in robotic technology, will create a different look. The changes could have something to do with the packaging process. Many variations – such as the majority of the Johnny Lightning changes in the Topper era — are easily explained as the result of cost-saving moves.

Many times you'll find that veteran expert collectors have graduated into specializing in variations. The expert collector will have accumulated such an extensive collection that the real thrill comes in finding something that nobody else has.

Many hobbyists will base their collection on themes: commemorative versions, cars with Hot Wheels logos on them, year of release, color of the car, etc.

Color – The most common variation is color and it's also a great way to collect. Many Hot Wheels collectors will just chase pink or purple cars, looking for all the variations and models on the market. This method works well for collectors who want to cross brands by grabbing your favorite color replicas from Hot Wheels, Matchbox, Johnny Lightning and other manufacturers.

Number – Matchbox has had a numbering system in place for five decades, while Mattel has been giving Hot Wheels numbers since 1989.

Series – Collecting by series can involve a wide variety of hunting options. Johnny Lightning, for instance, just came out with a series of James Bond die-cast cars from vehicles featured in the movie series. It's a well-defined series, complete with checklist. Another great example is the four-part series that Hot Wheels started producing in 1995. But these series would be relatively easy to collect compared to the Hot Wheels Grand Prix Series in 1969.

Blister packs – Many variations are created when a die-cast car is packaged. Some collectors only want cars that are still in the original blister pack, thus ensuring them the best condition possible. While this is an easy way to collect current releases, it can get difficult when hunting for vintage models.

Some collectors like to buy 1:64 scale cars, while others enjoy larger scales. Still others will get the same model in as many sizes as possible.

Scale – Scales are usually expressed as a ratio (1:64) or as a fraction (1/64). The larger the second number, or denominator, the smaller the scale. A 1:1 would be a regular sized car, while a 1:12 is twice the size of 1:24 car.

A good rule of thumb is the larger the scale, the more the detail. Trends have turned most large scale cars into expensive collector's editions. They're not really toys, but more like statues of cars. The larger scales also can be a challenge to display.

Many collections are built around a certain brand or line of replicas, such as this Major Pack line from Matchbox.

The most popular scale for manufacturers and beginning collectors is 1:64. Most Hot Wheels, Matchbox and Johnny Lightning vehicles are this size, though all three brands have extended their lines to other sizes at times.

Another popular size is 1:43, primarily because this scale works with many of the popular train sets. Companies such as Danbury Mint and Franklin Mint frequently use a 1:24 scale, while 1:18 is popular with auto enthusiasts who collect the die-cast cars to reflect their love for real cars that are out there on the streets and highways.

No matter what car scale you collect or what criteria you choose to make your want list, make sure to have fun. Your collection should reflect your personality and the things that you enjoy. Go out and collect the way you want to so that you can have fun.

Hot Cars Value Guide

Supply, demand and condition drive the value of your collectible cars

Two factors go into determining the value of your die-cast car: the supply vs. demand equation and its condition.

The supply of a certain car depends on a variety of items. Quite simply, more 1999 Johnny Lightning replicas will be available than any casting of a 1956 Matchbox.

Production numbers are a big supply factor, though attrition is just as important. Matchbox has made cars during six decades, so there are plenty to go around. Mattel produced its billionth Hot Wheels long ago. But many of these cars were long ago chewed up by lawn mowers or your neighborhood's version of Dennis the Menace.

And when it comes to a certain toy car casting, many factors come into play. Some types were limited to one year of production, while others were produced

The best way to keep the value of a die-cast car is to keep it in the original packaging.

Variations, such as Italian versions of a replica, will impact value because they change the dynamics between supply and demand.

over a decade. Sometimes molds or casting tools break, ending a car's production run before its schedule time. For the most part, the rarer the car the better. Of course, this also means that the rarer the variation the better. One gray version of the 1977 Z-Whiz car from Hot Wheels is common, but a white one is extremely rare. The difference in value? The white one is worth 50 times more.

But of course, even a rare car has to be desired by someone. If no one really wants a one-of-a-kind variation, it's not going to be valuable in the marketplace. Trends come and go, but it's hard to predict how long they might last. Take the Zamac cars available at the 1998 National Hot Wheels Convention. These pieces were hot at the beginning of 1999, but that's because they just hit the market.

Will their popularity last? Who knows?

There are some safe bets. Spectraflames and Redlines from Hot Wheels have stood the test of time. They've been bolstered by the fact that they are 25 to 30 years old and the first cars from what would become one of the best selling brands in history. They continue to fan the flames of fond childhood memories for a nation full of middle-aged men with disposable income.

Good examples of supply and demand working together to make cars valuable are the hot pink Spectraflames by Hot Wheels. Not many of these cars exist today. Either few were made or the boys in the late 1960s felt free to readily destroy any toys that color. But as the hobby heads into the next millenium, hot pink is indeed a hot color. It is in demand. Consequently, pink cars from this era usually demand a premium.

Hot Wheels '71 Sizzler Barracuda

Besides supply and demand, the condition of your die-cast car will go a long way in establishing its value. Even the rarest of Hot Wheels, if it is beat up and obviously child-used, won't be in big demand.

Obviously, the better condition of your car, the more it will be valued by collectors near and far. But it's tough to find many older cars in mint condition, the hobby's highest designation, simply because the majority of them were played with.

Not even cars kept untouched in a blister pack can be designated as mint. In fact, many toy cars already had blemishes before they left the manufacturer. Mattel officials understand the distinction. In company literature, they have defined four types of conditions just for cars in blister packs to help collectors.

A car "New in Blister" is the original package and has no visible flaws, with the package being undamaged. No flaws can be found on the car even upon close examination.

A car with no visible flaws but in an original package that is distressed is called "New in Damaged Blister." A close inspection of the car shows no flaws but the package has curls, creases, rips, discoloration, stains, cracks or a variety of other problems.

Mattel uses "Almost New in Blister" for a car that has visible flaws in mint original packaging. Possible flaws include discoloration, chips in the paint, flaking and a bubbling of the paint. These cars can even contain nicks, almost as if someone on the assembly line had accidentally dropped it on the floor before putting it in the blister pack

Finally, Mattel uses the designation of "Almost New in Damaged Blister" if both the car and the packaging has flaws. The imperfections on the car can be spotted even though it is still in the package, while the blister pack also shows visible signs of wear and tear.

The hobby as a whole has not adopted any one system of grading die-cast cars, though two or three have become popular.

Mattel Hot Wheels expert Michael Thomas Strauss and several Matchbox authors have published point systems. While the details vary from one method to the other, the main idea is to evaluate a car by adding up the points as listed for any defects found on the vehicle. Different defects have various point values.

This 1959 Ruston Shovel from Matchbox and its packaging are a little banged up, but they are still in pretty good shape for a 40-year-old toy.

Minor defects include:
- small, barely-noticeable scratch,
- slight wear on decal,
- slightly tarnished base, and
- minor wear on wheel.

More serious flaws, which commonly deduct twice or three times as many points as a minor defect, include:
- up to three barely-noticeable scratches,
- noticeable wear on decals,
- slightly crooked tampo or decal,
- clearly crooked tampo,
- substantial wear on decals,
- tarnished base, and
- wheels show considerable wear.

Major defects include:
- small, but noticeable scratches,
- more than one small dark spot,
- even one very noticeable dark spot,
- obvious scratches,
- paint missing, and
- parts missing.

Sets such as this GranToros Speed Strip will lose their value over the years if parts and pieces have been lost.

Some scales rank from 1 to 10, while others scale up to 50. If no points are deducted, you might have a perfect 10, or a mint condition car. But most beginning collectors are quick to tag a car with a mint designation when it is far from being so.

Of course, this is even more true for older cars such as the Topper Johnny Lightnings or the Redline era of Hot Wheels. Many cars from the 1990s that went straight from a toy store to a collector's closet have a much better chance of getting a high grade than any vintage vehicle.

Dave Williamson, an avid car collector, has created his own definition for several condition terms. Williamson keeps these on his web site (www.toycollector.com) and usually posts them in clear view when he sets up at shows or at the Hot Wheels National Convention. He established these guidelines for Redline Hot Wheels made between 1968 and 1973, but they make a good starting point for any kind of toy car.

Mint – This is a condition that wonderful, little toy cars can almost never be found in. Most did not even come from the factory in a true mint (or, in other words, unblemished condition).

Williamson says that just five percent of all Hot Wheels from 1968 to 1973 fall into the mint category. He rarely refers to anything as mint and doesn't believe any car is mint until he has seen it with his own eyes.

Mint minus – This describes a really nice car, recently taken out of the original packaging. Most cars in their original packaging are in this condition. They have a small nick or too but are beautiful cars. Williamson says that he occasionally finds loose cars in this condition, but that most are being hoarded like gold. He claims 10 percent of all 1968 to 1973 Redlines are mint minus.

Near mint – Near mint or NM describes cars that have been well taken care of. Minor imperfections, such as three to four small chips or rubs. Possibly light spotting. Williamson estimates that 15 percent of the Redline Hot Wheels are near mint. He also says that just a few haphazard trips in those old plastic collectors cases will turn a mint minus into a near mint.

Excellent – You say you played with your Hot Wheels. Well, if you kept them in a nice case and did not let that mean kid next door or your younger brother play with them, then chances are your cars are excellent. There are signs of play wear, small chips and a little tarnish on the base.

The Toy Collector, Mr. Williamson, believes that 30 percent of these Redlines fall into this condition and that this grade of car satisfies most collectors.

Good – Most of these cars have provided a lot of fun to some collectors. The paint wear is evident, maybe having been placed on those orange tracks and shot through the Super Charger.

Poor – These are not pretty, but not really junk either. Lots of paint wear, some damage, or parts missing. Makes a nice fixer upper or space filler.

Williamson estimates that 20 percent of Redlines are in good condition and another 20 percent in poor condition.

Maintaining Hot Cars

Collectors have many options for storing, displaying, protecting, restoring and even insuring their cars

Collecting die-cast cars can be addictive.

Before you know it, those first few cars have turned into an ever-growing fleet that's too large to park on the corner of your desk.

Or perhaps you've hit it lucky. You've picked up a big collection at a garage sale, yet the quality of the pieces vary from junkyard dogs to immaculate recent releases. How do you sort through this mess and what do you do with each car?

Most collectors do not remove cars from their original packaging to maintain optimum value to the piece. What you do with your cars can be more important than how you find and acquire them. Here are some of the basics.

STORAGE AND DISPLAY

Veteran hobbyist Mark Winkelman has given his die-cast collection a room of its own. In addition, he helps his young son build a collection of his own cars so that he won't be tempted to play with daddy's cars.

Several manufacturers make plastic and wooden display cases just for die-cast cars. Any issue of a toy collector's magazine will include several ads for such display cases. Of course, any carpenter can create a custom case to fit your own needs. Many collectors will just use thumbtacks to hang blister packs to a bulletin board or wall. If you are going to have fun collecting, displaying your collection needs to be a priority.

"You just have to display some of your cars," Winkelman says. "If you keep them all in boxes stored away some place, you won't enjoy them as much. If you got them displayed, just looking at them will get you excited about your collection.

Cases of all kinds can be used to display a collection.

Even accessories such as collectors buttons can have their specific storage containers.

"Sometimes I move them around in the case just to give them a different look, and I always get fired up about my collection."

Shifting your display also helps protect against long-term direct sunlight that will fade a car's color.

Caring for your cars is important in retaining their value to you and for their future value to others. So no matter which route you go with a piece – display or storage – the less a car is handled, the better off it will be.

Some collectors use cotton gloves when they handle unpackaged or loose vintage and prized pieces. Always wash your hands thoroughly before touching your cars with your bare hands. Avoid touching bare die-cast metal with your fingers, as the oils, acids and salts from your skin will cause them to tarnish over time. The chemicals in your hand can have the same effect on your car as the salt placed on snowy and icy roads decays real cars. Decals are more easily damaged than the metal of a car, so try to avoid touching them.

Some collectors have found that jewelry boxes make great transportation boxes, with one car fitting nicely in each compartment.

Collectors should spend a few dollars to protect those cars destined for longtime storage. Plastic clam shells for blister packs and small plastic boxes for even 1:64 scale loose cars are popular storage options. The plastic clam shells for blister packs store nicely in a copier paper box. If nothing else, collectors can use small plastic bags to help keep their cars safe.

Don't store your car collection in the attic. Cars should be kept in a dry and dust-free environment, where the temperatures don't vary greatly. Dust can easily scratch or damage their finish. Moisture and temperature changes can easily cause the metal in your cars to deteriorate.

Some types of cars may need special handling. Sizzlers, for instance, have built-in batteries that should be removed. The batteries tend to not only corrode the

Die-cast cars of all kinds should be kept in something, from molded plastic cases just for cars to multi-use plastic bags, to protect them from the elements.

car's paint, but also the ones around them. And Matchbox cars need to be separated from their original boxes. The very collectible boxes weren't built to stand the test of time and were printed on high-acidity card stock. The acid in paper will turn decals yellow and eventually even disintegrate rubber treads. One alternative is to use a small plastic bag as a liner, and keep the car in the box.

RESTORATION

Not every car you add to your collection will be in mint condition, but there are means to improving the appearance of your die-cast car.

Some cars will need cleaning, but be careful. You don't really want to open a miniature car wash and run your car through jet streams of water. Generally, the less water the better. Sometimes you'll pick up a vintage car that has been played with and your only choice is to give it a quick bath. No matter how much water you use, soft bristle toothbrushes can be used to get into the cracks and crevices. The older the toothbrush, the better as the bristles will get even softer with age and use. Keep your toothbrushes away from decals, however.

Companies make plastic containers specifically to hold cars in their blister packages.

Many collectors will use a little bit of glass cleaner on their car, which will give their toy vehicles a new shine. Polishing compounds and even car wax — yes, the same polishing compound used on the car you drive to work each day — is also used by many collectors on their cars. The wax really does help restore die-cast cars to their original brilliance, though you might want to give a wax job to the least valuable pieces of your collection until you are satisfied with the process. Most collectors use a cotton swab to apply the wax, moving lightly and in a circular motion.

Some die-cast vehicles, especially some of the older Matchbox, have parts that can break or fall off. You can use a little glue to fix these pieces, but the less glue used the better. If you try to sell or trade a repaired car, be sure to mention the fix-it job. Many collectors will value the piece less if it has been broken.

Cars often can be repaired using pieces from donor cars, and the combination can drastically increase the condition and value of the remaining car. If a collector has a good spectraflame Hot Wheels car that has bad tires but is in good condition, this can be easily remedied by finding a badly scratched spectraflame with good tires. Tires are the best donor parts, though sometimes pieces such as movable hoods and trunks will work, too.

Collectors are free to go beyond cleaning and repairing, but it's important to keep your goals in mind when making decisions about major restoration.

For instance, cars can be touched up with a paint job, making small chips and nicks disappear. It can be expensive, but you can even give your die-cast car an entirely new paint job and make it look practically brand new. Of course, unless a collector is experienced at painting die-cast cars, odds are their paint job will do more damage than good.

Most paint jobs, if done by an outside party, would cost more than the value of the vast majority of die-cast cars. Paint jobs are probably best for those collectors who have a car that they have a great attraction to and plan to keep forever, such as the original cars they used and abused as a child or the car that got them into collecting.

Collectors who are interested in eventually selling their collection should probably stay away from paint jobs. If they do sell or trade their cars, they need to let the potential new owner know of the restoration steps taken.

Some replicas, such as this Model of Yesteryear, have parts that will occasionally need to be glued back together.

CUSTOMIZING

Of course, collectors can do whatever they want to with their cars, especially if little consideration is given to reselling the vehicles.

With that in mind, many collectors will detail their collectible cars just as they would their street cars. Many hobbyists will even perform major customizing work on their cars, giving them one-of-a-kind looks. When it comes to restoration and customizing, anything that can be done with a big car, can be done to a small car.

In fact, customizing jobs often make the die-cast car look just like a particular big car that a collector uses each day on the streets of his hometown (or the first car he ever owned, or the one used on his honeymoon, etc.).

INSURANCE

No matter how big or small the size of your collection, you should consider insuring your valuables in case of theft, fire, flood or any other kind of destruction. Cherished collectibles usually can't be replaced in the heart, but that doesn't mean the disaster has to be an entire loss.

Collectors often can get a new lease on life if they have had the proper insurance on their collection. A well-funded collector can get right back in the hunt, often with a much better idea of chasing down all those items on the new want list.

Obtaining insurance on your collection isn't difficult, especially if you house your collectibles at your home. Talk to your agent about the specifics of your collection. In many cases, a small collection will already be covered under your current homeowners insurance. But the bigger and more valuable the collection, the more insurance you'll need.

Many policies insure specific categories of items, such as a toy car collection, only up to a certain amount. If your collection's value is above that amount, you can "schedule" out specific items and insure those separately. Some companies even offer special collector's insurance that requires a professional appraisal. If your collection is big enough, going through this process can be well worth it. Even if you have to get an addendum or rider added to your current policy, it is easily done and affordable.

Renters who keep their collection at home should make sure they have renter's insurance.

Collectors should keep accurate records of their collection, including purchase prices and receipts. In addition, maintain an inventory checklist and photograph your collection. Keep these in a safe place, away from the collection, so that you will have your records if disaster strikes.

Collector Clubs, Publications and Surfing the Web

Beginner and hard core collectors can benefit from networking, reading and exploring the information superhighway

COLLECTOR CLUBS

Collector clubs have been around almost as long as die-cast cars. In fact, they've been around longer than some brands of toy cars.

Matchbox, for instance, offered a club in the early 1960s before the brains at Mattel had dreamed up their Hot Wheels line. But when Mattel revved up its toy line, it quickly introduced a club geared for kids of any age who wanted to be a part of the Hot Wheels phenomenon. Mattel effectively used the back of its blister packs to advertise its clubs with every purchase.

Early on, the clubs boosted their membership by offering special die-cast cars as a membership privilege. The chrome club-only Hot Wheels cars of the late 1960s remain some of the hobby's most desirable pieces. Both of these trends continue today. Hot Wheels' collectors club offers a wide variety of benefits including a newsletter, exclusive merchandise, T-shirts, bumper stickers and more.

Matchbox not only offers a collectors club — it boasts two. The company founded the Premiere Collector Club in the summer of 1998 for those hobbyists with an interest in its Premier Series. Among the treats members received were a club-only 1957 Chevy and a poster.

Johnny Lightning also offers a club – NewsFlash – offering several types of memberships depending on the amount of dues you want to pay. The first NewsFlash car for members only was a 1954 Corvette Nomad.

All great collector clubs aren't formed by manufacturers. Car collectors from around the world network together to share resources and to boost collecting. Non-manufacturer-operated clubs help members keep abreast of the latest releases, share secrets of collecting, trade pieces and organize shows and are an invaluable sources of information for the beginning collector.

Clubs can be a useful tool for collectors.

If you know of a group of potential members in your community interested in collecting cars, you can benefit from coming together as a club. Many clubs have created Internet home pages on which they can share their tips and secrets with collectors outside their neighborhood or city. Some of these include the Space City Hot Wheels Club, Central California Hot Wheels, Connecticut Hot Wheels Club, Illinois Matchbox Collectors and Kiddie Kar Kollectibles.

The largest clubs were founded by collecting experts years ago. These large, international clubs offer something different than your local variety. Most large clubs publish newsletters written by veteran collectors with connections all over the world.

One such example is Matchbox USA, which was founded in 1977 by Charlie Mack. Another is Michael Thomas Strauss' club in San Carlos, Calif., which helps organize the Hot Wheels National Convention each year.

Here's a list of car collectors club that should help point you in the right direction. If you can't find a club close to your home, consider organizing a couple of other collectors and creating your own.

CLUBS

Hot Wheels Collector Club
1-800-852-1075
Matchbox Club
1-800-524-TOYS

Diecast Toy Collectors Association
(DTCA)
Dana Johnson
P.O. Box 1824
Bend, OR 97709-1824

Illinois Matchbox Collectors
Michael Sarlitto
681 Paxton Place
Carol Stream, IL 60188
630-681-1537

Kiddie Kar Kollectibles
Mike Appnel
1161 Perry St.
Reading, PA 19604
610-375-4780

Matchbox Collectors Club
Everett Marshall
P.O. Box 977
Newfield, NJ 08344
609-697-2800

Matchbox Forum Club
John Yanouzas
7 North Bigelow Rd.
Hampton, CT 06422

Matchbox International Collectors
Association (MICA)
North America Chapter
P.O. Box 28072
Waterloo, Ontario, Canada N2I 6J8
519-885-0529

Matchbox USA
Charlie Mack
62 Saw Mill Rd.
Durham, CT 06422
203-349-1655

National Hot Wheels Newsletter
Mike Strauss
26 Madera Ave.
San Carlos, CA 94070

Salt Flat Hot Wheelers
Rees Piper
3685 South 2200 West #88
West Valley City, UT 84119

Southern California/Orange County
Hot Wheelin'
5903 Cerritos Ave.
Cypress, CA 90630
Treasure Valley Die Cast
8198 W. Sloan St.
Boise, ID 83703

Here's my $1.00. Send me my BOSS HOSS™ car, Club Mag and Membership Kit. Money back guaranteed if not satisfied.

Name_____ Age_____
(Please print clearly)

Address_____

City_____ State_____ Zip_____

Calif. residents add 5¢ State Tax.

Hot Wheels CLUB

Mattel, Inc.
P.O. Box 2828
Hollywood, California
90028

Join the new Hot Wheels™ CLUB today! Look at all you get:

YOU GET the HOT WHEELS Annual, see the new 1970 cars and sets in big color pictures! 28 pages of news, offers, FUN!
YOU GET big Membership Kit with HOT WHEELS Racing Stickers, club patch, your own membership card and certificate!

Fill out coupon and send just $1.00 now!

New!
Silver Anniversary Special
Every club member gets one Free!

Even the earliest blister packs featured club applications.

HOT CAR PRICE GUIDES AND PUBLICATIONS

Can't keep up with what's going on in the world of die-cast car collecting? Don't be surprised. Hot car collectors can enjoy a library of price guides and publications aimed at providing news, checklists, pricing and information

Mattel claims to have produced more than a billion vehicles since it started producing Hot Wheels in 1968. That's more than Ford, Chevy and Chrysler combined for that same time period. Throw in the fact that Matchbox has been producing die-cast toys for almost 20 years longer than Mattel — and that these two big companies are far from the only players in the hobby — and what do you have? The need for some help.

Price guides and other publications are a must for car collectors. These resources can help you keep up with what's new on the market, what's hot in the hobby and whether or not that 1998 First Edition sitting on that dealer's table begging to be bought is really work the price tag. In addition, price guides and publications can help you catalogue the decades' worth of cars that are already out there just waiting to be added to your collection.

One good source is *Beckett Hot Toys*, a magazine from Beckett Publications. It contains the most comprehensive monthly Hot Wheels price guide in the market and frequently offers bonus prices of Matchbox and Johnny Lightning issues. *Beckett Hot Toys* also profiles the latest releases and the issues that are finding their way on every collector's want list.

Beckett Hot Toys not only runs a monthly column on die-cast cars, but it also frequently contains features on die-cast cars including redline variations and industry issues.

Several good sources that cover the Hot Wheels segment of the hobby are published by Mattel, the manufacturer of the popular toy cars.

The company has produced several publications over the years that can help out collectors: catalogues for toy buyers, collector club newsletters and several issues of Hot Wheels Collectors Book. These collector books included of photo of each model car produced by year and frequently featured collectors tops sprinkled through the photo checklists.

These tips offered jewels such as "The green Jeep vehicle from the 1982 line was a prototype color and was produced in very limited production runs." Or "The Pontiac J-2000 in alternate green was produced for distribution in the United States in 1984. When the first production run was complete, an error in shipping sent the entire series to Canada. The car was never sold in the U.S."

Mattel issued the *Hot Wheels Interactive Official Collector's Guide CD-ROM* for computer-savvy collectors. The CD was released in conjunction with the 30th anniversary of Hot Wheels in 1998 and includes a section on the special releases from Mattel to celebrate the milestone.

The CD offers a guide to Hot Wheels releases by year, complete with more than 5,000 photos. It also offers a detailed history, a section for fun facts, stories from designers and checklists and videotaped interviews with two top designers from Hot Wheels.

The CD also offers software that aids collectors in keeping track of their history, grading their collection and calculating values of individual pieces. Collectors can then compile and print out a number of reports, sorted by a variety of options.

Hot Wheels publications, such as this club magazine, are a must for collectors.

Collectors with computer skills can always find the late books on die-cast cars by surfing the Internet. Check out Barnes and Noble or amazon.com and execute a topic search. Many of these sites will also include reader reviews that may help you select the book that fits your needs.

Several die-cast collecting experts have made a name for themselves by writing books on their hobby. Bob Parker is one such Hot Wheels collector, having written two books: *The Complete Book of Hot Wheels with Price Guide* and *Hot Wheels: A Collector's Guide*. Edward Force has written several books on Matchbox and Lledo toys, while Douglas R. Kelly is another expert turned author. Nancy Schiffer wrote *Matchbox Toys*.

Dana Johnson has authored *Collectors Guide to Diecast Toys and Scale Models and Matchbox Toys: 1948 to 1993, Identification and Value Guide*. Among Charlie Mack's list of books on die-cast cars is a trilogy that breaks down the history of Matchbox cars into three parts plus the Encyclopedia of Matchbox Toys.

Michael Thomas Strauss is the author of *Tomart's Price Guide to Hot Wheels*. In addition, Strauss publishes the quarterly Hot Wheels Newsletter.

Strauss' publication is just one periodical that covers die-cast cars. *Collecting Toys* is one; *Diecast Toy Collector* is another. White's and Lee's both publish several monthly price guides, some of which contain some form of die-cast listings.

Collectors with an interest in not only Hot Wheels but racing die-cast cars should check out *Beckett Racing & Motorsports Marketplace* (P.O. Box 7649, Red Oak, IA, 51591-0649).

HUNTING THE INTERNET

So, you're having trouble finding the latest hot Treasure Hunt. You'd also like to go back and fill in a couple of gaps in your Redline collection. Maybe you need a couple of the more common cars to complete a run of castings. Or you're really a

Johnny Lightning collector, but you've also heard that Matchbox made a Dodge Caravan in 1984 that looks just like your old family car.

Collectors once were forced to let their fingers do the walking to find many of their prized possessions. A few minutes spent paging through the phone book, followed by a couple of calls, and they'd be just a trip to the hobby shop away from finding that rare First Edition.

That method can still work. So will making the trip to your local toy car show and actually letting your feet do the walking from table to table. But as the hobby heads into the next millenium, your fingers don't have to walk. They instead can climb on board your computer's mouse and go surfing for hot cars on the Information Highway. If you can't find what you want on the Internet, then it's probably not out on the market.

Of course, you need to have access to a computer that is wired to the World Wide Web, but there's one as close as your local library. And the possibilities are virtually endless. Using any of the popular search engines will reveal thousands of Internet sites that include information on die-cast cars. For instance, a recent search on "Hot Wheels" with Alta Vista resulted in 13,564 matches. Another effort on "Matchbox" with the Infoseek search engine produced 13,564 matches. Using Snap to look for "Johnny Lightning," collectors provided 19,239 sites to explore.

Sure, not all of these matches will be good hits. You'll have to sort out some real car sites with the miniature vehicle pages. But you'll quickly learn how to pick out the good ones without wasting too much time. Chances are you'll quickly find hundreds of sites trying to sell the cars you're looking for, or perhaps a slight variation. Hard-to-find items may remain rare, but you'll have a better chance than the local hobby shop or that show at the VFW Hall.

For collectors, these virtual dealers offer several advantages to the local hobby shop. First, hard-to-find pieces become a little easier to locate. Collectors can find a better inventory with a wider range of choices by visiting several stores, even if the stop is electronic. In addition, collectors get a chance to enjoy comparison shopping, checking out where in the World Wide Web to get the best price.

An ever-increasing number of businesses now utilize an Internet site to help them do business. Many collectors have built their home pages dedicated to their hobby, and these often provide great sources of information. Many dealers and mail-order suppliers also feature sites to reach their collector consumers.

Dean Dierschow produces a great site that provides a link to almost any die-cast car site you can find at www.bamca.org.toylinks.html.

Another good die-cast link is the home page of the Kentucky Hot Wheels Association, which can be found at www.wwd.net/user/jcb/info.htm.

Almost any search engine can also zoom you to a Hot Wheels web ring of home pages linked together. As you become more involved in the hobby, you may even decided to build your own page and link it to a ring. The Original Hot Wheels Web Ring, for example, joins 233 sites together and almost all of them are fun to surf.

As you surf, you'll find many die-cast car collectors clubs sites. These are not only a great source of information, but can lead you to more resources that may turn up that car you're dreaming of.

Many of these clubs post bulletin boards where you can swap information. Several Internet chat groups only allow you to asks questions and share your hobby. These chat groups can help you find other collectors to trade with or buy from. One of the best chat groups for car collectors is rec.toys.cars.

Before you know it, you'll be making on-line friends who can help you with your hobby. Of course, like with any purchase, the buyer should beware.

If you are going to make a trade or purchase from an e-mail pal, several steps can help you avoid getting burned. First, ask for at least three references. Most of these references will be other collectors with e-mail accounts. Drop them a line and get a reading on the person you're considering trading with.

Get a complete description, including condition, of the car or cars to be traded. Always trade pictures of high-dollar or rare cars.

Get the person's complete mailing, home or business address. Don't settle for a post office box.

Get the person's phone number and give him or her a call.

As with any deal, don't be afraid to back out if you aren't comfortable with it.

Another great source for any collectible is the Beckett Publications site at www.beckett.com. Beckett Collectibles Xchange which offers three distinct services that make it easy for online users to buy, sell or trade their collectibles.

Beckett Auction, with Beckett employees doing all the work, allows collectors to bid on a variety of items in a low-risk and ethical environment. Or you can consign your collectibles to sell. Collector-to-Collector Auction offers Beckett Collectibles Online members the opportunity to reach the same audience by hosting and maintaining their own auctions. The Beckett Buy/Sell/Trade area is the original Beckett marketplace for buying, selling and trading. Here, collectors post their own messages that can be read by the more than 270,000 members of Beckett Collectibles Online.

Another virtual collectibles show is held 24 hours a day on eBay at www.ebay.com. The site holds continuous auctions for just about anything, and this includes your favorite collectible car. A recent visit found cars dating back from the 1940s to the latest Hot Wheels set, with a total of 44,871 die-cast cars up for auction. There were 13,235 Hot Wheels, 4,452 Matchbox replicas and 1,854 Johnny Lightnings for sale, plus die-cast cars from Corgi, Franklin Mint and Ertl. You can search among these items by key words, using "Redline" or "Premier" to narrow down the listings.

Of course, you won't be able to go over these cars with a magnifying glass or be sure of their exact condition. First-time buyers should probably limit themselves to bidding on just items that are pictures on-line and don't expect everything to be in mint condition. In addition, most Internet auction services offer feedback ratings on sellers, allowing buyers to judge just how happy they are with their purchases. If you see a seller with a history of unhappy transactions, stay away from them.

Almost all of the companies that produce die-cast cars post their own Internet sites. Not only can you obtain bytes and bytes of information about their products, but you can join a collectors club and even buy certain products direct from Hot Wheels (www.hotwheels.com), Matchbox (www.matchbox.com) and Johnny Lightning (www.johnnylightning.com).

Of course, you avoid the problem by just buying new releases from virtual retailers. A major player is eToy, which is located at, not surprisingly, www.etoy.com.

So, get out the mouse, grab your want list, and put on your virtual wet suit. Time to go surfing. If you can't find that Superfast Matchbox or that Spectraflame variation autograph on the Internet, odds are you aren't going to find it.

Collectible Car Shows

A day at a collectible car show should include a game plan for filling your want list while staying within your budget and having fun

So you finally made it to the Hot Wheels National Convention, or maybe the annual Matchbox Toy Show that's held each summer in Hershey, Pa. Or perhaps you're taking a small plunge first, hitting a show at your local Holiday Inn for your first big excursion.

You're pumped up for the show, but are you really ready to go?

To some collectors, attending a large show can be perhaps the most exciting part of their hobby. But for beginners and folks that are naturally shy, dealing with large crowds, some of the biggest die-cast car experts in the world and a wide variety of collectibles can be an overwhelming task.

Questions shoot out like a Hot Wheels car flying through a double loop:

- Am I prepared?
- What should I have brought?
- Is there a proper way to cover all the tables?
- Is negotiating different than other collectibles?
- What if I miss something?

Whether your goal for the event is a peaceful stroll down Memory Lane or a quick fix of wheelin' and dealin', you need to prepare before you go.

For some collectors, preparation means little more than packing a wallet full of cash. For others, more equipment is necessary: updated checklists, perhaps a supply of cars that you'd like to trade or sell, and the current Hot Wheels Price Guide from the latest issue of *Beckett Hot Toys* to help guide you through the maze of collectibles.

Die-cast car shows have something for every collector, no matter the age.

Shows offer collectors more variety than retail stores and hobby shops.

A game plan will also help. What items are you looking for? What is your goal? How much money can you spend?

Once the doors open, the race for top-notch collectibles is on. If you're after a rare Matchbox, you should have your buying price in mind before you get there. When you see the vehicle for that price, buy it right away. Sure, have some fun and try to negotiate. Maybe even walk a few tables away, but if you see that the rest of the tables are full of current Hot Wheels and an abundance of NASCAR replicas, beat it back to that first table in a hurry. If the piece is really that rare and the price is good, odds are it won't be around long.

If you're not sure what a fair price is, walk around and get a feel for the market. Keep in mind, however, that the show is the market. Price guides are just that — guides. If the car you want is listed at $15 in a couple of guides and there are

Collectors can get the most out of a show if they know what they are looking for before hand.

CAR SHOW CHECKLIST

1. **Be prepared.** Get your want list and any of your trade bate organized. Don't wait until you get to the show to plan your strategy.

2. **List your top 10 wants and what you expect to pay for each particular item.**

3. **Plan how you are going to cover the show.** Try to set up a route that lets you cover as many tables as possible without repeating visits.

4. **Take a notepad.** Write down where you saw a particular piece, and your collectible will be easier to find later.

5. **Take supplies.** Pack plenty of storage bags or cases for your purchases.

6. **Talk to dealers.** They are helpful and knowledgeable about the products they sell. If you have questions, ask them.

7. **Stay alert to trends and listen for the "buzz."** Read between the lines when a dealer talks about different products.

8. **Check with the promoter or some of the dealers ahead of time.** You are looking for an edge, any edge. See if any unusual collections are scheduled for display. Perhaps a heavy-hitting dealer with a large and unique inventory is coming, or maybe it is just a part-time shower who happens to have the same interests that you do.

9. **Dress comfortably.** A good, comfortable pair of tennis shoes is a must.

10. **Have fun.** After all, collecting is a hobby, not a job.

none in the room for less than $25, it is up to you to determine just how badly you want that car. The going rate is obviously more than $15, no matter what it says in black and white.

Oh, you can refuse to pay more than guide that day, but be prepared to deal with your emotions if that car is listed higher in the next guide. Did you do the right thing by passing?

The key is to base your purchases on what you like. After all, collecting is a hobby. A collectible's value is different for each collector. Let your own sense of value be the determining factor.

Don't be afraid to walk away from a deal.

One way to get the first crack at that desired piece is to attack the show in a different way than the rest of the crowd. Odds are – especially if the show is at a local recreation or civic center, a small hotel or something like a VFW Hall – that the traffic has a pattern.

Many collectors seem to take the same general path through the show — starting at the entrance and moving counterclockwise. Try going the other way. Or instead of starting at the door and working your way back, start at the back and work your way to the door.

If you're lucky, you'll find a variety of items on your want list. Here's where you need to set limits for the amount of time and money you're willing to spend. If not, you might find yourself hobby rich but out of gas on your way back home.

If you plan to search for unique items, say a variation of a Hot Wheels redline, try to attend the show when it opens on the first day. Your odds of finding that rare gem clearly improve the earlier you start your search (and before another collector has the chance to buy it first).

As you're walking the showroom floor, you might overhear talk about a particular car or perhaps even a certain dealer. Maybe you'll see a collector and a dealer in animated negotiations. You can feel it. Something's up. Something's hot. Something's got everybody on edge.

The end of the day can be great for hot wheeling and dealing.

Collectors call it a "buzz."

Most of the big shows seem to have it. Sometimes you know before hand what is going to be the star attraction of the show, perhaps an out-of-town dealer with a large vintage selection of Matchbox or a complete run of Johnny Lightning Toppers. There usually are no indicators what will be the hot product before a show opens.

You want to get to the point where you will be able to recognize trends within a few hours of watching and listening or perhaps even a few minutes.

Maybe a Hot Wheels dealer is showing a large number of Treasure Hunts or First Editions. Perhaps a table is blowing out a bunch of the new Johnny Lightnings from Playing Mantis at below wholesale costs.

Watch for dealer-to-dealer transactions, but also beware of getting caught up in the hype. Cars will start selling for more than their guide prices, and before you know it, no more are left. Or perhaps you wind up with a hot traded commodity — that doesn't even fit into your collection.

Sometimes by the end of the show's last day, as dealers are packing up, you may be able to succeed with offers they balked at earlier. A dealer who specializes in the tough-to-get vintage vehicles won't care about taking his stuff home and saving it for a future show. But someone stocking cases of the latest product that didn't sell too well might be willing to lighten his load before he leaves.

Be respectful of the merchant and his merchandise and know what is and what is not being discounted.

As you negotiate, never offer your cars for sale without knowing how much you want. When a dealer is selling replicas at his table, it is his responsibility to say what he wants for them. When you offer to sell to him, it is your responsibility to say how much you want. You can shop around some, but don't be surprised if the original dealer isn't in a buying mood when you get back.

Chasing cars should be a stress-free experience, no matter how big the show is. Be prepared to walk away from any deal, unless it is a good one for you.

Make sure your accomplish your main goal – which is to have fun.

Hot Wheels

'69 Beach Bomb

A Southern California dreamer conceived the most successful line of collectible cars in the world

Elliot Handler turned his thoughts to cars and soon found himself California dreaming.

This really wasn't surprising. Beach music and custom cars were hot in the mid-1960s. Handler lived in Southern California, then known as the informal show car, muscle car and drag racing headquarters of the world.

But Handler was thinking of die-cast cars. Elliot and his wife, Ruth Handler, had founded the toy maker Mattel. The two had watched their grandchildren play with Matchbox vehicles, which at the time dominated the toy car market.

But Matchbox cars were imports, made in England by the Lesney Corporation. While die-cast vehicles were an American innovation, first made popular by Tootsietoys, collecting the cars first flourished overseas. Matchbox's popularity then spread to the Northeast United States, making the cars a booming, zooming success in big cities such as Philadelphia, Boston and New York.

Handler wanted to enter the die-cast market, but he thought the best way to get into the field was to create something entirely different. He did, and the results were more than an immediate success. Mattel created a product that not only took the United States with a rush, but has since become an icon of American youth.

First, Handler bought a small die-cast manufacturing plant that had been producing parts for some of Mattel's toys. He then instructed Jack Ryan, head of Mattel's research and development department, to give him something cool.

Ryan hired a couple of famous car designers, Bill Cushenberry and Big Daddy Ed Roth, who regularly built custom hot rod cars.

Hot Wheels debuted in 1968, but soon cars and sets were poppin' up everywhere.

The influence of California cool on Hot Wheels custom cars can be seen even with the 1999 releases.

The result was Hot Wheels, the first truly "hot" line of die-cast cars. The original 16 models, released in 1968 and pushed with extensive television advertising, came packaged in bright colors with metal buttons. The cars came in 14 vivid colors, spectraflame paint jobs that were ahead of their time. In addition, the cars featured mag wheels with redline tires and torsion-bar suspension. Several of the most popular cars were not replicas of real vehicles that could be had at a local car dealership, but dream machines.

The California Customs were not only attractive to look at, but were also lightning quick. The cars rolled so much better than Matchbox that the English brand had to eventually change the way it manufactured their tires and axles. Matchbox also was forced to spice up its line, adding fun, custom cars to their line of realistic, but boring, vehicles such as milk trucks, delivery vans and family sedans.

Before 1968 ended, Mattel found itself months behind in fulfilling orders. Though Hot Wheels may have been inspired by Matchbox, the brand's place atop the marketplace was undeniable.

And Hot Wheels has stayed on top. According to Mattel, the toy maker produced two billion Hot Wheels in the brand's first three decades. The actual production date of car No. 2 billion was Feb. 4, 1998. Placed front to rear, all the vehicles produced in the first 30 years of Hot Wheels would circle the earth almost four times.

Hot Wheels sells two cars every second, three track sets every minute and 230 play sets every hour. The lines' top production rate occurred in May of 1989, when Mattel was making two million Hot Wheels Color Racers a week.

Kids and collectors grab Hot Wheels by the dozen.

THE MAKING OF A HOT WHEEL

Wonder how your favorite Hot Wheel was constructed? Here's Mattel's eight-step process for driving a vehicle from a designer's dream to hobby reality.

Mattel has made more than one billion Hot Wheels since the first vehicle was produced in 1968, with more than 3,500 variations. Mattel officials estimate that the process of making a die-cast car, from concept to shipping, takes from 10 to 12 months. Mattel breaks down the production process into eight steps.

1. A vehicle's concept first comes to life through the imagination of Mattel's designers. To keep up with the latest trends, the designers visit auto shows, attend many categories of auto races and even study auto magazines.

2. The ideas are then sketched onto an artist's drawing board. The designers may sketch hundreds of versions during this step. The best drawings are then test-marketed with focus groups who help Mattel decide which design will come to life.

3. Reality cars, such as Mattel's race cars, are photographed for details, such as interior and exterior components, closeups of the grill. Manufacturers and owners also are consulted in the reproduction.

4. Precise measurements of the original are taken. The photographs and "specs" are sent to the engineering department, which translates the data into mechanical drawings.

5. The drawings are then sent to a pattern maker, who makes a wooden model of the car four times larger than an actual Hot Wheels car. The models must faithfully reproduce the details of the cars, including emblems, logos, door handles, headlight shape and instrumental panels.

6. Molds are made from the models. The die-cast is injected into the molds, and the body of the vehicle emerges.

7. The body is polished and washed, then spray-painted. Letters, logos, and other details such as pin striping are printed on.

8. Finally, all of the parts, including wheels, chassis and engine, are assembled.

Despite the large volume of cars produced, Hot Wheels remains a strong collectible for two reasons. Mattel has produced a wide variety of vehicles while at the same time creating demand for the cars among a huge population — anybody who was ever a kid and played with toy cars.

More than 15 million boys, ages 3 to 10, are avid collectors, owning an average of more than 30 cars each. These numbers skyrocket when you expand the age bracket. According to Mattel, 41 million adults grew up "driving" Hot Wheels, and the average adult collector owns 1,500 Hot Wheels vehicles.

These collectors chase more than 10,000 variations that have been created. While Hot Wheels began as a line of 1:64 scale die-cast cars, the line has been expanded to include all sizes of anything that rolls, flies or floats. Through the variety of models, the Corvette stands as the most popular vehicle in Hot Wheels history.

Over the years, Mattel has become increasingly aware of collectors. For the first few years of production, the cars came with collector's buttons, with the idea

Hot Wheels catered to collections from the beginning, producing this Rally Case in 1968.

being that kids could play with the cars while collecting the buttons with the pictures of the cars. The company almost immediately started a collector's club after the Hot Wheels line was produced, complete with special edition cars for members.

In 1989, Mattel started giving each model a number and putting collector tips on the back of packaging. The company also developed First Editions, another way for hobbyists to collect. In 1995, Mattel introduced Treasure Hunt cars, limited-edition chase cars sprinkled throughout regular case shipments. The company also started its line of four-car series, vehicles tied together by a theme.

The company helped advanced collectors complete defined checklists of the brand, making legendary designer Larry Wood available for interviews to help create hobby lore.

One such tale is the popular story of the 1969 Volkswagen Beach Bomb, which has a rare variation that includes surfboards sticking out the rear window. The regular variation of the car has slots on the side for the surfboards. Legend has it among collectors that the car needed the extra width to zoom through Hot Wheels Superchargers. In any version, the VW Beach Bomb remains a favorite with collectors.

In Mattel promotional material, the company touts the return of investment on the rare Beach Bomb. Mattel tracks several sales, including one that traded hands via the prestigious Christie's auction house for $1,250. The rear-version Beach Bomb has also been sold at prices ranging from $4,000 to $10,000. Hot Wheels employees like to point out that this car originally sold for 69 cents and that the base series cars can still be bought for under a dollar.

The company also has created an upscale Hot Wheels Collectibles line, trying to appeal to those kids who played with the 69-cent Hot Wheels as a youngster but are ready for better, more expensive cars now.

The collectible line broke out in a big way in 1998 to celebrate Hot Wheels 30th anniversary with a limited edition of 30 historic cars. The Hot Wheels Collectibles line also produced sets that year to celebrate the 25th anniversary of the film "American Graffiti," the 50th anniversary of the Porsche and the 45 anniversary of the Corvette. In addition, Mattel unveiled 1:24 Hot Wheels Legends to Life line. It kicked off with an exclusive replica of Don "the Snake" Prudhomme's yellow 1970 Plymouth Barracuda funny car. The car not only contained more than 135 die-cast parts, but also includes the roar of the engine and the actual smoking of tires.

Mattel promises bigger and better things for the future, for both adult collectors and children ready to play. Hot Wheels has extended far beyond its California roots, but the dream of Elliot Handler lives on.

The Snake and The Mongoose

Don "The Snake" Prudhomme and Tom "The Mongoose" McEwen drive Hot Wheels into the world of racing

In 1969, drag racing still was in its infancy. The darlings of the sport drove cars that burned massive quantities of nitromethane and carried the driver's fancy nicknames on the side, but mainstream popularity had not yet found the sport.

A couple of young Southern California racers, Don "The Snake" Prudhomme and Tom "The Mongoose" McEwen, were among the biggest names in the sport.

Friends off the track, their racing rivalry quickly became one of the most recognized match-race duos in the country.

In 1969, McEwen and Prudhomme both raced Top Fuel dragsters, but primarily were running on empty. The two lived from race to race, from exhibition to exhibition, reaping the big-money sponsorship of many of today's competitors.

But a chance comment McEwen uttered while visiting his mother and stepfather changed everything. Both McEwen's mother and Joe Ball, her husband, worked for Mattel Toys. Taking into account the popularity of Hot Wheels' recently released inaugural line, Tom wondered out loud if a set featuring "The Snake" and "The Mongoose" wouldn't sell well.

One thing led to another and, eventually, the California hot rods hooked up with the makers of California Custom die-cast cars starting in 1970. Mattel not only agreed to produce die-cast cars of the two drivers, but also signed up to sponsor them under the Hot Wheels banner in both the Top Fuel and Funny Car divi-

'70 Snake Funny Car

'70 Mongoose Funny Car

sions. Mattel officials especially wanted the pair to race Funny Car for two reasons: the vehicles more closely resembled a production car, which Mattel thought would sell better, and the real Funny Cars offer more room to display the Hot Wheels logo.

The combination of Hot Wheels and the Snake-Mongoose rivalry accomplished two significant feats. First, the drag racing team became one of the earliest to enjoy major sponsorship outside of automotive industries, complete with coordinated uniforms and television exposures. Also, "The Snake" and "The Mongoose" Hot Wheels models became two of the first mass-produced die-cast cars to become racing collectibles. Children spent time in their youth playing with the cars, then continued to chase them as collectibles as adults. While Matchbox cars were already being widely collected, Matchbox cars were predominately vehicles that drove up and down city streets, not the booming and zooming machines of the race track.

'71 Mongoose Funny Car

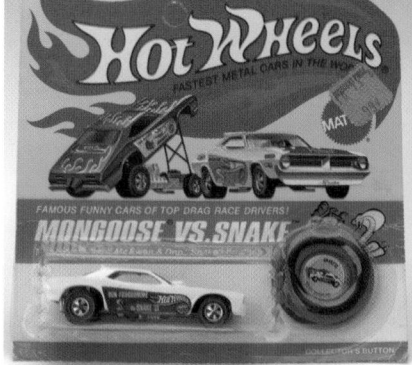

'71 Snake Funny Car

Mattel sponsored "The Snake" and "The Mongoose" as a means to sell toys. With that in mind, the company not only produced blister packs of the two drivers' cars but also came out with a set featuring the pair's Funny Cars. The kit featured a Prudhomme yellow die-cast Plymouth Duster and a McEwen die-cast red car. The cars featured flip-top bodies, and they were launched down

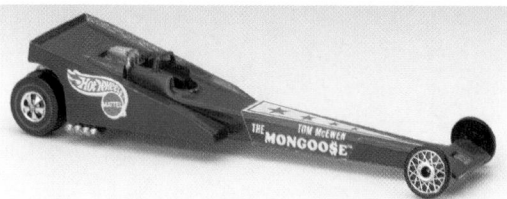

'72 Snake Rear Engine Dragster

'72 Mongoose Rear Engine Dragster

a plastic track with a thumb-activated, rubber band-powered launcher. The track also included a checkered flag that popped up at the end of the course to signal the winner.

The following year Mattel issued two sets: one with Funny Cars and a new game featuring the dragsters. The only differences between the 1970 and 1971 Funny Car kits were the color of the cars, with the 1971 game featuring McEwen in a blue car and Prudhomme's painted white. The dragster kit featured front-

'71 Snake Dragster

motored racers that could do wheelstands. Eventually, Mattel would make a version that had a parachute fly out to slow the toys, just like the real dragsters.

In 1972, Mattel once again issued games for both the dragsters and the Funny Cars. But this time the dragsters were the rear-engined, wedge-bodied cars popular at the time. In 1973, Mattel again issued a game with two cars. The cars retained the blue and white paint of the 1971-72 issues, but the body styles were Plymouth Barracudas without windows. This issue may be the most rare of all of the die-cast "The Snake and The Mongoose" series.

'73 Mongoose Funny Car

Mattel continued to issue Prudhomme and McEwen Hot Wheel cars throughout the 1970s. In 1978, the company issued the Prudhomme Arrow car showing his Army sponsorship. The car, mostly white, came without windows. Hot Wheels also produced a McEwen issue, a replica of the silver Corvette "The Mongoose" drove to victory in the 1978 U.S. Nationals. The final car in the series is the yellow 1982 Pepsi Challenger car of Prudhomme.

In the 1990s, Mattel again turned to racing to boost its Hot Wheels line. The company not only returned to "The Snake" for help, but also enlisted the aid of the legendary Pettys, the first family of NASCAR.

First, Mattel sponsored Jack Baldwin on the Trans-Am circuit to help celebrate the first 25 years of Hot Wheels. The company also produced versions of Baldwin's Camaro.

Then in 1994, to honor Prudhomme on his retirement tour and to celebrate 25 years of the relationship, Mattel re-issued a version of the 1970 Hot Wheels game. The 1994 game used a gravity launch instead of a thumb-activated launcher and also featured a loop in the middle of the track that wasn't part of the original game. In a new twist, the parachutes blossom from the current cars as they pass through the finish line.

According to Mattel, 25,000 of the games were produced.

'73 Snake Funny Car

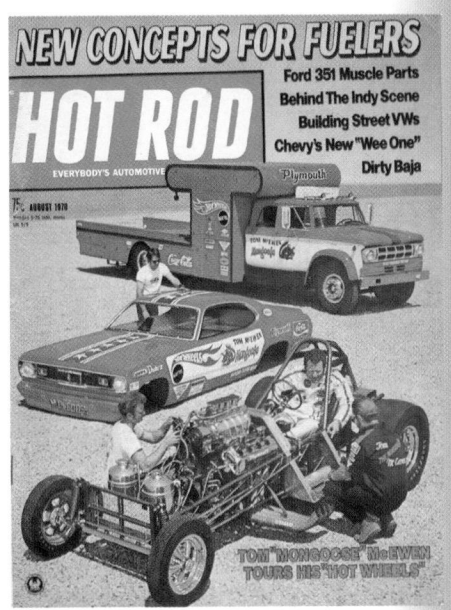

At about this same time, NASCAR racing team die-cast collectibles were becoming a booming business. Mattel decided to join the competition, squaring off with other racing die-cast makers such as Action Performance Companies, Racing Champions and the Winner's Circle line from Hasbro. Not only did Mattel begin production of replicas of race cars driven by NASCAR drivers, but also CART and Formula One teams.

In the late 1990s, Mattel sponsored Kyle Petty's No. 44 on NASCAR's Winston Cup circuit. In addition, the company came out with a Pro Racing line of Hot Wheels featuring NASCAR's top stars, drivers such as Bill Elliott, Mark Martin, Ricky Rudd and Terry Labonte.

'70 Mongoose & Snake Dragster Set

'71 Mongoose & Snake Dragster Set

'99 DAYTONA 500

Mattel also produced Kyle Petty and Daytona 500 sets for Hot Wheels, plus used its top-selling girls' brand to release a NASCAR Barbie. Hot Wheels also became one of the main sponsors for the 1999 Daytona 500, with a Mattel toy car given out to fans who bought a program for the race.

But Mattel didn't forget one of the drag racing legends that helped boost its popularity in the beginning. During the middle of this racing die-cast boom, Hot Wheels came out with one of its most expensive new releases ever. This 1:24 scale car in the Hot Wheels Legends to Life series honors Prudhomme and actually smokes, roars its engine and spins its tires. The Snake and Hot Wheels have come full circle.

Variations

Collectors love hunting down Hot Wheels featuring variations in castings, paint and other details

Collectors love variations.

The longer a Hot Wheels hobbyist has been chasing his die-cast vehicles, the more he treasures finding one that stands out from the rest. And in the 30 years Mattel has been cranking out Hot Wheels, the company has provided collectors with more than 10,000 variations to collect.

And more are being discovered every day. Collectors can find no greater joy than to find something unique about their car, daring to obtain the ultimate goal — a one-of-a-kind Hot Wheels. Even the most casual collector needs to be familiar with some of the most common variations, if simply to know the general value of the car.

Here's a variety of variations.

'74 El Rey

'75 Vega Bomb

Several Hot Wheels have been produced in alternate colors, meaning that fewer were produced in that color and those rare versions are more valuable. The 1975 Vega Bomb, for instance, comes in both orange and an alternate green (pictured). The alternate green version is worth as much as 10 times the orange version. Likewise, the 1974 El Rey Special came in alternate dark blue (pictured) and green. The green version routinely sells for less than $50, while the dark blue is regularly priced at $350 or more.

Several variations even occurred during the production run of a single Hot Wheels casting. The earliest of the 1968 Cougar, such as the car on the left that was probably made in the first four weeks of production, had the center of its grill painted the same color as the body paint. Later versions, such as the one on the right, featured an entirely silver grill. The early run car, shown on the left and in the profile photos, also featured "deep dish" wheels with the center of the wheel being inset. The later version on the right sports flush wheels.

Several variations among Hot Wheels resulted from where the cars were made. Hong Kong versions generally feature more details than the versions produced in the United States. Just a glance at the bottom of these two 1968 Custom Barracudas demonstrates how the Hong Kong version on the right, displays more lines and details.

The 1968 Mustang came with a variety of variations, helping to increase the popularity of the Hot Wheels release. One difference are the hood scoops, with the earliest versions of the Hong Kong casting (shown on the left) sporting an open scoop. This variation only occurred in the first month or two of production. Later versions had a closed scoop like the car on the right.

A different type of variation occurred in the casting from the United States. Late in the production run, a limited number of Mustangs were produced with ribbed rear windows as shown on the right. The variation on the left has a flat rear window. The hard-to-find ribbed versions, also called louvered, could be worth as much as $450 or more in mint condition.

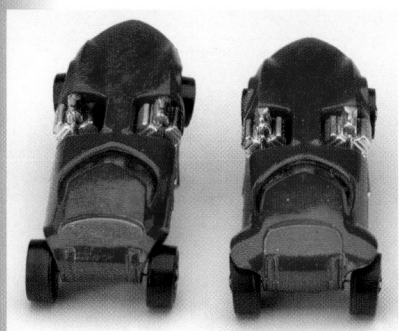

Prototype versions that make it to the hobby often have many differences from the production Hot Wheels. This 1969 Twinmill prototype, shown on the left, has cut-out rear fenders. In the production version on the right, the fenders are much larger.

Hot Wheels prototypes often made it into Mattel commercials and this Twinmill version was a star. It appeared in a 1969 Hot Wheels commercial zooming down the track, with its cut-out fenders clearly showing up on camera from a side shot.

The 1968 Fleetside featured several variations on its Hong Kong casts, with the differences coming with the bumper paint. The version on the left was produced in the first month or two and had the front and rear bumper painted the same color as the body. Then Hot Wheels stopped painting the front bumper, as shown by the car on the right, and left it a natural metal. After another four or five months of production, Hot Wheels stopped painting the rear bumper, leaving it, too, just natural metal.

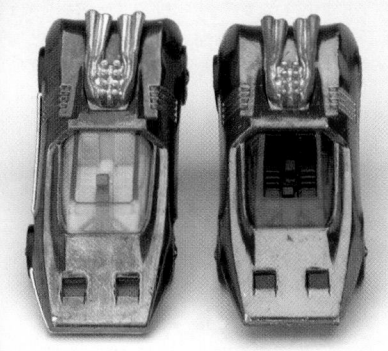

The prototype of the 1969 Peeping Bomb (left) was much different than the production version. The prototype included a white interior and a red headlight handle. The production model (right) featured a black interior, a black headlight handle and a different type of rivet underneath the car. The headlight handle can actually be pulled, changing the color of the plastic headlights to give the impression that the lights have come on. The car on the left was made in Hong Kong, but the clear windows are strong indicators that it's a prototype. Hot Wheels made in Hong Kong almost always came with blue-tinted windows.

Sometimes Hot Wheels variations were the result of tampo painting, a process used to apply stripes and other marks after the body had already been painted. The 1974 Mustang Stocker on the left displays a rare alternative tamp paintings consisting of red and blue markings. The Mustang on the right shows the more common version, with magenta and orange tampo.

Sometimes paint can make an extreme difference in the value of a die-cast car. The 1975 P911 is an extreme example. The white version shown on the left is very rare, with less than a dozen having shown up in public collections or shows. These white P911 cars in mint condition have been sold for more than $2,000. The normal yellow version, found in plentiful numbers, can be bought for less than $50.

Much like the 1975 P911, the white version of the Z-Whiz car was produced in very limited numbers. The gray enamel version, however, remains plentiful. One possible explanation for the rarity of the white versions is that Mattel occasionally ran out of gray paint, then switched to white for the remainder of the day so as not to halt production. The difference in supply shows up in the value, with the gray version commonly selling for around $40 and the white Z-Whiz regularly valued at more than $2,000. When one of the white Z-Whiz sold for $2,200 at an auction in 1997, Hot Wheels collector Mark Winkelman had a whim. He looked up the prices of real 1977 Datsun Z cars — which the Z-Whiz is based on — in *Auto Trader* magazine. The only one listed was selling for $1,800.

The 1970 Carabo rarely came with a white interior. A Hot Wheels variation usually occurs at just one production site. That combination makes these two Carabos unique, as both have white interiors yet the car on the left was made in Hong Kong and the one on the right in the United States.

Most of the Ford J-Cars were made in the United States, while almost all of the limited number from Hong Kong came in white enamel. This J-Car is a rare exception, being a red version from Hong Kong. But beware if you're shopping for one. The red version is common with U.S. casting. One way to tell the two J-Cars castings apart is the natural base of the U.S. casting, while the base and body of J-Cars from Hong Kong were painted the same color.

Less than two dozen of these in-house cars, produced just for Mattel designers on the Hot Wheels team in 1978, are thought to exist. The car includes the names of all of the Hot Wheels designers, plus the words, "El Diablo wants you." Larry Wood, who has been designing Hot Wheels from almost their conception in 1968, says the El Diablo tampo refers to a local restaurant the designers used to frequent.

One general misconception in the Hot Wheels hobby is that white interiors are harder to find. While that is true for some castings, it is not a rule a thumb for the majority of models. It is true for these four 1969 Indy cars, which usually came with black interiors.

This Italian packaging of Hot Wheels, translated "Brucia Pista," features a version of Hong Kong casting not seen in the United States. While the creamy pink 1968 Hot Heap often was found in U.S. castings, it is thought that this Hong Kong pink was only shipped out in international versions.

This German "Heisse Rader" is one of the few known examples of the chrome 1970 King Kuda in a blister pack, believed to have shown up just in Germany. The only way you could get this car in the United States was to join Mattel's Hot Wheels Club in the mail or buy a club kit in stores, and it wouldn't come in a blister pack.

The 1969 Ford Mark IV usually came with a sticker sheet that turned the Hot Wheels into a No. 1 race car. But this Canadian blister pack has a No. 5, leading many experts to believe that the international packaging carried a different sticker sheet.

This Canadian blister pack of the 1972 Mercedes C111 features a collector's button, which were dropped from United States packaging in 1972. These Northern button versions were different than the previous versions, which featured the name and picture of the car. These Canadian buttons were just mag wheels.

This blister pack contains a rare version of the 1969 Classic '32 Ford Vicky, one with a wrinkled paint job on the black roof. Most Vickys came with a smooth top. The Vicky's sister car, the 1969 Classic '31 Ford Woody, came in both smooth and wrinkled versions, but production of the two was split almost evenly.

Almost any variation of the 1971 Olds 442 is rare, as the car is thought to have one of the lowest production runs of any of the early Hot Wheels. To find the Olds 442 in a blister pack is even rarer.

This 1970 Porsche 917 has a couple of interesting variations. First, the packaging reads "Racing Car Series" while all of the United States blister packs call the line the "Grand Prix Series." In addition, this car is pink and has Hong Kong castings. Plenty of pink Porsche 917 Hot Wheels could be found in the United States, but they were all made in the U.S.A. Pink versions never reached the United States from Hong Kong.

The AOK Real Rider variation is one of the most popular variations in Hot Wheels history. The model debuted in 1978, with this green version from that year worth less than $50. This price of this 1981 red version with basic wheels would be a little bit less, say $5 worth, than the 1978 replica. But the value of the 1983 red AOK with Real Rider wheels jumps to as much as $700. The mold of the car broke when they were making the Real Rider version and was never replaced, making it rare because of a short production run.

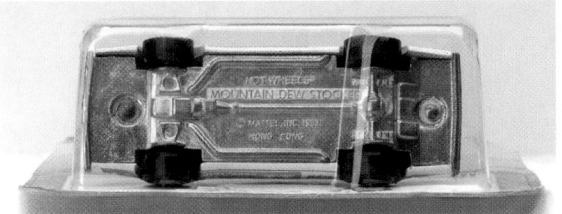

This 1983 NASCAR Stocker came with three bases, a common worth about $35 and the other two valued at four times as much. The production runs of the first two stopped due to copyright obligations with the sponsor's name.

This French version can draw a premium from collectors because its interior is much rarer than the one most commonly found in the United States. The French version is worth as much as $125, three times that of the U.S. versions.

GT Racers from 1989 aren't that special, with savvy collectors being able to pick up one for around $5. But this rare version with blue metal flake paint can fetch up to 10 to 12 times the price of the common GT Racer.

Hot Wheels' 1965 Mustang, released in 1990, most frequently came in an aqua color with tan or black interior. This white Mustang was a short run valued at more than 10 times the common color.

This 1983 Real Rider Cobra gets a price boost for just being in German packaging. It is worth twice as much than the U.S. versions.

This 1995 Porsche was sold two different ways. One variation came in a set, had knobby wheels that made sounds on the Hot Wheels track and can be found for under $20. The version that comes in blister packs had regular wheels and is worth five times as much.

This 1984 Frito Lay delivery van didn't come in a blister pack in the United States, adding extra value to this Canadian version.

WHEEL VARIATIONS

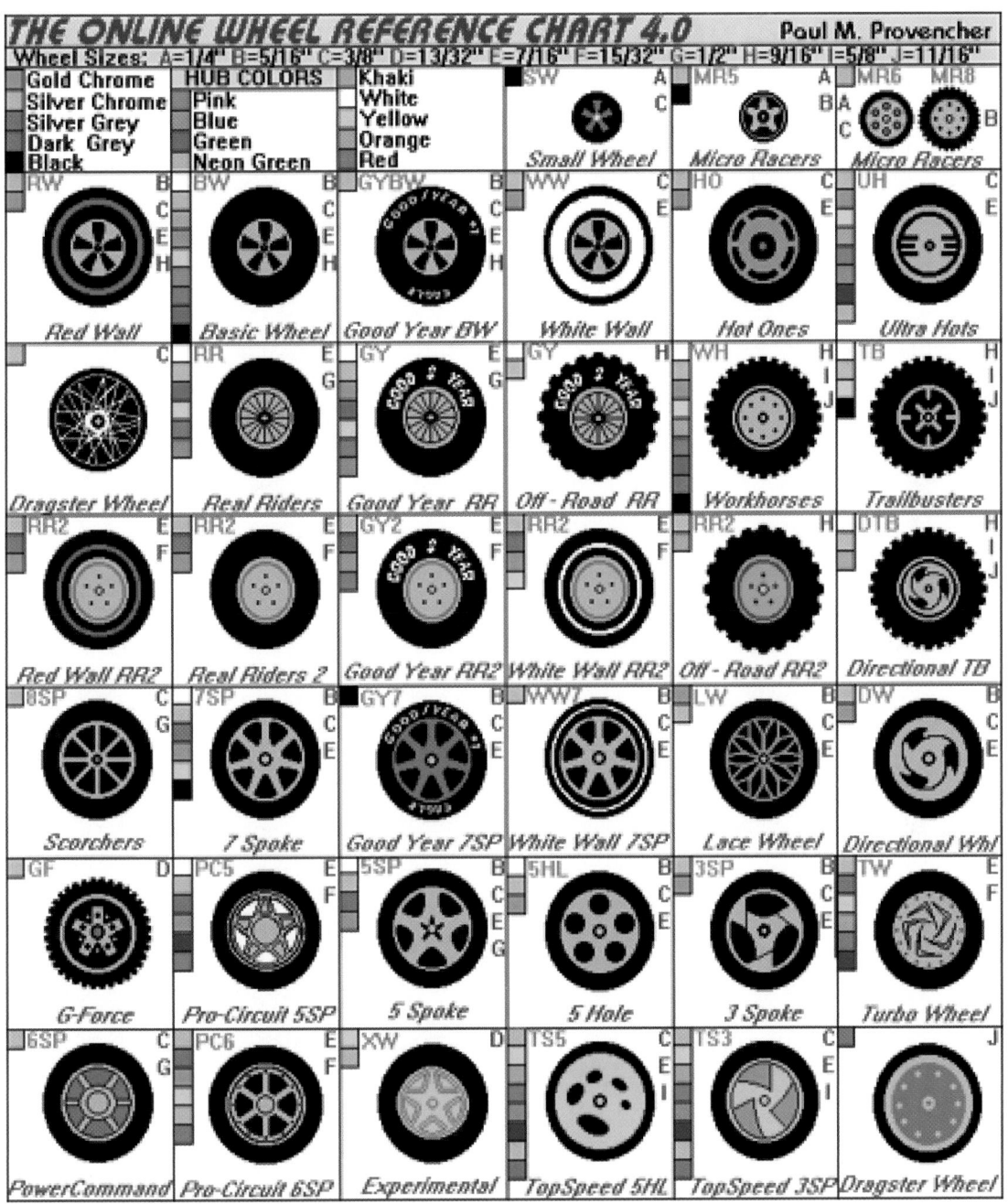

The Online Wheel Reference Chart 4.0 courtesy of: Paul M. Provencher and Timothy P. Voak @ http://whitemetal.com/

HOT WHEELS COLOR LEGEND

AF	Anti-Freeze
BLA	Black
BLU	Blue
BR	Brown
BRON	Bronze
CHR	Chrome
CP	Creamy Pink
CRE	Cream
COP	Copper
GOL	Gold
GOLP	Gold Plated
G	Green
GR	Gray
HP	Hot Pink
IB	Ice Blue
LB	Light Blue
LG	Light Green
LI	Lime
MAG	Magenta
MAR	Maroon
OL	Olive
OR	Orange
ORE	Orange Enamel
PI	Pink
PUR	Purple
R	Red
RO	Rose
SIL	Silver
SILP	Silver Plated
T	Tan
WH	White
Y	Yellow

HOT WHEELS LEGEND

HW	Heavyweights
RL	Redlines
MW	Metal Wheels
PW	Plastic Wheels
SFW	Super Fast Wheels
GP	Gift Pack
HH	Helpful Hauler

1968 Hot Wheels

	LOOSE	IN PKG.
Beatnik Bandit AF	35.00	75.00
Beatnik Bandit AQ	40.00	80.00
Beatnik Bandit BLU	35.00	70.00
Beatnik Bandit BR	40.00	90.00
Beatnik Bandit COP	50.00	100.00
Beatnik Bandit CP	125.00	300.00
Beatnik Bandit G	40.00	80.00
Beatnik Bandit GOL	35.00	70.00
Beatnik Bandit HP	200.00	500.00
Beatnik Bandit LB	40.00	80.00
Beatnik Bandit LG	50.00	100.00
Beatnik Bandit MAG	40.00	80.00
Beatnik Bandit OL	40.00	80.00
Beatnik Bandit OR	35.00	70.00
Beatnik Bandit PUR	40.00	80.00
Beatnik Bandit R	35.00	70.00
Beatnik Bandit RO	50.00	100.00
Beatnik Bandit Y	35.00	70.00
Custom Barracuda AF	150.00	350.00
Custom Barracuda AQ	80.00	250.00
Custom Barracuda BLU	80.00	250.00
Custom Barracuda COP	100.00	275.00
Custom Barracuda CP	500.00	1500.00
Custom Barracuda G	80.00	250.00
Custom Barracuda GOL	80.00	250.00
Custom Barracuda LB	150.00	350.00
Custom Barracuda OR	150.00	350.00
Custom Barracuda PUR	200.00	500.00
Custom Barracuda R	200.00	500.00
Custom Barracuda RO	200.00	500.00
Custom Barracuda Y	150.00	350.00
Custom Camaro AF	140.00	300.00

1968 CUSTOM BARRACUDA (AQUA)

1968 CUSTOM BARRACUDA (PURPLE)

1968 CUSTOM BARRACUDA (ROSE)

1968 BEATNIK BANDIT (ANTIFREEZE)

1968 BEATNIK BANDIT (ORANGE)

1968 BEATNIK BANDIT (ORANGE)

1968 BEATNIK BANDIT (UNPAINTED PROTOTYPE)

	LOOSE	IN PKG.
Custom Camaro AQ	110.00	275.00
Custom Camaro BLU	110.00	275.00
Custom Camaro BR	110.00	275.00
Custom Camaro COP	150.00	350.00
Custom Camaro CP	500.00	1000.00
Custom Camaro GOL	110.00	275.00
Custom Camaro GR	110.00	275.00
Custom Camaro LB	250.00	600.00
Custom Camaro OL	110.00	275.00
Custom Camaro OR	110.00	275.00
Custom Camaro PUR	275.00	700.00
Custom Camaro R	110.00	275.00
Custom Camaro RO	150.00	350.00
Custom Camaro WH	1200.00	
Custom Camaro Y	110.00	275.00
Custom Corvette AF	125.00	350.00
Custom Corvette AQ	100.00	300.00
Custom Corvette BLU	100.00	300.00
Custom Corvette COP	150.00	350.00
Custom Corvette CP	400.00	1000.00
Custom Corvette G	100.00	300.00
Custom Corvette GOL	100.00	300.00
Custom Corvette IB	200.00	400.00
Custom Corvette LB	200.00	400.00
Custom Corvette MAG	200.00	450.00
Custom Corvette OL	100.00	325.00
Custom Corvette OR	100.00	325.00
Custom Corvette PUR	150.00	350.00
Custom Corvette R	100.00	300.00
Custom Corvette RO	150.00	350.00
Custom Corvette Y	100.00	300.00
Custom Cougar AF	125.00	400.00
Custom Cougar AQ	90.00	350.00

1968 CUSTOM CAMARO (BLUE)

1968 CUSTOM CAMARO (BLUE)

1968 CUSTOM CAMARO (BROWN)

1968 CUSTOM CORVETTE (ROSE)

1968 CUSTOM CAMARO (GREEN WITH BLUE GLASS)

	LOOSE	IN PKG.
Custom Cougar BLU	90.00	350.00
Custom Cougar BR	250.00	700.00
Custom Cougar G	125.00	400.00
Custom Cougar GOL	125.00	400.00
Custom Cougar IB	200.00	500.00
Custom Cougar LG	200.00	400.00
Custom Cougar OL	125.00	400.00
Custom Cougar OR	125.00	400.00
Custom Cougar PUR	200.00	500.00
Custom Cougar R	250.00	700.00
Custom Cougar Y	90.00	350.00
Custom Eldorado AF	75.00	175.00
Custom Eldorado AQ	60.00	150.00
Custom Eldorado BLU	60.00	150.00
Custom Eldorado BR	75.00	175.00
Custom Eldorado COP	100.00	200.00
Custom Eldorado G	60.00	150.00
Custom Eldorado GOL	60.00	150.00
Custom Eldorado HP	125.00	250.00
Custom Eldorado IB	75.00	200.00
Custom Eldorado LB	150.00	300.00
Custom Eldorado LG	75.00	175.00
Custom Eldorado MAG	60.00	150.00
Custom Eldorado OL	60.00	150.00
Custom Eldorado OR	60.00	150.00
Custom Eldorado PI	125.00	250.00
Custom Eldorado PUR	60.00	150.00
Custom Eldorado R	60.00	150.00
Custom Eldorado RO	75.00	175.00
Custom Eldorado Y	60.00	150.00
Custom Firebird AF	80.00	200.00
Custom Firebird AQ	80.00	200.00
Custom Firebird BL	80.00	200.00

1968 CUSTOM CORVETTE (BLUE)

1968 CUSTOM COUGAR (BLUE)

1968 CUSTOM CORVETTE (LIME GOLD)

1968 CUSTOM COUGAR
(BLUE WITH BLUE INTERIOR)

1968 CUSTOM COUGAR (OLIVE)

1968 CUSTOM VW (RED)

1968 CUSTOM COUGAR (PURPLE)

1968 DEORA (PURPLE)

1968 DEORA (LIME GOLD)

1968 ELDORADO (MAGENTA)

	LOOSE	IN PKG.
Custom Firebird BLU w/BLU interior	125.00	350.00
Custom Firebird BR	100.00	250.00
Custom Firebird G	80.00	200.00
Custom Firebird GOL	80.00	200.00
Custom Firebird LB	150.00	300.00
Custom Firebird OL	80.00	200.00
Custom Firebird OR	80.00	200.00
Custom Firebird PUR	100.00	250.00
Custom Firebird R	80.00	200.00
Custom Firebird R w/R interior	125.00	350.00
Custom Firebird RO	175.00	400.00
Custom Firebird Y	80.00	200.00
Custom Fleetside AF	75.00	200.00
Custom Fleetside AQ	60.00	150.00
Custom Fleetside BLU	100.00	250.00
Custom Fleetside COP	100.00	250.00
Custom Fleetside G	100.00	250.00
Custom Fleetside GOL	60.00	150.00
Custom Fleetside IB	200.00	500.00
Custom Fleetside LB	200.00	400.00
Custom Fleetside OR	60.00	150.00
Custom Fleetside PUR	60.00	150.00
Custom Fleetside R	75.00	200.00
Custom Mustang AF	125.00	400.00
Custom Mustang AQ	90.00	350.00
Custom Mustang BLU	90.00	350.00
Custom Mustang BLU w/louv. rear window	300.00	1000.00
Custom Mustang COP	150.00	450.00
Custom Mustang CP	300.00	600.00
Custom Mustang G	150.00	450.00

1968 DEORA (PURPLE)

1968 ELDORADO (PURPLE)

	LOOSE	IN PKG.
Custom Mustang GOL	90.00	350.00
Custom Mustang GOL w/open hood scoops	400.00	1200.00
Custom Mustang LB	225.00	500.00
Custom Mustang OL	150.00	450.00
Custom Mustang OR	90.00	350.00
Custom Mustang OR w/louv. rear window	300.00	1000.00
Custom Mustang PUR	300.00	700.00
Custom Mustang R	90.00	350.00
Custom Mustang R w/louv. rear window	300.00	1000.00
Custom Mustang R w/open hood scoops	400.00	1200.00
Custom Mustang RO	150.00	450.00
Custom Mustang Y	90.00	350.00
Custom Mustang Y w/louv. rear window	300.00	1000.00
Custom T-Bird AF	70.00	225.00
Custom T-Bird AQ	70.00	225.00
Custom T-Bird BLU	70.00	225.00
Custom T-Bird COP	90.00	250.00
Custom T-Bird CP	200.00	400.00
Custom T-Bird G	70.00	225.00
Custom T-Bird GOL	70.00	225.00
Custom T-Bird OL	90.00	250.00
Custom T-Bird OR	70.00	225.00
Custom T-Bird PI	200.00	450.00
Custom T-Bird PUR	175.00	350.00
Custom T-Bird R	125.00	300.00
Custom T-Bird Y	70.00	225.00
Custom VW AF	60.00	125.00
Custom VW AQ	40.00	75.00

1968 ELDORADO (RED)

1968 CUSTOM FIREBIRD (RED)

1968 CUSTOM FIREBIRD (GREEN DOOR OUTLINE)

1968 CUSTOM FIREBIRD (BLUE)

1968 CUSTOM FLEETSIDE (PURPLE)

1968 CUSTOM FIREBIRD (RED)

1968 FORD J CAR (RED; HONG KONG CASTING)

1968 FORD J CAR (WHITE)

1968 FORD J CAR (WHITE)

1968 HOT HEAP (RED)

	LOOSE	IN PKG.
Custom VW BLU	40.00	75.00
Custom VW BLU no sunroof	750.00	
Custom VW BR	40.00	75.00
Custom VW COP	60.00	125.00
Custom VW CP	200.00	400.00
Custom VW G	40.00	75.00
Custom VW G no sunroof	750.00	
Custom VW GOL	40.00	75.00
Custom VW HP	250.00	450.00
Custom VW IB	125.00	250.00
Custom VW LB	125.00	250.00
Custom VW MAG	60.00	125.00
Custom VW OL	40.00	75.00
Custom VW OR	40.00	75.00
Custom VW PI	300.00	500.00
Custom VW PUR	125.00	250.00
Custom VW R	40.00	75.00
Custom VW RO	125.00	250.00
Custom VW Y	40.00	75.00
Deora AF	60.00	200.00
Deora AQ	50.00	175.00
Deora BLU	350.00	800.00
Deora G	100.00	325.00
Deora GOL	50.00	175.00
Deora OR	50.00	175.00
Deora PUR	50.00	175.00
Deora R	125.00	400.00
Deora Y	50.00	175.00
Ford J-Car AQ	30.00	60.00
Ford J-Car BLU	30.00	60.00
Ford J-Car BR	30.00	60.00
Ford J-Car CP	50.00	100.00
Ford J-Car G	30.00	60.00

1968 CUSTOM FLEETSIDE (BLUE)

1968 CUSTOM FLEETSIDE (PURPLE)

	LOOSE	IN PKG.
Ford J-Car GOL	30.00	60.00
Ford J-Car LB	30.00	60.00
Ford J-Car MAG	50.00	100.00
Ford J-Car OL	30.00	60.00
Ford J-Car OR	30.00	60.00
Ford J-Car PI	125.00	250.00
Ford J-Car PUR	35.00	80.00
Ford J-Car R	30.00	60.00
Ford J-Car RO	50.00	100.00
Ford J-Car WE	50.00	100.00
Ford J-Car Y	30.00	60.00
Hot Heap AF	50.00	100.00
Hot Heap AQ	35.00	75.00
Hot Heap BLU	35.00	75.00
Hot Heap BR	60.00	125.00
Hot Heap COP	60.00	125.00
Hot Heap G	35.00	75.00
Hot Heap GOL	35.00	75.00
Hot Heap HP	250.00	450.00
Hot Heap LB	75.00	150.00
Hot Heap LG	60.00	125.00
Hot Heap MAG	100.00	200.00
Hot Heap OL	35.00	75.00
Hot Heap OR	35.00	75.00
Hot Heap PI	200.00	450.00
Hot Heap PUR	60.00	125.00
Hot Heap R	35.00	75.00
Hot Heap RO	75.00	150.00
Hot Heap Y	35.00	75.00
Python AF	30.00	70.00
Python AQ	25.00	60.00
Python BLU	25.00	60.00
Python BR	75.00	175.00

1968 HOT HEAP (HOT PINK)

1968 CUSTOM MUSTANG (RED)

1968 CUSTOM MUSTANG (COPPER)

1968 HOT HEAP (ORANGE)

1968 CUSTOM MUSTANG (PURPLE)

1968 HOT HEAP (PURPLE)

1968 PYTHON (HOT PINK)

	LOOSE	IN PKG.
Python COP	50.00	100.00
Python CP	150.00	300.00
Python G	25.00	60.00
Python GOL	25.00	60.00
Python HP	300.00	600.00
Python LB	75.00	175.00
Python MAG	60.00	125.00
Python OL	50.00	100.00
Python OR	25.00	60.00
Python PI	200.00	400.00
Python PUR	50.00	100.00
Python R	25.00	60.00
Python Y	25.00	60.00
Silhouette AF	25.00	60.00
Silhouette AQ	20.00	50.00
Silhouette BLU	20.00	50.00
Silhouette CP	75.00	150.00
Silhouette G	20.00	50.00
Silhouette GOL	20.00	50.00
Silhouette HP	125.00	225.00
Silhouette IB	25.00	60.00
Silhouette LB	50.00	100.00
Silhouette LG	75.00	150.00
Silhouette MAG	75.00	150.00
Silhouette OL	20.00	50.00
Silhouette OR	20.00	50.00
Silhouette PI	75.00	150.00
Silhouette PUR	20.00	50.00
Silhouette R	20.00	50.00
Silhouette RO	50.00	100.00
Silhouette Y	20.00	50.00

1968 PYTHON (RED)

1968 SILHOUETTE (MAGENTA)

1968 CUSTOM MUSTANG (RED)

1968 SILHOUETTE (PURPLE)

1968 PYTHON (BLUE)

1969 Hot Wheels

	LOOSE	IN PKG.
'31 Ford Woody AF	50.00	100.00
'31 Ford Woody AQ	35.00	70.00
'31 Ford Woody BLU	35.00	70.00
'31 Ford Woody CP	100.00	200.00
'31 Ford Woody G	35.00	70.00
'31 Ford Woody GOL	35.00	70.00
'31 Ford Woody LB	75.00	200.00
'31 Ford Woody MAG	50.00	100.00
'31 Ford Woody OL	75.00	200.00
'31 Ford Woody OR	35.00	70.00
'31 Ford Woody PI	200.00	400.00
'31 Ford Woody PUR	35.00	70.00
'31 Ford Woody R	35.00	70.00
'31 Ford Woody RO	50.00	100.00
'31 Ford Woody Y	75.00	200.00
'32 Ford Vicky AF	40.00	100.00
'32 Ford Vicky AQ	35.00	80.00
'32 Ford Vicky BLU	35.00	80.00
'32 Ford Vicky BR	35.00	80.00
'32 Ford Vicky COP	50.00	125.00
'32 Ford Vicky G	35.00	80.00
'32 Ford Vicky GOL	35.00	80.00
'32 Ford Vicky LB	60.00	150.00
'32 Ford Vicky MAG	60.00	150.00
'32 Ford Vicky OL	35.00	80.00
'32 Ford Vicky OR	80.00	200.00
'32 Ford Vicky PI	550.00	1000.00
'32 Ford Vicky PUR	40.00	80.00
'32 Ford Vicky R	35.00	80.00
'32 Ford Vicky RO	50.00	125.00
'32 Ford Vicky Y	35.00	80.00
'36 Ford Coupe AF	60.00	150.00

1968 SILHOUETTE (PURPLE)

1968 CUSTOM T-BIRD (PINK)

1968 CUSTOM T-BIRD (ORANGE)

1968 CUSTOM T-BIRD (RED)

1968 CUSTOM VW (MAGENTA)

1968 CUSTOM T-BIRD (AQUA)

1969 VOLKSWAGEN BEACH BOMB (BLUE)

1969 VOLKSWAGEN BEACH BOMB (BLUE)

1969 VOLKSWAGEN BEACH BOMB (ORANGE)

1969 BRABHAM-REPCO F1 (OLIVE)

	LOOSE	IN PKG.
'36 Ford Coupe AQ	40.00	100.00
'36 Ford Coupe BLU	40.00	100.00
'36 Ford Coupe BR	40.00	100.00
'36 Ford Coupe G	40.00	100.00
'36 Ford Coupe GOL	40.00	100.00
'36 Ford Coupe LB	150.00	275.00
'36 Ford Coupe MAG	100.00	250.00
'36 Ford Coupe OL	50.00	125.00
'36 Ford Coupe OR	40.00	100.00
'36 Ford Coupe PI	250.00	500.00
'36 Ford Coupe PUR	40.00	100.00
'36 Ford Coupe R	40.00	100.00
'36 Ford Coupe RO	60.00	150.00
'36 Ford Coupe Y	40.00	100.00
'57 T-Bird AF	60.00	150.00
'57 T-Bird AQ	50.00	125.00
'57 T-Bird BLU	50.00	125.00
'57 T-Bird BR	50.00	125.00
'57 T-Bird G	50.00	125.00
'57 T-Bird GOL	50.00	125.00
'57 T-Bird LB	60.00	150.00
'57 T-Bird LG	75.00	175.00
'57 T-Bird MAG	75.00	175.00
'57 T-Bird OL	60.00	150.00
'57 T-Bird OR	50.00	125.00
'57 T-Bird PI	250.00	750.00
'57 T-Bird PUR	50.00	125.00
'57 T-Bird R	50.00	125.00
'57 T-Bird RO	75.00	175.00
'57 T-Bird Y	50.00	125.00
Brabham-Repco F1 AQ	25.00	60.00
Brabham-Repco F1 BLU	25.00	60.00
Brabham-Repco F1 COP	30.00	75.00

1968 CUSTOM VW (ORANGE)

1969 '31 WOODY
(LIME GOLD; WITHOUT BLACK ROOF)

	LOOSE	IN PKG.
Brabham-Repco F1 G	25.00	60.00
Brabham-Repco F1 OL	25.00	60.00
Brabham-Repco F1 OR	30.00	75.00
Brabham-Repco F1 PUR	25.00	60.00
Brabham-Repco F1 R	25.00	60.00
Chapparral 2G AF	40.00	75.00
Chapparral 2G AQ	25.00	50.00
Chapparral 2G BLU	25.00	50.00
Chapparral 2G BR	25.00	50.00
Chapparral 2G G	25.00	50.00
Chapparral 2G GOL	25.00	50.00
Chapparral 2G LB	35.00	70.00
Chapparral 2G LG	25.00	50.00
Chapparral 2G MAG	40.00	75.00
Chapparral 2G OL	40.00	75.00
Chapparral 2G OR	25.00	50.00
Chapparral 2G PI	150.00	300.00
Chapparral 2G PUR	40.00	75.00
Chapparral 2G R	25.00	50.00
Chapparral 2G RO	40.00	75.00
Chapparral 2G WH	40.00	75.00
Chapparral 2G Y	25.00	50.00
Continental Mark III AQ	50.00	125.00
Continental Mark III BLU	50.00	125.00
Continental Mark III G	50.00	125.00
Continental Mark III GOL	50.00	125.00
Continental Mark III LB	50.00	125.00
Continental Mark III LG	50.00	125.00
Continental Mark III MAG	60.00	150.00
Continental Mark III OL	75.00	150.00
Continental Mark III OR	50.00	125.00
Continental Mark III PI	125.00	250.00
Continental Mark III PUR	50.00	125.00

1969 BRABHAM-REPCO F1 (GREEN ENAMEL)

1969 CHAPPARRAL 2G (WHITE ENAMEL)

1969 CUSTOM CHARGER (HOT PINK)

1969 CUSTOM AMX (SALMON)

1969 FORD MK IV (RED ENAMEL)

1969 CONTINENTAL MARK III (BLUE)

1969 LOLA GT70 (GREEN ENAMEL)

1969 MASERATI MISTRAL (BLUE)

1969 McLAREN MG (ORANGE ENAMEL)

1969 MERCEDES 280 SL (OLIVE)

	LOOSE	IN PKG.
Continental Mark III R	50.00	125.00
Continental Mark III Y	50.00	125.00
Custom AMX AF	75.00	150.00
Custom AMX AQ	60.00	125.00
Custom AMX BLU	60.00	125.00
Custom AMX G	60.00	125.00
Custom AMX GOL	60.00	125.00
Custom AMX HP	200.00	350.00
Custom AMX LG	75.00	150.00
Custom AMX MAG	60.00	125.00
Custom AMX OR	60.00	125.00
Custom AMX PI	125.00	250.00
Custom AMX PUR	75.00	150.00
Custom AMX R	60.00	125.00
Custom AMX RO	60.00	125.00
Custom AMX SAL	125.00	250.00
Custom AMX Y	60.00	125.00
Custom Charger AF	125.00	250.00
Custom Charger AQ	100.00	225.00
Custom Charger BLU	100.00	225.00
Custom Charger BR	400.00	800.00
Custom Charger G	100.00	225.00
Custom Charger GOL	100.00	225.00
Custom Charger LG	100.00	225.00
Custom Charger MAG	125.00	250.00
Custom Charger OR	125.00	250.00
Custom Charger PI	250.00	400.00
Custom Charger PUR	125.00	250.00
Custom Charger R	100.00	225.00
Custom Charger RO	125.00	250.00
Custom Charger Y	100.00	225.00
Ford MK IV AQ	20.00	50.00
Ford MK IV BLU	20.00	50.00

1969 INDY EAGLE (GOLD CHROME)

	LOOSE	IN PKG.
Ford MK IV BR	30.00	60.00
Ford MK IV G	20.00	50.00
Ford MK IV GOL	20.00	50.00
Ford MK IV LB	20.00	50.00
Ford MK IV OL	20.00	50.00
Ford MK IV OR	20.00	50.00
Ford MK IV PUR	20.00	50.00
Ford MK IV R	20.00	50.00
Ford MK IV R En.	30.00	60.00
Ford MK IV Y	20.00	50.00
Indy Eagle AQ	25.00	60.00
Indy Eagle BLU	25.00	60.00
Indy Eagle COP	35.00	80.00
Indy Eagle G	25.00	60.00
Indy Eagle GOLP	125.00	250.00
Indy Eagle OL	30.00	70.00
Indy Eagle OR	25.00	60.00
Indy Eagle PUR	25.00	60.00
Indy Eagle R	25.00	60.00
Lola GT70 AF	30.00	60.00
Lola GT70 AQ	20.00	50.00
Lola GT70 BLU	20.00	50.00
Lola GT70 BR	20.00	50.00
Lola GT70 CP	50.00	100.00
Lola GT70 Dk.G En.	20.00	50.00
Lola GT70 G	20.00	50.00
Lola GT70 GOL	20.00	50.00
Lola GT70 LB	30.00	60.00
Lola GT70 OL	20.00	50.00
Lola GT70 OR	20.00	50.00
Lola GT70 PUR	20.00	50.00
Lola GT70 R	20.00	50.00
Lola GT70 Y	20.00	50.00

1969 POLICE CRUISER (PROTOTYPE)

1969 POLICE CRUISER (OPAQUE RED LIGHT)

1969 ROLLS ROYCE SILVER SHADOW
(GRAY ENAMEL)

1969 POLICE CRUISER (CLEAR RED LIGHT)

1969 SHELBY TURBINE (RED)

1969 SHELBY TURBINE (PROTOTYPE)

1969 TORERO (HOT PINK)

1969 TURBO FIRE (ROSE)

1969 TWIN MILL (ANTIFREEZE)

	LOOSE	IN PKG.
Lotus Turbine AQ	25.00	60.00
Lotus Turbine BLU	25.00	60.00
Lotus Turbine BR	25.00	60.00
Lotus Turbine G	25.00	60.00
Lotus Turbine MAG	50.00	100.00
Lotus Turbine OL	40.00	80.00
Lotus Turbine OR	25.00	60.00
Lotus Turbine PUR	25.00	60.00
Lotus Turbine R	25.00	60.00
Maserati Mistral AQ	70.00	150.00
Maserati Mistral BLU	70.00	150.00
Maserati Mistral BR	70.00	150.00
Maserati Mistral G	70.00	150.00
Maserati Mistral OL	100.00	200.00
Maserati Mistral OR	70.00	150.00
Maserati Mistral PUR	70.00	150.00
Maserati Mistral R	70.00	150.00
McLaren MGA AF	30.00	75.00
McLaren MGA AQ	25.00	50.00
McLaren MGA BLU	25.00	50.00
McLaren MGA BR	25.00	50.00
McLaren MGA G	25.00	50.00
McLaren MGA GOL	25.00	50.00
McLaren MGA LB	25.00	50.00
McLaren MGA LG	25.00	50.00
McLaren MGA MAG	25.00	50.00
McLaren MGA OL	25.00	50.00
McLaren MGA OR	25.00	50.00
McLaren MGA OR	50.00	200.00
McLaren MGA PUR	25.00	50.00
McLaren MGA R	25.00	50.00
McLaren MGA RO	30.00	75.00
Mercedes 280SL AQ	30.00	60.00

1969 '31 WOODY (UNPAINTED PROTOTYPE)

1969 '31 WOODY (GOLD)

	LOOSE	IN PKG.
Mercedes 280SL BLU	30.00	60.00
Mercedes 280SL COP	50.00	100.00
Mercedes 280SL G	30.00	60.00
Mercedes 280SL LB	50.00	100.00
Mercedes 280SL OL	30.00	60.00
Mercedes 280SL OR	30.00	60.00
Mercedes 280SL PUR	30.00	60.00
Mercedes 280SL R	30.00	60.00
Police Cruiser WH w/red dome light	75.00	150.00
Police Cruiser WH w/R opaque dome light	75.00	150.00
Rolls Royce SS AQ	40.00	75.00
Rolls Royce SS BLU	40.00	75.00
Rolls Royce SS G	40.00	75.00
Rolls Royce SS GR	35.00	60.00
Rolls Royce SS LG	35.00	60.00
Rolls Royce SS OR	100.00	200.00
Rolls Royce SS PI	250.00	500.00
Rolls Royce SS PUR	150.00	300.00
Rolls Royce SS R	40.00	75.00
Rolls Royce SS Y	40.00	75.00
Shelby Turbine AQ	20.00	50.00
Shelby Turbine BLU	20.00	50.00
Shelby Turbine COP	40.00	80.00
Shelby Turbine G	20.00	50.00
Shelby Turbine LG	50.00	100.00
Shelby Turbine OL	40.00	80.00
Shelby Turbine OR	20.00	50.00
Shelby Turbine PUR	20.00	50.00
Shelby Turbine R	20.00	50.00
Splittin Image AF	40.00	100.00
Splittin Image AQ	30.00	75.00
Splittin Image BLU	30.00	75.00

1969 '36 FORD COUPE (ANTIFREEZE)

1969 '36 FORD COUPE (HOT PINK)

1969 '36 FORD COUPE (LIME GOLD)

1969 '31 FORD WOODY (HOT PINK)

1969 '36 FORD COUPE (UNPAINTED PROTOTYPE)

1969 '32 FORD VICKY (HOT PINK)

1969 '57 T-BIRD (HOT PINK)

	LOOSE	IN PKG.
Splittin Image BR	30.00	75.00
Splittin Image G	30.00	75.00
Splittin Image GOL	30.00	75.00
Splittin Image LB	30.00	75.00
Splittin Image MAG	30.00	75.00
Splittin Image OL	30.00	75.00
Splittin Image OR	30.00	75.00
Splittin Image PI	30.00	75.00
Splittin Image PUR	30.00	75.00
Splittin Image R	30.00	75.00
Splittin Image RO	40.00	100.00
Torero AF	40.00	100.00
Torero AQ	25.00	60.00
Torero BLU	25.00	60.00
Torero BR	25.00	60.00
Torero CP	100.00	200.00
Torero G	25.00	60.00
Torero GOL	25.00	60.00
Torero LB	30.00	75.00
Torero LG	30.00	75.00
Torero MAG	30.00	75.00
Torero OL	25.00	60.00
Torero OR	25.00	60.00
Torero PI	150.00	250.00
Torero PUR	30.00	75.00
Torero R	25.00	60.00
Torero RO	40.00	100.00
Torero Y	25.00	60.00
Turbofire AF	30.00	60.00
Turbofire AQ	20.00	50.00
Turbofire BLU	20.00	50.00
Turbofire BR	20.00	50.00
Turbofire G	20.00	50.00

1970 AMBULANCE (WHITE ENAMEL)

1970 BOSS HOSS (CHROME)

1970 CARABO (LIGHT GREEN; WHITE INTERIOR)

1970 CARABO (HOT PINK)

1970 CARABO (RED; WHITE INTERIOR)

	LOOSE	IN PKG.
Turbofire GOL	20.00	50.00
Turbofire LB	20.00	50.00
Turbofire LG	20.00	50.00
Turbofire MAG	40.00	75.00
Turbofire OL	20.00	50.00
Turbofire OR	20.00	50.00
Turbofire PI	150.00	250.00
Turbofire PUR	20.00	50.00
Turbofire R	20.00	50.00
Turbofire RO	60.00	125.00
Twinmill AF	30.00	75.00
Twinmill AQ	25.00	60.00
Twinmill BLU	25.00	60.00
Twinmill CP	100.00	250.00
Twinmill G	25.00	60.00
Twinmill GOL	25.00	60.00
Twinmill LB	40.00	80.00
Twinmill LG	40.00	80.00
Twinmill MAG	50.00	100.00
Twinmill OL	40.00	80.00
Twinmill OR	25.00	60.00
Twinmill PI	200.00	500.00
Twinmill PUR	30.00	75.00.
Twinmill R	25.00	60.00
Twinmill RO	50.00	100.00
Twinmill Y	25.00	60.00
Volkswagen Beach Bomb AQ	150.00	400.00
Volkswagen Beach Bomb BLU	150.00	400.00
Volkswagen Beach Bomb COP	200.00	500.00
Volkswagen Beach Bomb G	150.00	400.00
Volkswagen Beach Bomb LG	175.00	450.00
Volkswagen Beach Bomb OL	150.00	400.00

1970 DUMP TRUCK (RED)

1970 DUMP TRUCK (YELLOW)

1970 FERRARI 312P (RED)

1970 CEMENT MIXER (LIGHT GREEN)

1970 FIRE CHIEF CRUISER (DARK RED)

1970 CEMENT MIXER (PURPLE)

1970 FIRE CHIEF CRUISER (RED)

	LOOSE	IN PKG.
Volkswagen Beach Bomb OR	200.00	500.00
Volkswagen Beach Bomb PUR	175.00	450.00
Volkswagen Beach Bomb R	175.00	450.00
Volkswagen Beach Bomb Y	175.00	450.00

1970 Hot Wheels

Boss Hoss CHR	75.00	
Carabo BLU	60.00	150.00
Carabo G	60.00	150.00
Carabo LG	60.00	150.00
Carabo MAG	60.00	150.00
Carabo PI	150.00	250.00
Carabo R	60.00	150.00
Carabo Y	60.00	150.00
Classic Nomad AQ	75.00	150.00
Classic Nomad BLU	75.00	150.00
Classic Nomad G	75.00	150.00
Classic Nomad LG	75.00	150.00
Classic Nomad MAG	100.00	200.00
Classic Nomad OL	100.00	200.00
Classic Nomad OR	75.00	150.00
Classic Nomad PI	125.00	250.00
Classic Nomad PUR	75.00	150.00
Classic Nomad R	75.00	150.00
Classic Nomad RO	100.00	200.00
Classic Nomad Y	75.00	150.00
Demon AQ	40.00	100.00
Demon BLU	40.00	100.00
Demon COP	50.00	125.00
Demon G	40.00	100.00
Demon LG	40.00	100.00
Demon OL	40.00	100.00

1970 FIRE ENGINE (RED ENAMEL)

1970 FIRE ENGINE (RED)

1970 HEAVY CHEVY (BROWN)

1970 HEAVY CHEVY (BLUE)

1970 HEAVY CHEVY (CHROME)

	LOOSE	IN PKG.
Demon OR	40.00	100.00
Demon PUR	40.00	100.00
Demon R	40.00	100.00
Demon Y	40.00	100.00
Ferrari 312P AQ	30.00	60.00
Ferrari 312P BLU	30.00	60.00
Ferrari 312P COP	50.00	100.00
Ferrari 312P G	30.00	60.00
Ferrari 312P LG	30.00	60.00
Ferrari 312P MAG	30.00	60.00
Ferrari 312P OL	30.00	60.00
Ferrari 312P OR	30.00	60.00
Ferrari 312P PI	60.00	125.00
Ferrari 312P PUR	40.00	75.00
Ferrari 312P R	30.00	60.00
Ferrari 312P R En.	30.00	60.00
Ferrari 312P R w/WH interior	200.00	350.00
Ferrari 312P RO	50.00	100.00
Ferrari 312P Y	30.00	60.00
Fire Chief Cruiser Dk. R	40.00	100.00
Fire Chief Cruiser R	30.00	80.00
Heavy Chevy AQ	75.00	200.00
Heavy Chevy BLU	75.00	200.00
Heavy Chevy BR	75.00	200.00
Heavy Chevy G	75.00	200.00
Heavy Chevy OL	150.00	300.00
Heavy Chevy OR	75.00	200.00
Heavy Chevy PUR	125.00	250.00
Heavy Chevy R	75.00	200.00
Jack Rabbit Special WH w/BLA int.	25.00	60.00
Jack Rabbit Special WH w/WH int.	25.00	60.00

1970 KING CUDA (ANTIFREEZE PROTOTYPE)

1970 KING CUDA (AQUA; BLACK ROOF)

1970 KING CUDA (CHROME)

1970 JACK RABBIT SPECIAL (WHITE)

1970 JACK RABBIT SPECIAL (BLUE TINTED WINDOWS)

1970 KING CUDA (BLUE)

71

1970 KING CUDA (ORANGE)

1970 LIGHT MY FIREBIRD (BLUE)

1970 LIGHT MY FIREBIRD (BLUE)

	LOOSE	IN PKG.
King Cuda AQ	80.00	160.00
King Cuda BLU	80.00	160.00
King Cuda BR	100.00	175.00
King Cuda CHR	80.00	160.00
King Cuda COP	100.00	175.00
King Cuda G	80.00	160.00
King Cuda OL	100.00	175.00
King Cuda OR	80.00	160.00
King Cuda PUR	80.00	160.00
King Cuda R	80.00	160.00
Light My Firebird AQ	75.00	175.00
Light My Firebird BLU	75.00	175.00
Light My Firebird COP	100.00	200.00
Light My Firebird G	75.00	175.00
Light My Firebird OL	75.00	175.00
Light My Firebird OR	75.00	175.00
Light My Firebird PUR	75.00	175.00
Light My Firebird R	75.00	175.00
Mantis AQ	40.00	80.00
Mantis BLU	40.00	80.00
Mantis BR	40.00	80.00
Mantis COP	50.00	100.00
Mantis G	40.00	80.00
Mantis LG	40.00	80.00
Mantis MAG	40.00	80.00
Mantis OL	40.00	80.00
Mantis OR	40.00	80.00
Mantis PI	50.00	100.00
Mantis PUR	40.00	80.00
Mantis R	40.00	80.00
Mantis RO	50.00	100.00
Mantis Y	40.00	80.00
Mighty Maverick AQ	80.00	160.00

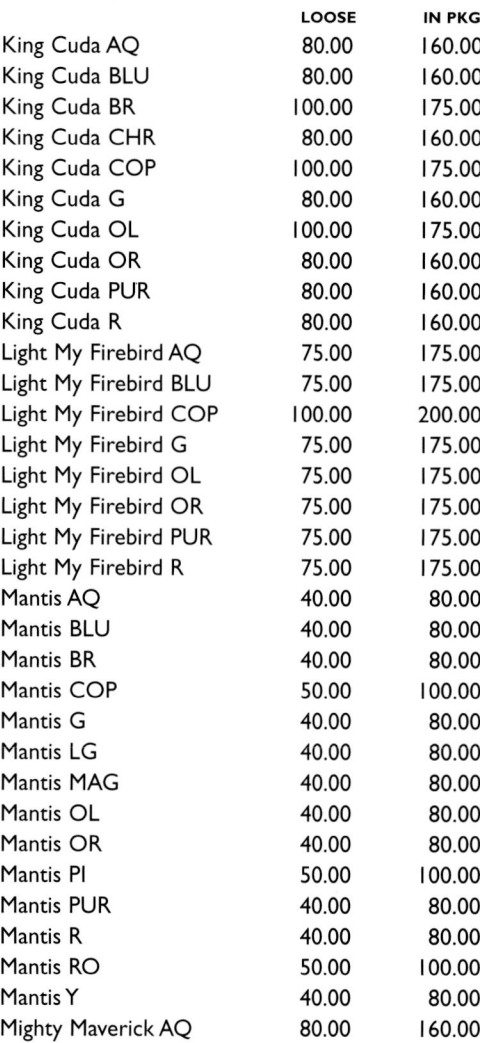

1970 MANTIS (ORANGE)

1970 MANTIS (MAGENTA)

1970 MIGHTY MAVERICK (COPPER; BROWN WING)

HOT WHEELS

	LOOSE	IN PKG.
Mighty Maverick BLU	80.00	160.00
Mighty Maverick COP	90.00	175.00
Mighty Maverick G	80.00	160.00
Mighty Maverick GOL	80.00	160.00
Mighty Maverick LG	80.00	160.00
Mighty Maverick MAG	80.00	160.00
Mighty Maverick OL	90.00	175.00
Mighty Maverick OR	100.00	175.00
Mighty Maverick PI	125.00	200.00
Mighty Maverick PUR	100.00	175.00
Mighty Maverick R	80.00	160.00
Mighty Maverick SAL	100.00	175.00
Mighty Maverick Y	80.00	160.00
Mod Quad BLU	40.00	100.00
Mod Quad G	40.00	100.00
Mod Quad GOL	40.00	100.00
Mod Quad LG	50.00	125.00
Mod Quad MAG	40.00	100.00
Mod Quad PI	125.00	250.00
Mod Quad PUR	40.00	100.00
Mod Quad R	40.00	100.00
Mod Quad SAL	60.00	150.00
Mod Quad Y	40.00	100.00
Mongoose Funny Car R Hong Kong	65.00	200.00
Mongoose Funny Car R U.S.	65.00	200.00
Nitty Gritty Kitty AQ	75.00	200.00
Nitty Gritty Kitty BLU	75.00	200.00
Nitty Gritty Kitty COP	100.00	225.00
Nitty Gritty Kitty G	75.00	200.00
Nitty Gritty Kitty OL	75.00	200.00
Nitty Gritty Kitty OR	75.00	200.00

1970 MOVING VAN (ORANGE)

1970 NITTY GRITTY KITTY (COPPER)

1970 MIGHTY MAVERICK (BLUE)

1970 NITTY GRITTY KITTY (PURPLE)

1970 MOD QUAD (PURPLE)

1970 NITTY GRITTY KITTY (BLUE; BLACK ROOF)

HOT CARS

1970 CLASSIC NOMAD (PURPLE)

1970 PADDY WAGON (BLUE ENAMEL)

1970 PEEPING BOMB (BLUE)

	LOOSE	IN PKG.
Nitty Gritty Kitty PUR	125.00	300.00
Nitty Gritty Kitty R	100.00	225.00
Paddy Wagon BLU Hong Kong	20.00	50.00
Paddy Wagon BLU w/GOL writing	20.00	50.00
Paddy Wagon BLU w/SIL writing	20.00	50.00
Peeping Bomb AQ	30.00	60.00
Peeping Bomb BLU	30.00	60.00
Peeping Bomb G	30.00	60.00
Peeping Bomb LG	30.00	60.00
Peeping Bomb MAG	30.00	60.00
Peeping Bomb OR	30.00	60.00
Peeping Bomb PI	75.00	150.00
Peeping Bomb PUR	40.00	70.00
Peeping Bomb R	30.00	60.00
Peeping Bomb Y	30.00	60.00
Porsche 917 AQ	40.00	75.00
Porsche 917 BLU	30.00	60.00
Porsche 917 G	30.00	60.00
Porsche 917 GR En.	50.00	100.00
Porsche 917 LG	30.00	60.00
Porsche 917 MAG	40.00	75.00
Porsche 917 PI	50.00	100.00
Porsche 917 PUR	50.00	100.00
Porsche 917 R	30.00	60.00
Porsche 917 RO	40.00	75.00
Porsche 917 SAL	50.00	100.00
Porsche 917 Y	30.00	60.00
Power Pad BLU	60.00	150.00
Power Pad G	60.00	150.00

1970 PORSCHE 917 (LIME GOLD)

1970 PORSCHE 917 (GREY ENAMEL)

1970 POWER PAD (HOT PINK)

HOT WHEELS

	LOOSE	IN PKG.
Power Pad LG	60.00	150.00
Power Pad MAG	60.00	150.00
Power Pad PI	125.00	250.00
Power Pad R	60.00	150.00
Power Pad RO	60.00	150.00
Power Pad Y	60.00	150.00
Red Baron R w/BLA interior	35.00	80.00
Red Baron R w/WH interior	300.00	
Sand Crab AQ	30.00	75.00
Sand Crab BLU	30.00	75.00
Sand Crab G	30.00	75.00
Sand Crab HP	70.00	150.00
Sand Crab LB	70.00	150.00
Sand Crab LG	30.00	75.00
Sand Crab MAG	30.00	75.00
Sand Crab OR	150.00	300.00
Sand Crab PI	60.00	125.00
Sand Crab R	30.00	75.00
Sand Crab RO	50.00	100.00
Sand Crab SAL	75.00	150.00
Sand Crab Y	30.00	75.00
Seasider BLU	100.00	250.00
Seasider G	75.00	200.00
Seasider LG	75.00	200.00
Seasider MAG	75.00	200.00
Seasider OR	100.00	250.00
Seasider PI	125.00	300.00
Seasider PUR	200.00	500.00
Seasider R	75.00	200.00
Seasider RO	100.00	200.00
Seasider Y	75.00	200.00
Snake Funny Car Y	75.00	300.00
Hong Kong		

1970 SAND CRAB (ORANGE)

1970 SEASIDER (BLUE)

1970 RED BARON (RED)

1970 SEASIDER
(ORANGE; WHITE INTERIOR PROTOTYPE)

1970 SKY SHOW FLEETSIDE (BLUE)

1970 SAND CRAB (BLUE; WHITE INTERIOR)

1970 SPLITTIN' IMAGE (ORANGE)

1970 SWINGIN' WING (HOT PINK)

**1970 SWINGIN' WING
(LIGHT GREEN; DARK INTERIOR)**

**1970 THE DEMON
(LIGHT GREEN; WHITE INTERIOR)**

	LOOSE	IN PKG.
Snake Funny Car Y U.S.	75.00	300.00
Sky Show Fleetside	75.00	
SS Fleetside w/ramp,plane AQ	400.00	
SS Fleetside w/ramp,plane BLU	400.00	
SS Fleetside w/ramp,plane LGF	400.00	
SS Fleetside w/ramp,plane OR	400.00	
SS Fleetside w/ramp,plane PI	500.00	
SS Fleetside w/ramp,plane PUR	400.00	
SS Fleetside w/ramp,plane R	400.00	
SS Fleetside w/ramp,plane RO	450.00	
Swingin' Wing AQ	25.00	60.00
Swingin' Wing BLU	25.00	60.00
Swingin' Wing G	25.00	60.00
Swingin' Wing LG	25.00	60.00
Swingin' Wing MAG	25.00	60.00
Swingin' Wing PI	50.00	100.00
Swingin' Wing PUR	30.00	75.00
Swingin' Wing RO	40.00	100.00
Swingin' Wing SAL	60.00	125.00
Swingin' Wing Y	25.00	60.00
TNT-Bird AQ	70.00	175.00
TNT-Bird BLU	70.00	175.00
TNT-Bird COP	100.00	200.00
TNT-Bird G	70.00	175.00
TNT-Bird LB	100.00	200.00
TNT-Bird OL	100.00	200.00
TNT-Bird OR	70.00	175.00
TNT-Bird PUR	100.00	200.00
TNT-Bird R	70.00	175.00
Tri-Baby AQ	50.00	100.00
Tri-Baby BLU	40.00	80.00
Tri-Baby G	40.00	80.00

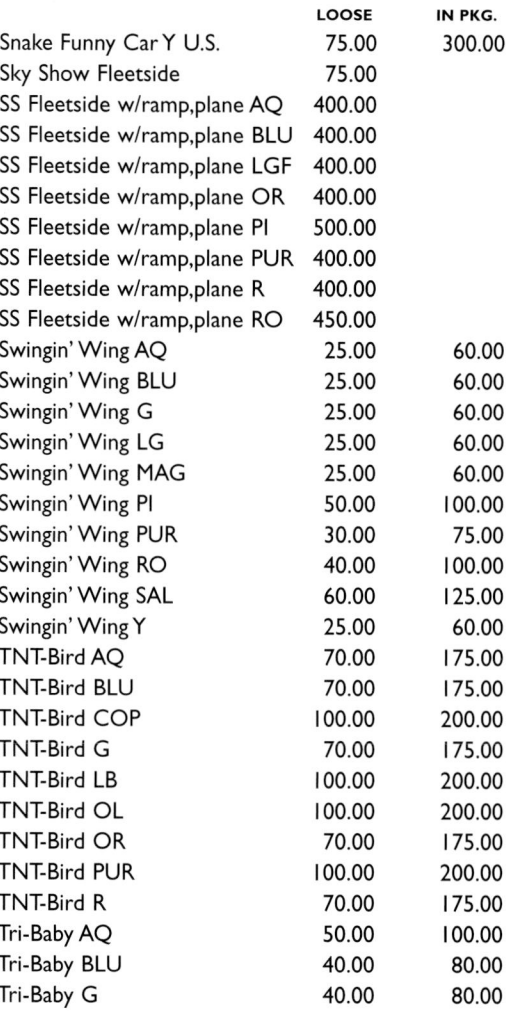

1970 THE DEMON (ORANGE)

1970 TOW TRUCK (ORANGE)

	LOOSE	IN PKG.
Tri-Baby LG	40.00	80.00
Tri-Baby LPI	75.00	150.00
Tri-Baby MAG	40.00	80.00
Tri-Baby PI	100.00	200.00
Tri-Baby R	40.00	80.00
Tri-Baby RO	60.00	125.00
Tri-Baby Y	40.00	80.00
Whip Creamer BLU	30.00	75.00
Whip Creamer G	30.00	75.00
Whip Creamer LG	30.00	75.00
Whip Creamer MAG	40.00	80.00
Whip Creamer PI	75.00	150.00
Whip Creamer PUR	75.00	150.00
Whip Creamer R	30.00	75.00
Whip Creamer RO	50.00	100.00
Whip Creamer Y	30.00	75.00

1970-71 Hot Wheels Heavyweights

Ambulance All WH	150.00	300.00
Ambulance AQ	50.00	100.00
Ambulance BLU	50.00	100.00
Ambulance COP	60.00	125.00
Ambulance G	50.00	100.00
Ambulance LG	50.00	100.00
Ambulance OL	50.00	100.00
Ambulance OR	60.00	125.00
Ambulance PI	150.00	300.00
Ambulance PUR	50.00	100.00
Ambulance R	50.00	100.00
Ambulance RO	60.00	125.00
Ambulance Y	50.00	100.00
Cement Mixer AQ	40.00	100.00

1970 TNT-BIRD (PURPLE)

1970 TNT-BIRD (OLIVE)

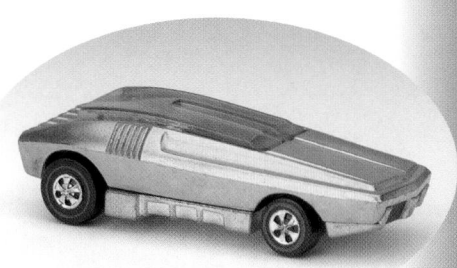

1970 WHIP CREAMER (LIGHT GREEN)

1970 TRI-BABY (LIGHT PINK)

1970 TRI-BABY (LIGHT GREEN)

1971 AMX I (BLUE)

1971 BOSS HOSS (OLIVE; BLACK ROOF)

1971 BOSS HOSS (AQUA)

1971 BOSS HOSS (PURPLE)

1971 BUGEYE (MAGENTA)

	LOOSE	IN PKG.
Cement Mixer BLU	40.00	100.00
Cement Mixer BR	40.00	100.00
Cement Mixer G	40.00	100.00
Cement Mixer LG	40.00	100.00
Cement Mixer OL	40.00	100.00
Cement Mixer OR	40.00	100.00
Cement Mixer PUR	50.00	125.00
Cement Mixer R	40.00	100.00
Cement Mixer WHE	150.00	300.00
Cement Mixer Y	40.00	100.00
Dump Truck AQ	50.00	125.00
Dump Truck BLU	50.00	125.00
Dump Truck BR	50.00	125.00
Dump Truck G	50.00	125.00
Dump Truck GOL	50.00	125.00
Dump Truck LG	50.00	125.00
Dump Truck OR	50.00	125.00
Dump Truck PUR	50.00	125.00
Dump Truck R	60.00	150.00
Dump Truck Y	50.00	125.00
Fire Engine R w/BLA int.	50.00	125.00
Fire Engine R w/WH int.	50.00	125.00
Fire Engine RE w/BLA int.	100.00	250.00
Fire Engine RE w/WH int.	100.00	250.00
Fuel Tanker WHE	75.00	175.00
Moving Van AQ	50.00	125.00
Moving Van BLU	50.00	125.00
Moving Van G	50.00	125.00
Moving Van LG	50.00	125.00
Moving Van OL	75.00	200.00
Moving Van OR	75.00	200.00
Moving Van PUR	75.00	200.00
Moving Van R	50.00	125.00

1971 BUGEYE (ROSE)

1971 BYE FOCAL (PURPLE)

	LOOSE	IN PKG.
Racer Rig R	75.00	250.00
Racer Rig WHE	75.00	250.00
S' Cool Bus Y	200.00	850.00
Scooper AQ	75.00	200.00
Scooper BLU	60.00	150.00
Scooper G	60.00	150.00
Scooper GOL	60.00	150.00
Scooper LG	60.00	150.00
Scooper OL	60.00	150.00
Scooper R	75.00	200.00
Scooper Y	60.00	150.00
Snorkel AQ	60.00	150.00
Snorkel BLU	60.00	150.00
Snorkel G	60.00	150.00
Snorkel GOL	60.00	150.00
Snorkel LG	60.00	150.00
Snorkel OL	60.00	150.00
Snorkel PI	125.00	250.00
Snorkel R	60.00	150.00
Snorkel WHE	125.00	250.00
Snorkel Y	60.00	150.00
Team Trailer R	75.00	175.00
Team Trailer WHE	75.00	175.00
Tow Truck AQ	50.00	100.00
Tow Truck BLU	50.00	100.00
Tow Truck BR	60.00	125.00
Tow Truck G	50.00	100.00
Tow Truck LG	50.00	100.00
Tow Truck OL	50.00	100.00
Tow Truck OR	50.00	100.00
Tow Truck PI	150.00	300.00
Tow Truck PUR	50.00	100.00
Tow Truck R	50.00	100.00

1971 CLASSIC CORD (PURPLE)

1971 CLASSIC CORD (MAGENTA)

1971 MONGOOSE RAIL DRAGSTER (BLUE)

1971 COCKNEY CAB (LIGHT PINK)

1971 COCKNEY CAB (LIGHT MAGENTA)

1971 SNAKE/MONGOOSE 2-PACK

1971 EEVIL WEEVIL (LIME GOLD)

	LOOSE	IN PKG.
Tow Truck Y	50.00	100.00
Waste Wagon AQ	60.00	125.00
Waste Wagon BLU	60.00	125.00
Waste Wagon G	60.00	125.00
Waste Wagon LG	60.00	125.00
Waste Wagon MAG	60.00	125.00
Waste Wagon OR	75.00	150.00
Waste Wagon R	75.00	150.00
Waste Wagon Y	60.00	125.00

1970-73 Hot Wheels Rrrumblers

Road Hog	30.00	75.00
High Tailer	30.00	75.00
Mean Machine	30.00	75.00
Rip Snorter	30.00	75.00
3-Squealer	30.00	75.00
Torque Chop	30.00	75.00
Straight Away	30.00	75.00
Devil's Duece	30.00	75.00
Roamin Candle	30.00	75.00
Bold Eagle	100.00	250.00
Choppin Chariot	30.00	75.00
Revolution	30.00	75.00
Preying Menace	150.00	400.00
Bone Shaker	150.00	400.00
Rip Code	150.00	400.00
Centurion	150.00	400.00

1971 Hot Wheels

AMX 2 BLU	75.00	100.00
AMX 2 G	45.00	100.00
AMX 2 LG	45.00	100.00

1971 EEVIL WEEVIL (RED)

1971 FUEL TANKER (WHITE ENAMEL)

1971 GRASS HOPPER (GREEN)

1971 FUEL TANKER (WHITE)

1971 HAIRY HAULER (MAGENTA)

	LOOSE	IN PKG.
AMX 2 MAG	45.00	100.00
AMX 2 PI	50.00	125.00
AMX 2 PUR	60.00	150.00
AMX 2 R	45.00	100.00
AMX 2 RO	50.00	125.00
AMX 2 Y	45.00	100.00
Boss Hoss AQ	125.00	275.00
Boss Hoss BLU	125.00	275.00
Boss Hoss COP	150.00	350.00
Boss Hoss G	125.00	275.00
Boss Hoss LMAG	200.00	500.00
Boss Hoss MAG	300.00	600.00
Boss Hoss OL	125.00	275.00
Boss Hoss OR	125.00	275.00
Boss Hoss PI	500.00	1000.00
Boss Hoss PUR	175.00	350.00
Boss Hoss R	125.00	275.00
Bugeye AQ	60.00	150.00
Bugeye BLU	60.00	150.00
Bugeye LG	60.00	150.00
Bugeye MAG	60.00	150.00
Bugeye PI	100.00	200.00
Bugeye R	60.00	150.00
Bugeye RO	100.00	250.00
Bugeye Y	60.00	150.00
Bye Focal AQ	125.00	300.00
Bye Focal BLU	125.00	300.00
Bye Focal G	125.00	300.00
Bye Focal LG	200.00	400.00
Bye Focal LI GOL	200.00	400.00
Bye Focal LMAG	150.00	400.00
Bye Focal MAG	125.00	300.00
Bye Focal PUR	300.00	600.00
Bye Focal R	400.00	1000.00

1971 MUTT MOBILE (MAGENTA)

1971 NOODLE HEAD (LIGHT PINK)

1971 NOODLE HEAD (MAGENTA)

1971 ICE T (YELLOW)

1971 RACER RIG (BLUE)

1971 JET THREAT (RED)

1971 OLDS 442 (BLUE)

1971 OLDS 442 (LIME GOLD)

1971 OLDS PREPRODUCTION
(RED; BLACK INTERIOR)

1971 PIT CREW (WHITE)

	LOOSE	IN PKG.
Classic Cord BLU	250.00	500.00
Classic Cord G	250.00	500.00
Classic Cord GOL	250.00	500.00
Classic Cord LG	250.00	500.00
Classic Cord MAG	250.00	500.00
Classic Cord PI	800.00	2000.00
Classic Cord PUR	400.00	1000.00
Classic Cord R	250.00	500.00
Classic Cord Y	250.00	500.00
Cockney Cab AQ	60.00	125.00
Cockney Cab BLU	60.00	125.00
Cockney Cab G	60.00	125.00
Cockney Cab LG	60.00	125.00
Cockney Cab LMAG	100.00	200.00
Cockney Cab MAG	75.00	150.00
Cockney Cab PI	150.00	300.00
Cockney Cab R	60.00	125.00
Cockney Cab Y	60.00	125.00
Eevil Weevil BLU	100.00	200.00
Eevil Weevil G	100.00	200.00
Eevil Weevil LG	100.00	200.00
Eevil Weevil MAG	125.00	250.00
Eevil Weevil PUR	125.00	250.00
Eevil Weevil R	100.00	200.00
Eevil Weevil Y	100.00	200.00
Grass Hopper AQ	40.00	75.00
Grass Hopper BLU	40.00	75.00
Grass Hopper G	40.00	75.00
Grass Hopper LG	40.00	75.00
Grass Hopper MAG	40.00	75.00
Grass Hopper PI	100.00	200.00
Grass Hopper PUR	50.00	100.00
Grass Hopper R	40.00	75.00
Grass Hopper RO	50.00	100.00

1971 PIT CREW (WHITE)

1971 PIT CREW (WHITE)

	LOOSE	IN PKG.
Grass Hopper SAL	50.00	100.00
Grass Hopper Y	40.00	75.00
Hairy Hauler BLU	35.00	70.00
Hairy Hauler G	35.00	70.00
Hairy Hauler LG	35.00	70.00
Hairy Hauler LB	40.00	75.00
Hairy Hauler MAG	35.00	70.00
Hairy Hauler PI	75.00	150.00
Hairy Hauler PUR	50.00	100.00
Hairy Hauler R	35.00	70.00
Hairy Hauler SAL	50.00	100.00
Hairy Hauler Y	35.00	70.00
Hood AQ	60.00	150.00
Hood BLU	60.00	150.00
Hood G	60.00	150.00
Hood GOL	60.00	150.00
Hood LG	60.00	150.00
Hood MAG	60.00	150.00
Hood OL	75.00	150.00
Hood PI	175.00	300.00
Hood PUR	75.00	175.00
Hood R	60.00	150.00
Hood RO	75.00	175.00
Hood Y	60.00	150.00
Ice T Y	60.00	175.00
Jet Threat AQ	60.00	150.00
Jet Threat BLU	60.00	150.00
Jet Threat G	75.00	175.00
Jet Threat GOL	60.00	150.00
Jet Threat LG	60.00	150.00
Jet Threat MAG	75.00	175.00
Jet Threat PUR	75.00	175.00
Jet Threat R	75.00	175.00
Jet Threat Y	60.00	150.00

1971 SCOOPER (WHITE ENAMEL)

1971 ROCKET BYE BABY (MAGENTA)

1971 SHORT ORDER (PURPLE)

1971 S'COOL BUS (YELLOW)

1971 STRIP TEASER (AQUA)

1971 S'COOL BUS (YELLOW)

1971 SIX SHOOTER (LIME)

1971 SIX SHOOTER (ICE BLUE)

1971 SNORKLE (ORANGE)

1971 SNORKLE (ORANGE)

	LOOSE	IN PKG.
Mongoose II BLU w/BLU windows Hong Kong	100.00	325.00
Mongoose II BLU U.S.	100.00	325.00
Mongoose Rail Dragster BLU	75.00	
Mongoose Rail Dragster BLU w/BLA front wheels	75.00	
Mutt Mobile AQ	75.00	150.00
Mutt Mobile BLU	75.00	150.00
Mutt Mobile GOL	75.00	150.00
Mutt Mobile LB	75.00	150.00
Mutt Mobile LMAG	125.00	200.00
Mutt Mobile MAG	125.00	275.00
Mutt Mobile R	125.00	275.00
Noodle Head AQ	60.00	175.00
Noodle Head BLU	60.00	175.00
Noodle Head GOL	75.00	200.00
Noodle Head LB	75.00	200.00
Noodle Head LG	60.00	175.00
Noodle Head MAG	60.00	175.00
Noodle Head PI	200.00	400.00
Noodle Head R	60.00	175.00
Noodle Head Y	60.00	175.00
Olds 442 BLU	450.00	750.00
Olds 442 G	450.00	750.00
Olds 442 LB	500.00	1000.00
Olds 442 LG	450.00	750.00
Olds 442 MAG	450.00	750.00
Olds 442 PI	800.00	2000.00
Olds 442 PUR	500.00	800.00
Olds 442 R	450.00	750.00
Olds 442 RO	500.00	800.00
Olds 442 Y	450.00	750.00
Pit Crew WH 6138	100.00	300.00

1971 SPECIAL DELIVERY (LIGHT BLUE)

1971 SPECIAL DELIVERY (LIGHT BLUE)

	LOOSE	IN PKG.
Rocket Bye Baby AQ	60.00	150.00
Rocket Bye Baby BLU	60.00	150.00
Rocket Bye Baby G	60.00	150.00
Rocket Bye Baby GOL	75.00	200.00
Rocket Bye Baby MAG	75.00	200.00
Rocket Bye Baby R	75.00	200.00
Rocket Bye Baby Y	60.00	150.00
Short Order AQ	60.00	150.00
Short Order BLU	125.00	250.00
Short Order G	60.00	150.00
Short Order GOL	60.00	150.00
Short Order LG	60.00	150.00
Short Order MAG	150.00	300.00
Short Order PUR	150.00	300.00
Short Order R	60.00	150.00
Short Order Y	60.00	150.00
Six Shooter AQ	100.00	200.00
Six Shooter BLU	100.00	200.00
Six Shooter GOL	100.00	200.00
Six Shooter LB	100.00	200.00
Six Shooter MAG	125.00	275.00
Six Shooter Y	100.00	200.00
Snake II 5953	100.00	300.00
Snake II WH U.S.	100.00	300.00
Snake II WH w/BLU windows Hong Kong	100.00	300.00
Snake Rail Dragster WH	75.00	
Snake Rail Dragster WH w/BLA front wheels	75.00	
Snake/Mongoose 2 Pk		1200.00
Special Delivery BLU	75.00	175.00
Special Delivery LB	75.00	175.00
Strip Teaser AQ	60.00	150.00
Strip Teaser BLU	60.00	150.00

1971 SUGAR CADDY (PURPLE)

1971 SUGAR CADDY (PURPLE)

1971 T-4-2 (MAGENTA)

1971 HOOD (HOT PINK)

1971 TEAM TRAILER (WHITE)

1971 HOOD (LIGHT GREEN)

1971 WASTE WAGON (BLUE)

1971 WASTE WAGON (LIME GOLD)

	LOOSE	IN PKG.
Strip Teaser GOL	100.00	200.00
Strip Teaser LB	150.00	300.00
Strip Teaser LG	100.00	200.00
Strip Teaser MAG	150.00	300.00
Strip Teaser Y	60.00	150.00
Sugar Caddy AQ	60.00	150.00
Sugar Caddy BLU	60.00	150.00
Sugar Caddy COP	100.00	250.00
Sugar Caddy G	60.00	150.00
Sugar Caddy LG	60.00	150.00
Sugar Caddy LMAG	100.00	250.00
Sugar Caddy OR	60.00	150.00
Sugar Caddy PI	150.00	300.00
Sugar Caddy PUR	60.00	150.00
Sugar Caddy R	60.00	150.00
Sugar Caddy Y	60.00	150.00
T-4-2 AQ	75.00	175.00
T-4-2 BLU	75.00	175.00
T-4-2 G	75.00	175.00
T-4-2 LG	75.00	175.00
T-4-2 LMAG	150.00	250.00
T-4-2 MAG	150.00	250.00
T-4-2 R	75.00	175.00
T-4-2 Y	75.00	175.00
What-4 AQ	100.00	200.00
What-4 BLU	100.00	200.00
What-4 G	100.00	200.00
What-4 GOL	100.00	200.00
What-4 MAG	150.00	300.00
What-4 PUR	150.00	300.00
What-4 R	100.00	200.00

1971 WHAT 4 (LIGHT GREEN)

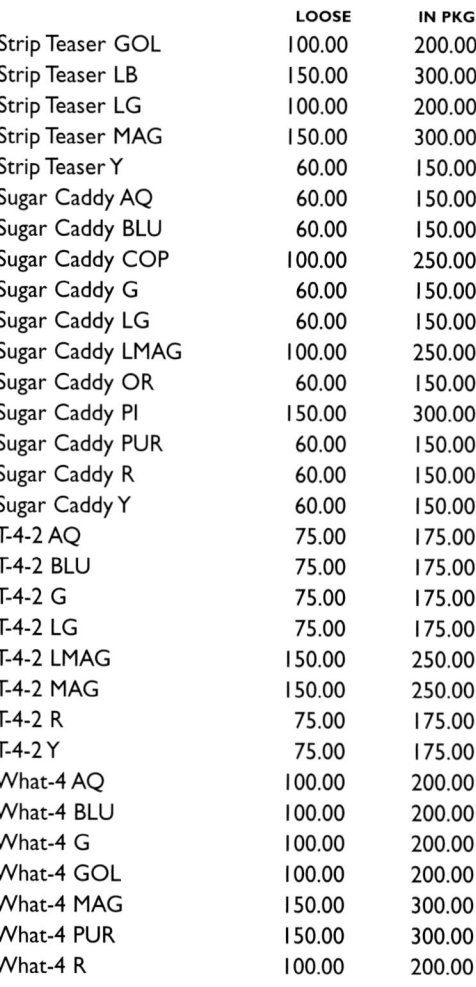

1972 FUNNY MONEY (GRAY)

1972 FERRARI 512S (BLUE)

1972 MERCEDES C111 (LIME GOLD)

1972 Hot Wheels

	LOOSE	IN PKG.
Ferrari 512S BLU	125.00	300.00
Ferrari 512S GOL	100.00	250.00
Ferrari 512S LG	100.00	250.00
Ferrari 512S MAG	100.00	250.00
Ferrari 512S R	100.00	250.00
Ferrari 512S Y	100.00	250.00
Funny Money GR	75.00	225.00
Mercedes C111 AQ	125.00	250.00
Mercedes C111 BLU	125.00	250.00
Mercedes C111 GOL	125.00	250.00
Mercedes C111 LG	125.00	250.00
Mercedes C111 MAG	125.00	250.00
Mercedes C111 R	125.00	250.00
Mercedes C111 Y	125.00	250.00
Open Fire BLU	175.00	350.00
Open Fire GOL	150.00	300.00
Open Fire MAG	150.00	300.00
Open Fire R	150.00	300.00
Open Fire Y	150.00	300.00
Rear Engine Mongoose BLU	140.00	500.00
Rear Engine Mongoose BLU w/BLA front wheels	140.00	500.00
Rear Engine Snake Y	140.00	500.00
Rear Engine Snake Y w/BLA front wheels	140.00	500.00
Side Kick AQ	125.00	350.00
Side Kick BLU	150.00	400.00
Side Kick GOL	125.00	350.00
Side Kick LG	125.00	350.00
Side Kick MAG	125.00	350.00
Side Kick R	125.00	350.00
Side Kick Y	125.00	350.00

1972 Hot Wheels Farbs

Hot Rodney 5854	30.00	75.00
Hy Gear 5850	30.00	75.00
Miles Ahead 5851	30.00	75.00
Red Catchup 5852	30.00	75.00

1972 OPEN FIRE (BLUE)

1972 OPEN FIRE (MAGENTA)

1972 SIDE KICK (MAGENTA)

1972 SIDE KICK (MAGENTA)

1973 Hot Wheels

	LOOSE	IN PKG.
Double Header	150.00	300.00
Superfine Turbine	350.00	750.00
Superfine Turbine PI	500.00	900.00
Sweet 16	200.00	500.00
Mercedes 280SL	100.00	250.00
Police Cruiser	200.00	400.00
Red Baron	30.00	100.00
Prowler	250.00	500.00
Paddy Wagon	40.00	125.00
Dune Daddy	100.00	200.00
Alive '55	150.00	400.00
Alive '55 OR	200.00	500.00
Alive '55 PUR	200.00	500.00
Snake	400.00	1000.00
Mongoose	400.00	1000.00
Street Snorter	150.00	400.00
Porsche 917	150.00	350.00
Porsche 917 PI	250.00	500.00
Ferrari 213P	200.00	500.00
Sand Witch	100.00	200.00
Double Vision	100.00	300.00
Double Vision PI	150.00	400.00
Buzz Off	100.00	250.00
Buzz Off HP	250.00	600.00
Xploder	125.00	300.00
Mercedes C111	250.00	500.00
Hiway Robber	110.00	225.00
Hiway Robber P	125.00	300.00
Hiway Robber PUR	125.00	300.00
Ice T	175.00	400.00
Odd Job	175.00	500.00
Show-off	200.00	500.00
Show-off PI	250.00	600.00
Show-off PUR	250.00	600.00

1973 Hot Wheels Revvers

Draggin' Dagger	25.00	60.00
Buzzin' Bomb	25.00	60.00
Stingin' Thing	25.00	60.00
Haulin' Horses	30.00	60.00
Burnin' Box	75.00	250.00
Jettin' Vette	50.00	125.00
Passin' Pride	25.00	60.00
Towin' Terror	100.00	300.00

'73 DOUBLE HEADER

'73 SUPER FINE TURBINE

'73 SWEET 16

1974 Hot Wheels

	LOOSE	IN PKG.
Road King Truck	150.00	
Road King Truck w/Trailer	750.00	
Rash I	40.00	75.00
Rash I LG	50.00	80.00
Rash I DB	300.00	500.00
Carabo	40.00	75.00
Carabo Y	300.00	500.00
Winnipeg	100.00	175.00
Heavy Chevy	110.00	175.00
Heavy Chevy LG	400.00	700.00
Volkswagen	50.00	100.00
Funny Money	60.00	150.00
Grass Hopper	40.00	80.00
Top Eliminator	90.00	200.00
Baja Bruiser	35.00	60.00
Baja Bruiser Yellow	300.00	500.00
Rodger Dodger	50.00	100.00
Steam Roller	40.00	70.00
Sir Rodney Roadster	60.00	125.00
Breakaway Bucket	50.00	100.00
El Rey Special	35.00	60.00
El Rey Special Light Green	60.00	125.00
El Rey Special Dark Blue	250.00	500.00
El Rey Special Light Blue	350.00	600.00

'74 BREAKAWAY BUCKET

1975 Hot Wheels

	LOOSE	IN PKG.
Dune Daddy	40.00	75.00
Mustang Stocker	125.00	250.00
Torino Stocker	40.00	100.00
P-911	40.00	80.00
P-911 WH	1500.00	
Super Van	40.00	80.00
Emergency Squad	20.00	35.00
Sand Drifter	50.00	100.00
Gremlin Grinder	25.00	50.00
Mighty Maverick	40.00	75.00
Warpath	40.00	100.00
Tough Customer	20.00	40.00
Vega Bomb	50.00	100.00
Vega Bomb LG	400.00	1000.00
Ramblin' Wrecker	20.00	35.00
Monte Carlo Stocker	50.00	125.00
Paramedic	20.00	35.00
American Victory	25.00	50.00
Gun Slinger	25.00	50.00
Chief's Special	35.00	60.00
Ranger Rig	20.00	40.00
Motorcross	100.00	200.00
Street Eater	75.00	175.00
Backwoods Bomb	35.00	70.00
Chevy Monza 2+2	35.00	60.00
Large Charge	25.00	40.00

'75 P-911 WH

'74 BAJA BRUISER

'74 HEAVY CHEVY

'74 TOP ELIMINATOR

'74 PROWLER

1975 Hot Wheels Super Chromes

	LOOSE	IN PKG.
Gremlin Grinder	30.00	50.00
Monza 2+2	30.00	50.00
Mustang Stocker	65.00	125.00
P-917	75.00	150.00
Super Van	30.00	50.00
P-911	30.00	60.00
Prowler	30.00	60.00
Steam Roller	30.00	60.00
Mighty Maverick	30.00	60.00
Alive '55	40.00	75.00
Large Charge	40.00	75.00
Heavy Chevy	50.00	100.00

1976 Hot Wheels

	LOOSE	IN PKG.
Formula P.A.C.K.	25.00	50.00
Rock Buster	25.00	40.00
American Tipper	25.00	50.00
Gun Bucket	25.00	40.00
American Hauler	25.00	50.00
Formula 5000	25.00	40.00
Cool One	45.00	75.00
Khaki Kooler	25.00	40.00
Maxi Taxi	40.00	75.00
Lowdown	35.00	60.00
Inferno	35.00	60.00
Poison Pinto	30.00	50.00
Corvette Stingray	60.00	125.00
Street Rodder	45.00	75.00
Aw Shoot	15.00	25.00
Neet Streeter	40.00	70.00
Staff Car	650.00	

1977 Hot Wheels

	LOOSE	IN PKG.
'57 Chevy	40.00	80.00
Z Whiz	15.00	40.00
Z-Whiz WH	1500.00	
Fire Eater	15.00	25.00
Spoiler Sport	20.00	40.00
Odd Rod	50.00	125.00
Letter Getter	15.00	30.00
Letter Getter RL	400.00	
Second Wind	50.00	100.00
GMC Motor Home	15.00	30.00
GMC Motor Home RL	400.00	
Show Hoss II	40.00	75.00
Show Hoss II RL	300.00	500.00
'56 Hi-Tail Hauler	25.00	50.00
T-Totaller	15.00	30.00
T-Totaller RL	500.00	
'31 Doozie	25.00	50.00
Thrill Drivers Torino	75.00	

1978 Hot Wheels

	LOOSE	IN PKG.
Jaguar XJS	15.00	25.00
'57 T-Bird	15.00	30.00
Hot Bird	25.00	75.00
Packin' Pacer	10.00	25.00
A-OK	20.00	35.00
Lickety Six	20.00	40.00
Science Friction	15.00	35.00
Highway Patrol	10.00	25.00
Stagefright	10.00	20.00
Race Bait 308	10.00	25.00
Baja Breaker	15.00	25.00
Army Funny Car	25.00	40.00
American Victory	15.00	35.00
Jet Threat II	15.00	30.00
Formula P.A.C.K.	20.00	40.00
Cool One	25.00	50.00
Prowler	15.00	30.00

1979 Hot Wheels

	LOOSE	IN PKG.
Corvette Stingray	20.00	35.00
Jaguar XJS	8.00	15.00
Up Front 924	10.00	20.00
Royal Flash	8.00	15.00
Greased Gremlin	20.00	35.00
Spacer Racer	10.00	20.00
Hare Splitter	6.00	15.00
Auburn 852	8.00	15.00
Flat Out	8.00	15.00
Dumpin' A	15.00	25.00
Vetty Funny	20.00	35.00
Bywayman	10.00	20.00
Inside Story	10.00	20.00
Bubble Gunner	8.00	15.00
Fire Chaser	8.00	15.00
The Incredible Hulk	45.00	75.00
Spider-Man	40.00	75.00
Motorcross Team	40.00	100.00
S.W.A.T. Van	60.00	120.00
Space Van	50.00	100.00
Spider-Man Van	40.00	80.00
Spoiler Sport	15.00	25.00
Hulk Spoiler Sport	25.00	60.00
Captain America	50.00	100.00
Thor	20.00	35.00
Human Torch	25.00	50.00
The Thing	25.00	50.00
Hot Bird	20.00	40.00
Ferrari 308	10.00	20.00
Torino Stocker	20.00	40.00
Toys R Us Pickup	20.00	40.00
Monte Carlo Stocker	30.00	50.00
California Cruisin'	8.00	15.00
Large Charge	10.00	20.00
Z-Whiz	12.00	20.00
Show Hoss II GR	40.00	70.00

'74 ROAD KING TRUCK

'74 RODGER DODGER

'74 RODGER DODGER

'74 TOP ELIMINATOR

'74 SIR RODNEY ROADSTER

'75 MAXI TAXI

1980 Hot Wheels

	LOOSE	IN PKG.
Turbo Mustang	15.00	30.00
Stutz Blackhawk	12.00	20.00
Greyhound MC-8	25.00	60.00
Super Scraper	8.00	15.00
Tricar X8	8.00	15.00
40's Woodie	15.00	40.00
3-Window '34	20.00	35.00
Dodge D-50	10.00	20.00
Turbo Wedge	8.00	15.00
'Vette Van	10.00	20.00
Split Window '63	15.00	25.00
CAT Forklift	15.00	25.00
Peterbilt Cement Mixer	6.00	12.00
CAT Dump Truck	5.00	10.00
CAT Bulldozer	5.00	10.00
CAT Wheeler Loader	10.00	20.00
Hiway Hauler	15.00	30.00
P-911 Turbo	20.00	40.00
'56 Hi-Tail Hauler	15.00	30.00

1981 Hot Wheels

	LOOSE	IN PKG.
Peterbilt Tank Truck	6.00	10.00
Bronco 4-Wheeler	6.00	12.00
Cannonade	6.00	10.00
Omni 024	6.00	12.00
Chevy Citation	8.00	15.00
Turismo	6.00	12.00
Old Number 5	10.00	20.00
'37 Bugatti	6.00	10.00
Minitrek	8.00	15.00
Cadillac Seville	6.00	12.00
Airport Rescue	12.00	20.00
Mirada Stocker	15.00	25.00
Sheriff Patrol	6.00	12.00
Firebird Funny Car	8.00	15.00
Jeep CJ-7	6.00	12.00
Silver Surfer	20.00	40.00
Iron Man	20.00	40.00
Circus Cats	60.00	125.00
Rescue Squad	50.00	100.00
Racing Team	50.00	100.00
Turbo Mustang	8.00	15.00
Chevy Citation	6.00	10.00
Dixie Challenger	15.00	30.00
Top Eliminator	20.00	40.00
Baja Bruiser	15.00	30.00
'31 Doozie	8.00	15.00

1982 Hot Wheels

	LOOSE	IN PKG.
Stutz Blackhawk	8.00	15.00
Vette Van	10.00	25.00
Split Window '63	10.00	20.00
'57 T-Bird	25.00	50.00

	LOOSE	IN PKG.
Packin' Pacer	8.00	15.00
Science Friction	15.00	25.00
Race Bait 308	8.00	15.00
Pepsi Challenger	25.00	60.00
Royal Flash	6.00	12.00
'35 Classic Caddy	8.00	15.00
Ford Dump Truck	6.00	12.00
Construction Crane	10.00	20.00
Rapid Transit	10.00	20.00
Aries Wagon	8.00	15.00
Land Lord	5.00	10.00
Mercedes 380 SEL	6.00	12.00
Peugeot 505	6.00	12.00
Turbo Mustang	8.00	15.00
Mercedes	8.00	15.00
Trash Truck	6.00	10.00
'55 Chevy	10.00	20.00
Taxi	8.00	15.00
Camaro Z28	10.00	25.00
Megadestroyer 2	20.00	35.00
Megadestroyer 1	20.00	35.00
Personnel Carrier	20.00	40.00
Battle Tank	15.00	30.00
Tac-Com	20.00	40.00
Mustang Stocker	40.00	100.00
P-911 Turbo	6.00	12.00
Malibu Grand Prix	8.00	15.00
Corvette Stingray	12.00	20.00
Z Whiz	12.00	20.00
Spoiler Sport	10.00	20.00

1982-85 Hot Wheels Real Riders

	LOOSE	IN PKG.
A-OK	250.00	400.00
Path Beater	20.00	35.00
Classic Cobra	20.00	50.00
'57 T-Bird	20.00	50.00
Rescue Ranger	25.00	50.00
Power Plower	15.00	35.00
Jeep CJ7	15.00	35.00
Thunderstreak	20.00	35.00
Jeep Scrambler	20.00	40.00
Baja Bug	20.00	40.00
BMW MI	30.00	60.00
Super Scraper	15.00	40.00
3-Window '34	25.00	50.00
Dodge D-50	20.00	40.00
'63 Split Window Vette	30.00	70.00
Bronco 4-Wheeler	20.00	40.00
Race Bait	25.00	50.00
Baja Breaker	15.00	35.00
Bywayman	20.00	40.00
Mercedes 380 SEL	15.00	35.00
Formula Fever	15.00	35.00
40's Ford 2-Door	40.00	80.00

'75 COOL ONE

'75 NEET STREETER

'75 MUSTANG STOCKER

'75 MUSTANG STOCKER

'75 SAND DRIFTER

'75 GREMLIN GRINDER

Beach Patrol	25.00	50.00
Lightning Gold	20.00	40.00
Malibu Grand Prix	15.00	35.00
Dodge Rampage	15.00	35.00
Dream Van XGW	20.00	40.00
Street Rodder	35.00	70.00
Good 'Ol Pick-Um-Up	40.00	80.00
Black Lightning	15.00	35.00

1983 Hot Wheels

	LOOSE	IN PKG.
Tricar X8	5.00	10.00
Hiway Hauler	15.00	30.00
Toys R Us Bronco	40.00	75.00
Omni 024	6.00	12.00
Minitrek	8.00	15.00
Up Front 924	6.00	12.00
Flat Out 442	8.00	15.00
Vetty Funny	20.00	35.00
Sunagon	12.00	25.00
Datsun 200SX	18.00	30.00
Front Runnin' Fairmont	15.00	25.00
Ford Escort	10.00	20.00
Pontiac J-2000	8.00	15.00
'80's Firebird	8.00	15.00
'40's Ford 2-Door	25.00	40.00
Long Shot	8.00	15.00
Classic Cobra BL BW	25.00	40.00
Thunder Roller	6.00	12.00
'82 Supra	8.00	15.00
'80's Corvette	10.00	20.00
Firebird Funny Car	8.00	15.00
Peterbilt Dump Truck	6.00	12.00
Ford Stake Bed Truck	6.00	12.00
'56 Hi Tail Hauler	8.00	15.00
Super Scraper	6.00	10.00
Bronco 4 Wheeler	8.00	15.00
BMW M1	15.00	25.00
Turbo Streak	6.00	12.00
Jeep Scrambler	10.00	20.00
P-928	10.00	20.00
Camaro Z28	15.00	30.00
Ramblin' Wrecker	12.00	25.00

1984 Hot Wheels

	LOOSE	IN PKG.
Tricar X8	5.00	10.00
CAT Forklift	8.00	15.00
Peterbilt Cement Mixer	5.00	10.00
CAT Dump Truck	5.00	10.00
CAT Bulldozer	5.00	10.00
Car Wheel Loader	5.00	10.00
Hiway Hauler	15.00	30.00
Tank Truck	6.00	12.00
Cannonade	5.00	10.00
Old Number 5	6.00	12.00
'37 Bugatti	5.00	10.00

Airport Rescue	8.00	15.00
T-Bird	8.00	15.00
Sheriff Patrol	5.00	10.00
Pepsi Challenger	25.00	50.00
Greased Gremlin	10.00	20.00
Auburn 852	6.00	12.00
Flat Out 442	5.00	10.00
Vetty Funny	20.00	35.00
Car Fire Chaser	5.00	10.00
Firebird Funny	8.00	15.00
'35 Classic Caddy	6.00	12.00
Construction Crane	10.00	20.00
Datsun 200SX	18.00	30.00
Team Bus	5.00	10.00
Front Runnin' Fairmont	8.00	15.00
Landlord	5.00	10.00
Ford Escort	10.00	20.00
Rolls Royce	5.00	10.00
Turbo Mustang	8.00	15.00
Dixie Challenger	10.00	20.00
Mercedes	5.00	10.00
Trash Truck	5.00	10.00
'67 Camaro	25.00	75.00
Rig Wrecker	5.00	10.00
Pontiac J-2000	5.00	10.00
80's Firebird	6.00	12.00
Classic Packard	12.00	30.00
Long Shot	5.00	10.00
Thunder Roller	5.00	10.00
'82 Supra	6.00	10.00
Racing Stocker	20.00	40.00
80's Corvette	6.00	12.00
Peterbilt Dump Truck	5.00	10.00
Ford Stake Bed Truck	6.00	12.00
Sunagon	10.00	20.00
'56 Hi Tail Hauler	6.00	12.00
'31 Doozie	6.00	12.00
Super Scraper	5.00	10.00
40's Woodie	10.00	20.00
'34 3 Window	8.00	15.00
Dodge D-50	6.00	12.00
'63 Split Window	15.00	30.00
Bronco 4-Wheeler	6.00	12.00
'57 T-Bird	8.00	15.00
Baja Breaker	8.00	15.00
Bywayman	6.00	12.00
Jeep CJ7	6.00	12.00
Turbo Streak	5.00	10.00
Formula Fever	8.00	15.00
40's Ford 2-Door	10.00	25.00
Beach Patrol	10.00	20.00
Classic Cobra	15.00	35.00
Jeep Scrambler	6.00	12.00
Lightning Gold	8.00	15.00
Battle Tank	5.00	10.00
Troop Convoy	5.00	10.00
'55 Chevy	8.00	15.00
Camaro Z28	10.00	20.00

'76 HEAVY CHEVY

'76 STAFF CAR

'76 HEAVY CHEVY

'76 STREET RODDER

'76 MAXI TAXI

'76 MUSTANG STOCKER

T-Bird Stocker	20.00	40.00
Blown Camaro	6.00	12.00
Sol-Aire CX4	5.00	10.00
Dodge Rampage	6.00	12.00
Good Humor Truck	10.00	20.00
Oshkosh Snow Plow	8.00	15.00
Phone Truck	10.00	20.00
Baja Bug	5.00	10.00
'65 Mustang	15.00	25.00
Dream Van	6.00	12.00
Blazer 4x4	6.00	12.00
Turbo Heater	6.00	12.00
Predator	6.00	12.00
Flame Runner	5.00	10.00
Quick Trick	5.00	10.00
Wind Splitter	5.00	10.00
Speed Seeker	6.00	12.00
Torino Stocker	10.00	20.00
P-911 Turbo	5.00	10.00
Emergency Squad	6.00	15.00
Ramblin' Wrecker	8.00	15.00
Corvette Stingray	10.00	20.00
Neet Steeter	20.00	40.00
'57 Chevy	12.00	25.00
Fire Eater	5.00	10.00
Delivery Van	10.00	20.00

1985 Hot Wheels 4-Car Gift Pack

	LOOSE	IN PKG.
Construction GP	15.00	25.00
Off-Road 4x4 GP	15.00	25.00
Battleground GP	15.00	25.00
Ultra Hots GP	15.00	25.00
Speed Busters GP	15.00	25.00

1985 Hot Wheels 6-Car Gift Pack

	LOOSE	IN PKG.
Weekend GP	25.00	50.00
City GP	100.00	150.00
Racer GP	40.00	100.00
60's Teen GP	40.00	100.00
Competition GP	60.00	125.00
Classic 6-Car GP	30.00	50.00

1985 Hot Wheels Action Command Military Vehicles

Command Tank	5.00	10.00
Big Bertha	5.00	10.00
Super Cannon	5.00	10.00
Tank Gunner	5.00	10.00
Roll Patrol Jeep CJ	5.00	10.00
Troop Convoy	4.00	8.00

1985 Hot Wheels Bash 'N Smash

Crash Patrol	2.00	5.00
Smak Bak	2.00	5.00
Stocker Smasher	2.00	5.00
Fire Smasher	2.00	5.00
Hatch Popper	2.00	5.00
Sport Crasher	2.00	5.00
Bang-Up Job	2.00	5.00
Sidebanger	2.00	5.00
Bumper Thumper	2.00	5.00
Top Bopper	2.00	5.00
Smash Hit	2.00	5.00
Smash Mobile	2.00	5.00
Speed Crasher	2.00	5.00
Super Blaster	2.00	5.00
Front Ender	4.00	8.00
Hood Basher	2.00	5.00

1985 Hot Wheels Originals

Tricar X8	5.00	10.00
Old Number 5	5.00	10.00
Auburn 852	5.00	10.00
Firebird Funny Car	5.00	10.00
Team Bus	4.00	8.00
Rolls Royce Phantom II	4.00	8.00
Dixie Challenger	10.00	20.00
Firebird Funny Car	5.00	10.00
Split Window '63	10.00	20.00
'65 Mustang	10.00	20.00
Blazer 4x4	6.00	10.00
Tall Ryder	5.00	10.00
XT-3	5.00	10.00
Gulch Stepper	4.00	8.00
Screamin'	15.00	40.00
'57 T-Bird	8.00	15.00
Flat Fendered '40	10.00	20.00
Turbo Heater	5.00	10.00
Corvette Stingray	8.00	15.00
Sheriff Patrol	5.00	10.00
Emergency Squad	6.00	15.00
'57 Chevy	10.00	20.00

1985 Hot Wheels The Hot Ones

Cannonade	5.00	8.00
Hot Bird	10.00	20.00
'80's Firebird	5.00	8.00
'82 Supra	8.00	15.00
Racing Stocker	12.00	30.00
'80's Corvette	6.00	10.00
Thunderbird Stocker	8.00	20.00
Blown Camaro Z-280	5.00	10.00
Fiero 2M4	5.00	10.00
Nissan 300 ZX	5.00	8.00
P-911 Turbo	5.00	10.00

'76 P-911

'76 ROCK BUSTER

'77 HI TAIL HAULER

'77 SHOW HOSS II

'77 SHOW HOSS II

'77 ODD ROD

Mustang S.V.O.	8.00	15.00
Camaro Z-28	6.00	10.00
Torino Tornado	20.00	35.00

1985 Hot Wheels Ultra Hots

Bronco 4-Wheeler	6.00	10.00
Baja Breaker	6.00	12.00
Bywayman	8.00	15.00
Lightning Gold	5.00	10.00
Sol-Aire CX-4	5.00	10.00
Dodge Rampage	5.00	10.00
Flame Runner	6.00	12.00
Speed Seeker	5.00	10.00
Jet Sweep	6.00	12.00
Redliner	5.00	10.00
Silver Bullet	5.00	10.00
Street Scorcher	15.00	40.00
Nightstreaker	6.00	12.00
Street Beast	10.00	20.00
Aggressor	6.00	10.00
Dodge D-50	6.00	12.00
Pavement Pounder	6.00	12.00
Jeep CJ-7	6.00	12.00
Black Lightning	6.00	10.00
Thunderstreak	6.00	10.00
Dream Van XGW	5.00	10.00
Jeep Scrambler	6.00	12.00
Baja Bug	6.00	10.00

1985 Hot Wheels Workhorses

CAT Forklift	4.00	8.00
Peterbilt Cement Truck	4.00	8.00
CAT Dump Truck	4.00	8.00
CAT Bulldozer	4.00	8.00
Rig Wrecker	5.00	10.00
Thunder Roller	4.00	8.00
Good Humor Truck	5.00	10.00
Oshkosh Snow Plow	5.00	10.00
Phone Truck	6.00	12.00
Hiway Hauler	15.00	30.00
Peterbilt Dump Truck	4.00	8.00
Ford Stake Bed Truck	5.00	10.00

1986 Hot Wheels 5-Car Gift Packs

Classic GP	15.00	25.00
Ultra Hots GP	15.00	25.00
Racers GP	15.00	25.00
Super Sportscars GP	15.00	25.00

1986 Hot Wheels Action Command

Shell Shocker	4.00	8.00
Combat Medic	5.00	10.00

Command Tank	4.00	8.00
Big Bertha	4.00	8.00
Super Cannon	4.00	8.00
Tank Gunner	4.00	8.00
Roll Patrol Jeep CJ	4.00	8.00
Troop Convoy	4.00	8.00

1986 Hot Wheels Crack-Ups

Slammer	2.00	5.00
Super Denter	2.00	5.00
Knocker Stocker	2.00	5.00
Slidegrinder	2.00	5.00
Bangster	2.00	5.00
Smash Mobile	2.00	5.00
Stocker Smasher	2.00	5.00
Fire Smasher	2.00	5.00
Sport Crasker	2.00	5.00
Crunch Chief	3.00	6.00
Blind Sider	2.00	5.00
Back Biter Vehicle	2.00	5.00
Bank Up Job	2.00	5.00
Sidebanger	2.00	5.00
Bumper Thumper	2.00	5.00
Top Bopper	2.00	5.00
Speed Crasher	2.00	5.00
Super Blaster	2.00	5.00
Front Ender	4.00	8.00
Hood Basher	2.00	5.00

1986 Hot Wheels Flip Outs

Road Flipper	5.00	10.00
Flipper Snapper	5.00	10.00
Vaultin' Van	5.00	10.00
Capsider	5.00	10.00
Flipbuster	5.00	10.00
Fliproarin'	5.00	10.00
Flippin' Frenzy	5.00	10.00
Drag Flip	5.00	10.00

1986 Hot Wheels Hot Ones

Hot Bird	8.00	15.00
Race Ace	10.00	25.00
Stock Rocket	10.00	25.00
'55 Chevy	20.00	40.00
Highway Heat	10.00	20.00
'80 Firebird	5.00	10.00
'82 Supra Vehicle	4.00	8.00
'80's Corvette	6.00	12.00
Thunderbird Stocker	10.00	20.00
Blown Camaro Z-28	5.00	10.00
Fiero 2M4	4.00	8.00
Nissan 300 ZX	4.00	8.00
P-911 Turbo	4.00	8.00
Corvette Stingray	8.00	15.00

'77 T-TOTALLER RL

'77 T-TOTALLER

'75 PROWLER

'77 Z WHIZ WH

'78 ARMY FUNNY CAR

'78 BAJA BRUISER

Sheriff Patrol	4.00	8.00
Mustang S.V.O.	6.00	15.00
Camaro Z-28	6.00	12.00
'57 Chevy	10.00	25.00

1986 Hot Wheels Originals

Tricar X8	4.00	8.00
'37 Bugatti	5.00	10.00
Auburn 852	4.00	8.00
Poppa Vette	25.00	40.00
Classic Caddy	8.00	15.00
40's Woody	10.00	25.00
Screamin'	20.00	40.00
'31 Doozie	5.00	10.00
Firebird Funny Car	6.00	15.00
Rolls Royce Phantom II	4.00	8.00
Mercedes 540K	5.00	10.00
3-Window '34	5.00	12.00
'63 Split Window	8.00	15.00
'65 Mustang Convertible	10.00	20.00
Blazer 4x4	4.00	8.00
Tall Ryder	4.00	8.00
XT-3	4.00	8.00
Gulch Stepper	4.00	8.00

1986 Hot Wheels Speed Demons

Double Demon	5.00	10.00
Cargoyle	6.00	12.00
Fangster	5.00	10.00
Vampyra	4.00	8.00
Turboa	5.00	10.00
Eevil Weevil	5.00	10.00

1986 Hot Wheels Ultra Hots

Flashfire	4.00	8.00
Back Burner	3.00	6.00
Jet Sweep X5	6.00	12.00
Sol-Aire CX4	4.00	8.00
Speed Seeker	4.00	8.00
Redliner	4.00	8.00
Silver Bullet	4.00	8.00
Nightstreaker	6.00	12.00
Street Beast	5.00	10.00
Wind Splitter	4.00	8.00

1986 Hot Wheels Workhorses

Peterbilt Cement Truck	4.00	8.00
CAT Dump Truck	4.00	8.00
CAT Bulldozer	4.00	8.00
CAT Wheel Loader	4.00	8.00
Old Number 5	5.00	10.00
Hiway Hauler	15.00	30.00

Peterbilt Tank Truck	5.00	10.00
Team Bus	4.00	8.00
Rig Wrecker	4.00	8.00
Thunder Roller	4.00	8.00
Good Humor Truck	4.00	8.00
Oshkosh Snow Plow	4.00	8.00
Peterbilt Dump Truck	4.00	8.00
Ford Stake Bed Truck	8.00	15.00
Fire Eater	4.00	8.00

1986 Hot Wheels X-V Racers

Ultimator	3.00	8.00
Mach 7	3.00	8.00
Proformer	3.00	8.00
Gyracer	3.00	8.00
Ultra-Sonix	3.00	8.00
Hyper Twister	3.00	8.00
Stunt Racer	3.00	8.00
Speed Spinner	3.00	8.00

'78 STREET RODDER

1987 Hot Wheels 5-Car Gift Packs

	LOOSE	IN PKG.
Classics GP	12.00	20.00
Ultra Hots GP	12.00	20.00
Racers GP	12.00	20.00
Body Swappers GP	25.00	40.00

1987 Hot Wheels Action Command

	LOOSE	IN PKG.
Shell Shocker	3.00	6.00
Combat Medic	4.00	8.00
Assault Crawler	6.00	12.00
Tail Gunner	4.00	8.00
Command Tank	4.00	8.00
Big Bertha	4.00	8.00
Tank Gunner	4.00	8.00
Roll Patrol	4.00	8.00
Troop Convoy	4.00	8.00
Super Cannon	4.00	8.00

1982 '57 T-BIRD

1987 Hot Wheels Classics

Corvette Stingray	5.00	10.00
Nissan 300ZX	4.00	8.00
Thunderburner	6.00	12.00
'80 Corvette	5.00	10.00
Fiero 2M4	4.00	8.00
3-Window '34	10.00	25.00
Firebird Funny Car	6.00	12.00
Split Window '63	10.00	20.00
Thunderstreak	4.00	8.00

'79 STREET RODDER

'79 STREET RODDER

Nightstreaker	5.00	10.00
Road Torch	5.00	10.00
Speed Seeker	4.00	8.00
'57 Chevy	10.00	20.00
'65 Mustang Convertible	15.00	35.00
Ferrari Testarossa	8.00	15.00
Hot Bird	6.00	12.00
'55 Chevy	6.00	12.00
Tricar X8	4.00	8.00
'37 Bugatti	4.00	8.00
Classic Caddy	5.00	10.00
'40 Woody	8.00	15.00
'31 Doozie	3.00	6.00
Classic Cobra	8.00	15.00
'57 T-Bird	3.00	6.00
Jet Sweep X5	5.00	10.00
Power Plower	4.00	8.00
Rolls Royce Phantom II	4.00	8.00
Chevy Nomad	5.00	10.00
Mercedes 540K	4.00	8.00
'80 Firebird	5.00	10.00
Blown Camaro Z28	5.00	10.00
Sol-Aire CX4	4.00	8.00
XT-3	4.00	8.00
P-911 Turbo	4.00	8.00
Camaro Z28	4.00	8.00
Silver Bullet	4.00	8.00
Street Beast	4.00	8.00

1987 Hot Wheels Flip Outs

Road Flipper	4.00	8.00
Flipper Snapper	4.00	8.00
Vaultin Van	4.00	8.00
Capsider	4.00	8.00
Flipbuster	4.00	8.00
Fliproarin	4.00	8.00
Flippin' Frenzy	4.00	8.00
Drag Flip	4.00	8.00

1987 Hot Wheels Speed Demons

Double Demon	5.00	10.00
Cargoyle	5.00	10.00
Fangster	5.00	10.00
Vampyra	4.00	8.00
Turboa	4.00	8.00
Eevil Weevil	5.00	10.00
Sharkruiser	4.00	8.00
Phantomachine	5.00	10.00
Zombot	4.00	8.00

1987 Hot Wheels Trailbusters

Gulch Stepper	4.00	8.00
Bronco 4-Wheeler	4.00	8.00
Path Beater	5.00	10.00

Jeep CJ-7	6.00	12.00
Jeep Scrambler	6.00	12.00
Baja Bug	6.00	12.00
Suzuki Quadracer	4.00	8.00
Monster Vette	6.00	12.00
Baja Breaker	5.00	10.00
Bywayman	5.00	10.00
Blazer 4x4	4.00	8.00
Tall Ryder	4.00	8.00

'82 BAJA BRUISER

1987 Hot Wheels Workhorses

Peterbilt Cement Truck	4.00	8.00
CAT Dump Truck	3.00	6.00
CAT Bulldozer	4.00	8.00
CAT Wheel Loader	4.00	8.00
Hiway Hauler	15.00	30.00
Old Number 5	5.00	10.00
Rescue Ranger	5.00	10.00
Peterbilt Tank Truck	5.00	10.00
CAT Vehicle	4.00	8.00
Team Bus	4.00	8.00
CAT Earth Mover	5.00	10.00
Rig Wrecker	4.00	8.00
Thunder Roller	4.00	8.00
Good Humor Truck	4.00	8.00
Oshkosh Snow Plow	4.00	8.00
Sheriff Patrol	4.00	8.00
Peterbilt Dump Truck	3.00	6.00
Fire Eater	5.00	10.00

1987 Hot Wheels X-V Racers

Excellerator	3.00	8.00
Velocitor	3.00	8.00
Ultimator	3.00	8.00
Mach 7	3.00	8.00
Proformer	3.00	8.00
Gyracer	3.00	8.00
Ultra-Sonix	3.00	8.00
Hyper Twister	3.00	8.00
Stunt Racer	3.00	8.00
Speed Spinner	3.00	8.00

'82 FAIRMONT — FOREIGN PACKAGING

1988 Hot Wheels 5-Car Gift Pack

	LOOSE	IN PKG.
Classics GP	10.00	15.00
Racers GP	10.00	15.00
Super Sportscars GP	10.00	15.00
Action Command GP	10.00	15.00
Workhorses GP	10.00	15.00
Trailbusters GP	10.00	15.00

'82 STREET RODDER

'82 FRENCH THREE-CAR PACK

1988 Hot Wheels Action Command

	LOOSE	IN PKG.
Combat Medic	6.00	12.00
Assault Crawler	5.00	10.00
Tail Gunner	4.00	8.00
Radar Ranger	5.00	10.00
Sting Rod	6.00	12.00
Command Tank	4.00	8.00
Big Bertha	4.00	8.00
Tank Gunner	3.00	6.00
Roll Patrol Jeep CJ	4.00	8.00
Troop Convoy	3.00	6.00
Rocketank	5.00	10.00

1988 Hot Wheels Classics

Nissan 300ZX	4.00	8.00
'80 Corvette	5.00	10.00
Fiero 2M4	4.00	8.00
'34 3-Window	3.00	6.00
'57 Chevy	8.00	15.00
'65 Mustang Convertible	6.00	12.00
'37 Bugatti	4.00	8.00
Classic Caddy	5.00	10.00
'40 Woody	5.00	10.00
'31 Doozie	3.00	6.00
Classic Cobra	6.00	12.00
Rolls Royce Phantom II	4.00	8.00
Talbot Lago	4.00	8.00
Ferrari Testarossa	4.00	8.00
Tricar X8	4.00	8.00
Firebird Funny Car	6.00	12.00
'80 Firebird	5.00	10.00
Blown Camaro Z28	5.00	10.00
Thunderburner	5.00	10.00
Mercedes 540K	4.00	8.00
Sol-Aire CX4	4.00	8.00
XT-3	4.00	8.00
Camaro Z28	4.00	8.00
Silver Bullet	3.00	6.00

1988 Hot Wheels Crack-Ups

Wreckin' Rig	4.00	8.00
Deformula I	4.00	8.00
Cab Cruncher	4.00	8.00
Indentor	4.00	8.00
Slammer	4.00	8.00
Super Denter	4.00	8.00
Side Grinder	4.00	8.00
Bangster	4.00	8.00
Crash Patrol	4.00	8.00
Stocker Smasher	4.00	8.00
Fire Smasher	4.00	8.00
Bumper Thumper	4.00	8.00

1988 Hot Wheels Speed Demons

Double Demon	4.00	8.00
Cargoyle	4.00	8.00
Fangster	5.00	10.00
Vampyra	3.00	6.00
Turboa	4.00	8.00
Sharkruiser	4.00	8.00
Phantomachine	5.00	10.00
Zombot	3.00	6.00
Rodzilla	4.00	8.00
Turborat	3.00	6.00
Eevil Weevil	4.00	8.00

'82 TURBO MUSTANG

1988 Hot Wheels Speed Fleet

Lamborghini Countach	5.00	10.00
Porsche 959	4.00	8.00
Shadow Jet	4.00	8.00
Alien	5.00	10.00

1988 Hot Wheels Trailbusters

Gulch Stepper	4.00	8.00
Bronco 4-Wheeler	3.00	6.00
Baja Bug	5.00	10.00
Suzuki Quadracer	4.00	8.00
Monster Vette	5.00	10.00
Baja Breaker	5.00	10.00
Bywayman	5.00	10.00
Nissan Hardbody	5.00	10.00
Power Plower	4.00	8.00
Jeep Scrambler	4.00	8.00
Blazer 4x4	4.00	8.00
Tall Ryder	3.00	6.00

1983 '40s FORD 2-DOOR

1988 Hot Wheels Workhorses

Peterbilt Cement Truck	3.00	6.00
Dump Truck	4.00	8.00
Bulldozer	3.00	6.00
Wheel Loader	4.00	8.00
Old Number 5	4.00	8.00
Peterbilt Tank Truck	5.00	10.00
Team Bus	3.00	6.00
Earth Mover	3.00	6.00
Road Roller	4.00	8.00
Rig Wrecker	3.00	6.00
Thunder Roller	3.00	6.00
Flame Stopper	4.00	8.00
Hiway Hauler	15.00	30.00
Rescue Ranger	4.00	8.00
Good Humor Truck	5.00	10.00
Oshkosh Snow Plow	4.00	8.00
Sheriff Patrol	3.00	6.00
Peterbilt Dump Truck	3.00	6.00

'84 DREAM VAN XGW

'85 BEACH PATROL

1989 Hot Wheels Action Command

	LOOSE	IN PKG.
Tail Gunner	3.00	6.00
Radar Ranger	4.00	8.00
Sting Rod	5.00	10.00
Command Tank	3.00	6.00
Big Bertha	3.00	6.00
Roll Patrol Jeep CJ	3.00	6.00
Troop Convoy	3.00	6.00
Rocketank	4.00	8.00

1989 Hot Wheels Classics

'65 Mustang Convertible	6.00	12.00
Classic Caddy	4.00	8.00
'37 Bugatti	4.00	8.00
'40's Woody	8.00	15.00
'31 Doozie	3.00	6.00
Classic Cobra	5.00	10.00
Rolls-Royce Phantom II	3.00	6.00
'34 3-Window	5.00	10.00
Talbot Lago	3.00	6.00
Mercedes 540K	3.00	6.00
'32 Ford Delivery	3.00	6.00
'57 Chevy	8.00	15.00

1989 Hot Wheels Speed Demons

Vampyra	3.00	6.00
Sharkruiser	3.00	6.00
Zombot	3.00	6.00
Ratmobile	3.00	6.00

1989 Hot Wheels Speed Fleet

Hot Bird	5.00	10.00
Nissan 300ZX	3.00	6.00
Thunderbird Stocker	5.00	10.00
Fiero 2M4	3.00	6.00
Ferrari F40	3.00	6.00
XT-3	4.00	8.00
Sol-Aire CX4	4.00	8.00
GT Racer	3.00	6.00
Chevy Stocker	5.00	10.00
Pontiac Banshee	4.00	8.00
Firebird Funny Car	4.00	8.00
Lamborghini Countach	5.00	10.00
'80 Corvette	5.00	10.00
Mercedes 380 SEL	4.00	8.00
Porsche 959	4.00	8.00
Shadow Jet	3.00	6.00
Alien	4.00	8.00
Ferrari Testarossa	4.00	8.00
Tricar X8	3.00	6.00
'80 Firebird	5.00	10.00

Custom Corvette	5.00	10.00
VW Bug	5.00	10.00
T-Bucket	5.00	10.00
Camaro Z28	3.00	6.00

1989 Hot Wheels Trailbusters

Gulch Stepper	3.00	6.00
Baja Breaker	5.00	10.00
Bywayman	4.00	8.00
Bronco 4-Wheeler	3.00	6.00
Baja Bug	4.00	8.00
Suzuki Quadracer	3.00	6.00
Monster Vette	4.00	8.00
Nissan Hardbody	4.00	8.00
Power Plower	3.00	6.00
Jeep Scrambler	4.00	8.00
Blazer 4x4	3.00	6.00
Tall Ryder	3.00	6.00

'85 GOOD OL' PIC-UM-UP

1989 Hot Wheels Workhorses

Peterbilt Cement Truck	3.00	6.00
Dump Truck	4.00	8.00
Bulldozer	3.00	6.00
Wheel Loader	3.00	6.00
Peterbilt Dump Truck	3.00	6.00
Old Number 5	4.00	8.00
Big Rig	4.00	8.00
Ambulance	3.00	6.00
School Bus	5.00	10.00
Peterbilt Tank Truck	5.00	10.00
Hiway Hauler	15.00	30.00
Delivery Truck	6.00	12.00
Earth Mover	3.00	6.00
Road Roller	3.00	6.00
Rig Wrecker	3.00	6.00
Thunder Roller	3.00	6.00
Flame Stopper	4.00	8.00
Rescue Ranger	4.00	8.00
Good Humor Truck	4.00	8.00
Oshkosh Snow Plow	3.00	6.00
Sheriff Patrol	3.00	6.00
Fire Eater	3.00	6.00

'85 POWER PLOWER

1990 Hot Wheels Action Command

	LOOSE	IN PKG.
Tail Gunner	2.00	6.00
Radar Ranger	2.00	6.00
Command Tank	2.00	6.00
Big Bertha	2.00	6.00
Tank Gunner	2.00	6.00
Roll Patrol	2.00	6.00
Troop Convoy	2.00	6.00
Rocketank	2.00	6.00

'86 NISSAN HARDBODY

'86 POWER PLOWER

1990 Hot Wheels California Customs

	LOOSE	IN PKG.
'40 Woody	5.00	15.00
Baja Bug	5.00	15.00
Mustang	5.00	15.00
Street Roader	10.00	25.00
Camaro	6.00	15.00
Cobra	6.00	15.00
'57 Chevy	6.00	15.00
'34 Ford	5.00	15.00
Corvette	5.00	15.00
Ferrari	5.00	12.00
Banshee	6.00	15.00
'63 Corvette	6.00	15.00
'59 Caddy	12.00	30.00
'55 Nomad	12.00	30.00
BMW Convertible	6.00	15.00
Corvette Funny Car	12.00	30.00
'67 Camaro	40.00	80.00
Firebird	6.00	15.00
Fast GT	6.00	15.00
Stutz Blackhawk	8.00	20.00
P-911 Turbo	6.00	15.00
Mercedes 380 SEL	6.00	15.00
Classic Caddy	6.00	15.00

1990 Hot Wheels Classics

'55 Chevy	3.00	8.00
Auburn	3.00	8.00
'57 T-Bird	4.00	10.00
'37 Bugatti	3.00	8.00
'31 Doozie	3.00	8.00
Classic Packard	3.00	8.00
Talbot Lago	3.00	8.00
Mercedes 540K	3.00	8.00
'32 Ford Delivery	3.00	8.00
Ford T-Bucket	5.00	15.00

1990 Hot Wheels Convertibles

Fab Cab	2.00	5.00
Odd Bod	2.00	5.00
Pick Up Trick	2.00	5.00
Shift Kicker	2.00	5.00
Vary Cool	2.00	5.00
Engine-Air	2.00	5.00
Doublin Duty	2.00	5.00
Shiftin' 50's	2.00	5.00
Black Ballet	2.00	5.00
Turnin T	2.00	5.00
Formula Fever	2.00	5.00
Lo Down Limo	2.00	5.00

1990 Hot Wheels Speed Demons

Vampyra	2.00	5.00
Sharkruiser	1.50	4.00
Zambot	1.50	4.00
Ratmobile	2.50	6.00

1990 Hot Wheels Speed Fleet

'80 Corvette	1.50	4.00
Porsche 959	2.00	5.00
'80 Firebird	3.00	8.00
Fiero 2M4	3.00	8.00
Ferrari F40	2.50	6.00
Peugeot	1.50	4.00
XT-3	1.50	4.00
GT Racer	2.00	5.00
Chevy Stocker	5.00	10.00
Hot Bird	1.50	4.00
Mini Truck	3.00	8.00
VW Bug	2.00	5.00
Buick Stocker	6.00	15.00
Purple Passion	2.00	5.00
Lamborghini Countach	2.00	5.00
Mercedes 380 SEL	1.50	4.00
Turbo Streak	1.50	4.00
Shadow Jet	1.50	4.00
T-Bird Stocker	5.00	15.00
Alien	1.50	4.00
Ferrari Testarossa	2.00	5.00
Funny Car	1.50	4.00
Nissan 300ZX	1.50	4.00
Camaro Z28	3.00	6.00
Thunderstreak	1.50	4.00
VW Golf	1.50	4.00

1990 Hot Wheels Trailbusters

Street Roader	2.00	5.00
Blazer 4x4	3.00	8.00
Gulch Stepper	2.00	5.00
Baja Breaker	4.00	10.00
Monster Vetter	2.00	5.00
Bywayman	2.00	5.00
Suzuki Quadracer	4.00	10.00
Bronco 4-Wheeler	4.00	10.00
Nissan Hardbody	4.00	10.00
Power Plower	4.00	10.00
Beach Patrol	2.00	5.00
Tall Ryder	5.00	15.00
Range Rover	2.00	5.00

1990 Hot Wheels Workhorses

Fork Lift	1.50	4.00
Peterbilt Cement Truck	1.50	4.00
Dump Truck	1.50	4.00

'89 WHEEL LOADER

'89 RESCUE RANGER

'89 RIG WRECKER

'89 THUNDER ROLLER

Bulldozer	1.50	4.00
Wheel Loader	1.50	4.00
Hiway Hauler	1.50	4.00
Sheriff Patrol	1.50	4.00
Peterbilt Dump Truck	1.50	4.00
Delivery Truck	3.00	8.00
Old Number 5	3.00	8.00
Big Rig	1.50	4.00
Ambulance	3.00	8.00
School Bus	1.50	4.00
Oshkosh Snow Plow	1.50	4.00
Peterbilt Tank Truck	1.50	4.00
Earth Mover	1.50	4.00
Road Roller	1.50	4.00
Rescue Ranger	1.50	4.00
Ramp Truck	1.50	4.00
Good Humor Truck	1.50	4.00
Ramblin Wrecker	1.50	4.00
Proper Chopper	2.00	5.00
Ford Stake Bed Truck	1.50	4.00
Fire-Eater	1.50	4.00

1991 Hot Wheels Action Command

	LOOSE	IN PKG.
Command Tank	2.00	5.00
Big Bertha	1.50	4.00
Rockettank	1.50	4.00
Roll Patrol	1.50	4.00

1991 Hot Wheels Billionth Car

Custom Corvette Convertible	5.00	12.00
Corvette Hard Top	5.00	12.00
Corvette Stingray	5.00	12.00
Split Window Corvette	5.00	12.00

1991 Hot Wheels Classics

Auburn	1.50	4.00
'37 Bugatti	1.50	4.00
'65 Mustang Convertible	1.50	4.00
Talbo Lago	1.50	4.00
Trailbuster	1.50	4.00
Street Beast	1.50	4.00
T-Bucket	3.00	8.00
Mercedes 540K	1.50	4.00
'32 Ford Delivery	3.00	8.00
Ranger Rover	1.50	4.00

1991 Hot Wheels Off Road

Gulch Stepper	1.50	4.00
Bywayman	1.50	4.00
Surf Patrol	2.00	5.00

Power Plower	1.50	4.00
Suzuki Quadracer	2.50	6.00

1991 Hot Wheels Speed Demons

Vampyra	1.50	4.00
Sharkruiser	1.50	4.00
Zombot	2.00	5.00
Ratmobile	1.50	4.00

1991 Hot Wheels Speed Fleet

'80 Firebird	1.50	4.00
XT-3	1.50	4.00
Sol-Air CX4	3.00	8.00
GT Racer	2.00	5.00
Chevy Stocker	2.00	5.00
Pontiac Banshee	3.00	8.00
Hot Bird	5.00	15.00
Mini Truck	2.00	5.00
VW Bug	2.00	5.00
Purple Passion	3.00	8.00
Lamborghini Countach	1.50	4.00
Ferrari Testarossa	1.50	4.00
Bird Stocker	1.50	4.00
Limozeen	4.00	10.00
Speed Shark	1.50	4.00
Mazda Miata MX-5	1.50	4.00
Classic Ferrari	1.50	4.00
Ferrari 348	1.50	4.00
Toyota MR2 Rally	1.50	4.00
Zender Fact 4	1.50	4.00
Chevy Lumina	1.50	4.00
Nissan Custom Z	1.50	4.00
Porsche 959	1.50	4.00
Turbo Streak	1.50	4.00
Camaro Z28	1.50	4.00
Fiero 2M4	1.50	4.00
VW Golf	4.00	10.00
Shadow Jet	1.50	4.00
Mercedes 380 SEL	2.00	5.00

1991 Hot Wheels Workhorses

Wheel Loader	1.50	4.00
Sheriff Patrol	1.50	4.00
Peterbilt Dump Truck	1.50	4.00
Ford Stake Bed Truck	1.50	4.00
Ambulance	1.50	4.00
School Bus	1.50	4.00
Road Roller	1.50	4.00
Rescue Ranger	1.50	4.00
Ramp Truck	1.50	4.00
Propper Chopper	1.50	4.00
Fire-Eater	1.50	4.00

'89 FIRE EATER FIRE TRUCK

'89 RADAR RANGER

'90 TRAILBUSTER

'90 SPEED SHARK

1991-92 Hot Wheels
Super California Custom Cars

E.Z. Duzzit	3.00	8.00
Catalina Cruz	3.00	8.00
Mean Machine	3.00	8.00
Turbular Turbo	3.00	8.00
Jack Flash	3.00	8.00
Beach Blaster	5.00	12.00
Race Ace	3.00	8.00
Laguna Lightning	3.00	8.00
Scorch Torch	3.00	8.00
Cool Duel	3.00	8.00
Big Sur-Prize	3.00	8.00
Bod-Acious	3.00	8.00

1992 Hot Wheels
5-Car Gift Packs

	LOOSE	IN PKG.
Classic Collection GP	6.00	12.00
Racing Team GP	5.00	10.00
Super Sportscars GP	5.00	10.00
Emergency Squad GP	5.00	10.00
Construction Crew GP	5.00	10.00
Off Road Explorers GP	5.00	10.00

1992 Hot Wheels
Action Command

	LOOSE	IN PKG.
Big Bertha	1.00	3.00
Command Tank	1.50	4.00
Roll Patrol	1.50	4.00
Hummer	1.50	4.00
Rockettank	1.00	3.00

1992 Hot Wheels
Cap Blastin Hot Wheels

Back Burner	2.00	5.00
Jet Threat	2.00	5.00
Velocitor	2.00	5.00
Sonic Special	2.00	5.00
Blast Trax	2.00	5.00
Road Torch	2.00	5.00

1992 Hot Wheels Classics

'67 Mustang Convertible	2.00	5.00
Talbot Lago	1.50	4.00
Mercedes 540K	1.50	4.00
Auburn 852	1.50	4.00
'56 Flashrider	2.00	5.00

'37 Bugatti	1.50	4.00
Classic Cobra	1.50	4.00
'57 Cadillac	2.00	5.00
'57 Chevy	3.00	8.00
Street Beast	1.50	4.00
T-Bucket	2.50	6.00
'32 Ford Delivery	2.00	5.00

1992 Hot Wheels Off Road

Suzuki Quadracer	1.50	4.00
Street Roader	1.50	4.00
Gulch Stepper	1.50	4.00
Bywayman	1.50	4.00
Surf Patrol	1.50	4.00
Trailbuster	1.50	4.00
Power Plower	1.50	4.00
Nissan Hardbody	1.50	4.00
Range Rover	1.50	4.00

'90 COMMANDO TANK

1992 Hot Wheels Speed Demons

Turboa	1.00	3.00
Sharkruiser	1.50	4.00
Zombot	1.00	3.00
Rodzilla	1.00	3.00
Ratmobile	1.00	3.00

1992 Hot Wheels Speed Fleet

'80 Firebird	2.00	5.00
GT Racer	1.50	4.00
Sol-Aire CX4	1.50	4.00
Chevy Stocker	1.00	3.00
VW Bug	1.50	4.00
Mazda MX-5 Miata	1.50	4.00
T-Bird Stocker	1.00	3.00
Limozeen	2.00	5.00
Ferrari 348	1.00	3.00
Lamborghini Diablo	1.50	4.00
Zender Fact 4	1.00	3.00
Hot Bird	1.50	4.00
Porsche 959	1.50	4.00
Fiero 2M4	1.50	4.00
Shadow Jet	1.00	3.00
VW Golf	2.00	5.00
Mercedes 380 SEL	2.00	5.00
Pontiac Stocker	1.00	3.00
Ferrari F40	1.00	3.00
XT-3	1.00	3.00
Pontiac Banshee	1.00	3.00
Mini Truck	1.50	4.00
Purple Passion	2.00	5.00
Flashfire	1.00	3.00
Shock Factor	1.00	3.00
Lamborghini Countach	1.00	3.00
Toyota MR2 Rally	1.00	3.00

1990 '80s FIREBIRD

'90 MERCEDES 380 SEL

'90 PROPER CHOPPER

'90 SHERIFF PATROL

Thundersteak	1.00	3.00
Alien	1.00	3.00
Ferrari Testarossa	1.00	3.00
Speed Shark	1.00	3.00
Classic Ferrari 250	1.00	3.00
BMW 850i	1.00	3.00
Chevy Lumina	1.50	4.00
Porsche 930	1.00	3.00
Nissan Custom Z	1.00	3.00
Turbo Streak	1.00	3.00
Camaro Z-28	1.50	4.00
BMW 323	1.00	3.00

1992 Hot Wheels Workhorses

Propper Chopper	1.50	4.00
Ford Aerostar	1.50	4.00
Ramp Truck	1.50	4.00
Goodyear Blimp	1.50	4.00
Sheriff Patrol	1.50	4.00
Peterbilt Dump Truck	1.50	4.00
Ford Stake Bed Truck	1.50	4.00
Kentworth Big Rig	1.50	4.00
Ambulance	1.50	4.00
School Bus	1.50	4.00
Recycling Truck	1.50	4.00
Oshkosh Cement Truck	1.50	4.00
Tank Truck	1.50	4.00
Tractor	1.50	4.00
Bulldozer	1.50	4.00
Hiway Hauler	1.50	4.00
Road Roller	1.50	4.00
Rescue Ranger	1.50	4.00
Mercedes Benz Unimog	1.50	4.00
Good Humor Truck	1.50	4.00
Fire-Eater	1.50	4.00

1993 Hot Wheels 5-Car Gift Pack

	LOOSE	IN PKG.
Classics Collection GP	7.00	14.00
Racing Team GP	5.00	10.00
Super Sportscar GP	5.00	10.00
Emergency Squad GP	5.00	10.00
Construction Crew GP	6.00	12.00
Off Road Explorers GP	5.00	10.00

1993 Hot Wheels Action Command

	LOOSE	IN PKG.
Big Bertha	2.00	5.00
Command Tank	2.00	5.00
Roll Patrol	2.00	5.00
Hummer	2.00	5.00
Troop Convoy	2.00	5.00

1993 Hot Wheels Classic

1993 Camaro	2.00	5.00
Jaguar XJ220	1.50	4.00
Oscar Mayer Wiener Mobile	1.50	4.00
Treadator	1.50	4.00
Pipe Jammer	2.00	5.00
Vector WX-3	1.50	4.00
Audi	1.50	4.00
Lexus SC 400	1.50	4.00
Nissan 300ZX	1.50	4.00

1993 Hot Wheels Classics Vintage

	LOOSE	IN PKG.
'65 Mustang Convertible	3.00	8.00
Mercedes 540 K	2.00	5.00
'56 Flashrider	2.00	5.00
'37 Bugatti	2.00	5.00
'34 3-Window	2.00	5.00
Classic Cobra	2.00	5.00
'57 Chevy	2.00	5.00
Street Beast	2.00	5.00
Auburn	2.00	5.00
'59 Cadillac	2.00	5.00
T-Bucket	2.00	5.00
'32 Ford Delivery	4.00	10.00

1993 Hot Wheels Key Force Cycles

	LOOSE	IN PKG.
Road Kill	2.00	5.00
Jet Threat	2.00	5.00

1993 Hot Wheels Off Road

Suzuki Quadracer	1.50	4.00
Vampyra	1.50	4.00
Turboa	1.00	3.00
Path Beater	1.50	4.00
Double Demon	1.00	3.00
Sharkruiser	1.00	3.00
Blazer 4x4	1.50	4.00
Street Roader	1.00	3.00
Gulch Stepper	1.00	3.00
Bywayman	1.00	3.00
Range Rover	1.00	3.00
Baja Bug	2.00	5.00
Zombot	1.00	3.00
Rodzilla	1.00	3.00
Nissan Truck	2.00	5.00

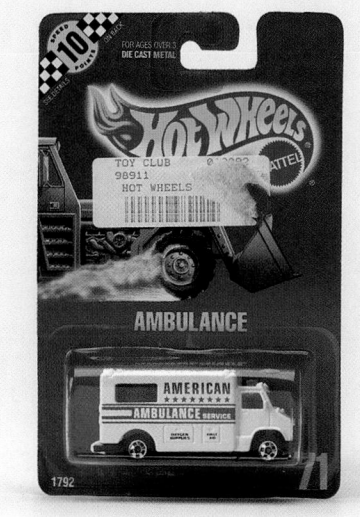

'90 AMBULANCE

'91 SPEED SHARK

1991 '32 FORD DELIVERY

'91 RECYCLING TRUCK

1993 Hot Wheels ReVealers

Sol-Aire	2.00	5.00
Ferrari 348	2.00	5.00
Lamborghini Diablo	2.00	5.00
Zender Fact 4	2.00	5.00
Mercedes 380 SEL	2.00	5.00
Ferrari F-40	2.00	5.00
Lamborghini Countach	2.00	5.00
Ferrari Testarossa	2.00	5.00
Porsche 930	2.00	5.00
Nissan Custom Z	2.00	5.00
Jaguar XJ220	2.00	5.00
Custom Corvette	2.00	5.00

1993 Hot Wheels Speed Fleet

GT Racer	1.00	3.00
Sol-Aire CX4	1.00	3.00
VW Bug	2.00	5.00
Mazda Miata	1.00	3.00
Shadow Jet	1.00	3.00
Mercedes 380 SEL	1.00	3.00
Ferrari F-40	1.00	3.00
Gleamer Patrol	2.00	5.00
Gleam Team T-Bird	2.00	5.00
Gleamer Aero Flash	2.00	5.00
Gleam Team Stingray	2.00	5.00
Gleam Team Porsche	2.00	5.00
Pontiac Banshee	1.00	3.00
Purple Passion	2.00	5.00
Custom Vette	1.00	3.00
'63 Split Window Vette	3.00	8.00
Flash Fire	1.00	3.00
Shock Factor	1.00	3.00
Limozeen	2.00	5.00
Ferrari 348	1.00	3.00
Lamborghini Diablo	1.00	3.00
Zender Fact 4	1.00	3.00
XT3	1.00	3.00
Lamborghini Countach	1.00	3.00
Toyota MR2	1.00	3.00
Nissan Custom	1.00	3.00
Ferrari Testarossa	1.00	3.00
Classic Ferrari	1.00	3.00
BMW 850i	1.00	3.00
Chevy Lumina	1.00	3.00
Porsche 930	1.00	3.00

1993 Hot Wheels Super Attack Pack

	LOOSE	IN PKG.
Blowtorch	1.50	4.00
Big Bones	1.50	4.00

1993 Hot Wheels Tattoo Machines

	LOOSE	IN PKG.
Spiderrider	3.00	8.00
Dragon Wagon	2.50	6.00
Road Pirate	2.50	6.00
Open Wide	2.50	6.00
Street Beast	2.50	6.00
Skull Rider	3.00	8.00
Eye-Gor	2.50	6.00
Hot Wheels	2.50	6.00
Street Dog	2.50	6.00
Bus Boys	2.50	6.00
Light Storm	3.00	8.00
Ammo	2.50	6.00

1993 Hot Wheels Workhorses

Propper Chopper	1.50	4.00
Goodyear Blimp	1.50	4.00
Sheriff Patrol	1.50	4.00
Peterbilt Dump Truck	1.50	4.00
Stake Truck	1.50	4.00
Kenworth Big Rig	1.50	4.00
School Bus	1.50	4.00
Recycling Truck	1.50	4.00
Oshkosh Cement Mixer	1.50	4.00
Tank Truck	1.50	4.00
Tractor	1.50	4.00
Bulldozer	1.50	4.00
Road Roller	1.50	4.00
Highway Hauler	1.50	4.00
Mercedes Benz Unimog	1.50	4.00
Dump Truck	1.50	4.00
Good Humor Truck	1.50	4.00
Fire-Eater	1.50	4.00

1994 Hot Wheels 5-Car Gift Pack

	LOOSE	IN PKG.
Speed Demons GP	5.00	10.00
Blimp/Support Team GP	7.00	14.00
Action Command GP	7.00	14.00
Classic Collection GP	5.00	10.00
Racing Team GP	5.00	10.00
Emergency Squad GP	5.00	10.00
Construction Crew GP	4.00	8.00
Off Road Explorers GP	4.00	8.00

1994 Hot Wheels Action Command

	LOOSE	IN PKG.
Big Bertha	1.50	4.00
Command Tank	1.50	4.00

'91 OSHKOSH CEMENT MIXER

'91 CORVETTE SPLIT WINDOW

'91 DOUBLE DEMON

'91 CUSTOM CORVETTE

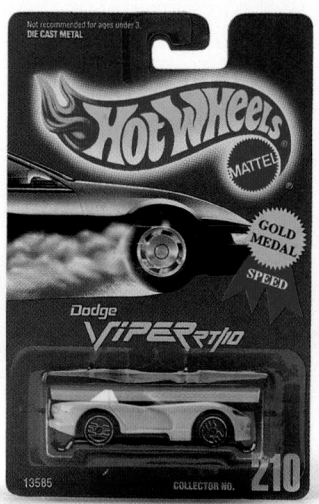

'91 DODGE VIPER RT

'91 RANGE ROVER

Roll Patrol	1.50	4.00
Hummer	1.50	4.00
Troop Convoy	1.50	4.00
Mercedes Benz Unimog	1.50	4.00

1994 Hot Wheels Attack Pack Monster Trucks

Slashcat	2.00	5.00
Slaughterhaws	2.00	5.00
The Darkclaw	2.00	5.00
Sandstinger	2.00	5.00
Taran-Chewa	2.00	5.00
Rip Rat	2.00	5.00
Toothslayer	2.00	5.00
Riptile	2.00	5.00
Wolverraider	2.00	5.00
King Hiss	2.00	5.00
Slash Cat	2.00	5.00
Sandstinger	2.00	5.00
Rip Rat	2.00	5.00
The Dark Claw	2.00	5.00

1994 Hot Wheels Classic

'65 Mustang Convertible	3.00	8.00
Talbot Lago	2.00	5.00
Mercedes 540K	2.00	5.00
'57 T-Bird	6.00	15.00
'57 Flashrider	2.00	5.00
'37 Bugatti	2.00	5.00
3-Window '34	4.00	10.00
Classic Cobra	5.00	12.00
'57 Chevy	4.00	10.00
Swingfire	2.00	5.00
Auburn 852	2.00	5.00
Fat Fender '40	2.00	5.00
'40's Woodie	2.00	5.00
'57 Cadillac	3.00	8.00
T-Bucket	4.00	10.00
'32 Ford Delivery	2.00	5.00

1994 Hot Wheels Color FX 2-Car Packs

Big Bertha/Hummer	4.00	8.00
Roll Patrol/Command Tank	4.00	8.00
GT Racer/Camaro Race	4.00	8.00
Funny Car/1993 T-Bird	4.00	8.00
Baja Bug/Aero Flash	4.00	8.00
Vampyra/Ferrari Testarossa	4.00	8.00
Tanker/1992 Camaro	4.00	8.00
Hiway Hauler/Lamborghini	4.00	8.00
Dragon Wagon/Double Demon	4.00	8.00
Bug Brain/Ratmobile	4.00	8.00

Octo-Blimp/Sharkcruiser	4.00	8.00
Skullmobile/Turboa	4.00	8.00
Killer Kopter/Eevil Weevil	4.00	8.00
Spyder Ryder/Cargoyle	4.00	8.00

1991 '93 CAMARO

1994 Hot Wheels Key Force Cycles

	LOOSE	IN PKG.
Swingshot	2.00	5.00
Cutthroat	2.00	5.00
Road Kill	2.00	5.00
Jet Threat	2.00	5.00

1994 Hot Wheels Key Force Leaders

	LOOSE	IN PKG.
Rocket Shot	2.00	5.00
Headlock	2.00	5.00
Keymander	2.00	5.00
Blader Raider	2.00	5.00

1994 Hot Wheels Off Road

Suzuki Quadracer	1.50	4.00
Path Beater	1.50	4.00
Street Roader	1.50	4.00
Gulch Stepper	1.50	4.00
Bywayman	1.50	4.00
Ranger Rover	1.50	4.00
Blazer 4x4	1.50	4.00
Baja Bug	1.50	4.00
Nissan Truck	1.50	4.00

'91 DRIVEN TO THE MAX

1994 Hot Wheels Speed Demons

Vampyra	2.00	5.00
Turboa	3.00	8.00
Double Demon	2.00	5.00
Sharkcruiser	2.00	5.00
Zombot	2.00	5.00
Rodzilla	2.00	5.00
Ratmobile	2.00	5.00

1994 Hot Wheels Speed Fleet

'80's Firebird	2.50	6.00
GT Racer	1.00	3.00
Sol-Aire CX-4	2.00	5.00
VW Bug	1.00	3.00
Mazda MX-5 Miata	1.00	3.00
Shadow Jet	1.00	3.00
'93 Hot Wheels Race Car	1.00	3.00
Stealth	1.50	4.00
Rigor Motor	1.50	4.00

'91 TWIN MILL II

'91 PORSCHE 959

	LOOSE	IN PKG.
Splittin' Image II	1.50	4.00
Ferrari F40	1.00	3.00
Pontiac Banshee	1.00	3.00
Purple Passion	2.00	5.00
Custom Corvette	1.00	3.00
Hot Wheels Camaro	1.50	4.00
1993 Camaro	1.00	3.00
Jaguar XJ220	1.50	4.00
Oscar Mayer Wiener Mobile	2.00	5.00
Treadator	1.00	3.00
Pipe Jammer	2.50	6.00
Vector WX-3	1.00	3.00
'63 Corvette Split Window	2.50	6.00
Flashfire	2.00	5.00
Shock Factor	1.50	4.00
Limozeen	2.50	6.00
Ferrari 348	1.00	3.00
Lamborghini Diablo	1.00	3.00
Zender Fact 4	1.00	3.00
Mercedes 380 SEL	1.00	3.00
XT-3	1.00	3.00
Mini Truck	1.50	4.00
Lamborghini Countach	1.00	3.00
Toyota MR2	1.00	3.00
Nissan Custom Z	1.00	3.00
Turbo Streak	1.00	3.00
Ferrari Testarossa	1.50	4.00
Avus Quattro	1.00	3.00
Twin Mill II	2.00	5.00
Silhouette II	1.00	3.00
Ferrari 250	1.00	3.00
BMW 850i	1.00	3.00
Chevy Lumina	1.00	3.00
Porsche 930	1.50	4.00
No Fear Race Car	2.00	5.00

1994 Hot Wheels Super Attack Pack

	LOOSE	IN PKG.
Talk Back Bone Beast	1.50	4.00
Blowtorch	1.50	4.00
Big Bones	1.50	4.00
Slim-inator	1.50	4.00

1994 Hot Wheels Vintage Collection

	LOOSE	IN PKG.
Red Baron	2.00	6.00
Paddy Wagon	2.00	6.00
Splittin' Image	2.00	6.00
Twin Mill	3.00	8.00
Beatnik Bandit	2.00	6.00
Silhouette	2.00	6.00

The Demon	2.00	6.00
Classic Nomad	3.00	8.00

1994 Hot Wheels Workhorses

Propper Chopper	1.00	3.00
Dump Truck	1.00	3.00
Goodyear Blimp	1.00	3.00
Sheriff Patrol	1.00	3.00
Peterbilt Dump Truck	2.00	5.00
Kenworth Big Rig	3.00	8.00
School Bus	1.00	3.00
Recycling Truck	2.00	5.00
Oshkosh Cement Mixer	1.00	3.00
Tractor	2.00	5.00
Oshkosh Snowplow	1.00	3.00
Bulldozer	1.00	3.00
Road Roller	1.00	3.00
Ford Aerostar	1.00	3.00
Ford Stake Bed Truck	2.00	5.00
Hiway Hauler	2.00	5.00
Good Humor Truck	2.50	6.00
Fire-Eater	1.00	3.00

'91 CHUCK E. CHEESE JEEP

1995 Hot Wheels 5-Car Gift Pack

	LOOSE	IN PKG.
Speed Demons GP	6.00	10.00
Blimp/Support Team GP	6.00	10.00
Action Command GP	6.00	10.00
Chevy GP	6.00	10.00
Ford GP	6.00	10.00
Ferrari GP	6.00	10.00
Super Cars GP	6.00	10.00
Muscle Cars '60's GP	8.00	12.00
Porsche GP	6.00	10.00
HW Race Team GP	6.00	10.00
Classic Collection GP	6.00	10.00
Racing Team GP	6.00	10.00
Emergency Squad GP	6.00	10.00
Construction Crew GP	6.00	10.00
Off-Road Explorers GP	6.00	10.00

'92 XT-3

1995 Hot Wheels Adventures Deluxe Vehicles

Jungle Ranger	2.00	5.00
Astro Rover	2.00	5.00
Reef Raider	2.00	5.00
Sky Stormer	2.00	5.00
Transylvania Express	2.00	5.00
Tunnel Runner	2.00	5.00
Time Travel Machine Vehicle	2.00	5.00

'92 TALBOT LAGO

'94 SPEED BLASTER

'94 HYDROPLANE

1995 Hot Wheels Color FX Vehicles

	LOOSE	IN PKG.
Swarmula I/Double Demon	2.00	5.00
Off-Roadent/Evil Weevil	2.00	5.00
Octo-Blimp/Shark Teeth	2.00	5.00
Grim Creeper/Turboa	2.00	5.00
Killer Kopter/Stinger	2.00	5.00
Arachnorod/Cargoyle	2.00	5.00

1995 Hot Wheels Crash Calvary Vehicles.

The Extinguisher	2.00	5.00
Nitrod	2.00	5.00
Wastelander	2.00	5.00
Big Jack	2.00	5.00
Lucky Edie	2.00	5.00
Gen. Buster O'Casey	2.00	5.00
Desert Hawk	2.00	5.00

1995 Hot Wheels Dark Rider Series

	LOOSE	IN PKG.
Twin Mill II	3.00	8.00
Rigor-Motor	2.50	6.00
Splittin Image II	2.50	6.00
Silhouette II	2.00	5.00

1995 Hot Wheels Hot Hubs Series

	LOOSE	IN PKG.
Cyber Cruiser	2.50	6.00
Vampyra	2.50	6.00
Shadow Jet	2.50	6.00
Suzuki Quad Racer	4.00	10.00

1995 Hot Wheels Krackle Car Series

	LOOSE	IN PKG.
Sharkcruiser	2.50	6.00
Turboa	2.00	5.00
'63 Split Window	2.50	6.00
Flashfire	2.00	5.00

1995 Hot Wheels Race Team Series

	LOOSE	IN PKG.
Lumina Stocker	2.00	5.00
Hot Wheels 500	2.00	5.00

Side-Splitter	2.00	5.00
Dragster	2.00	5.00

1995 Hot Wheels Model Series

'58 Corvette	3.00	8.00
Power Pipes	1.50	4.00
'94 Camaro Convertible	2.00	5.00
Speed-A-Saurus	1.50	4.00
Hydroplane	2.00	5.00
Dodge Ram 1500	2.00	5.00
Ferrari 355	1.00	3.00
Power Rocket	3.00	8.00
Snowmobile	2.50	6.00
Power Pistons	1.50	4.00
Speed Blaster	2.00	5.00
Mercedes SL	2.50	6.00

'94 TWIN MILL II

1995 Hot Wheels Pearl Driver Series

	LOOSE	IN PKG.
Passion Car	2.00	5.00
VW Bug	3.00	8.00
Jaguar X5220	2.50	6.00
Talbot Lago	2.00	5.00

1995 Hot Wheels Photo Finish Series

	LOOSE	IN PKG.
Hiway Hauler	2.50	6.00
Tank Truck	2.50	6.00
Ford Aerostar	2.00	5.00
Blimp	2.50	6.00

'94 VAMPYRA

1995 Hot Wheels Racing Metals Series

	LOOSE	IN PKG.
Ramp Truck	2.00	5.00
Race Truck	2.00	5.00
'93 Camaro	2.50	6.00
Dragster	2.00	5.00

1995 Hot Wheels Real Rider Series

	LOOSE	IN PKG.
Dump Truck	8.00	20.00
Mercedes Benz Unimog	8.00	20.00
'59 Caddy	12.00	35.00
Corvette Stingray	12.00	35.00

'94 SHADOW JET

'94 SUZUKI QUAD RACER

'94 PEARL PASSION

1995 Hot Wheels Roarin' Rods Series

	LOOSE	IN PKG.
Street Roader	2.00	5.00
Roll Patrol	2.00	5.00
Cobra	2.50	6.00
Cobra w/metal base	3.00	8.00
Mini Truck	2.00	5.00

1995 Hot Wheels Silver Series

Fire-Eater	2.00	5.00
Rodzilla	2.50	6.00
Propper Chopper	2.00	5.00
School Bus	3.00	8.00

1995 Hot Wheels Speed Gleamers Series

3-Window '34	2.50	6.00
T-Bucket	2.00	5.00
Ratmobile	1.50	4.00
Limozeen	3.00	8.00

1995 Hot Wheels Steel Stamp Series

	LOOSE	IN PKG.
'56 Flashsider	2.00	5.00
Steel Passion	2.00	5.00
'57 Chevy	2.50	6.00
Zender Fact 4	1.50	4.00

1995 Hot Wheels Treasure Hunt Series

COMPLETE SET	650.00	750.00
BOXED JC PENNEY SET (12)	750.00	900.00
JC PENNEY BOX/ CERTIFICATE	100.00	200.00
Olds 442	30.00	80.00
Gold Passion	35.00	85.00
'67 Camaro	100.00	225.00
'57 T-Bird	25.00	70.00
VW Bug	40.00	100.00
'63 Split Window Corvette	30.00	70.00
Stutz Blackhawk	20.00	50.00
Rolls Royce II	20.00	60.00
Classic Caddy	20.00	50.00
'55 Nomad	30.00	75.00
Cobra	50.00	100.00
'31 Doozie	20.00	50.00

1995 Hot Wheels Vintage Cars Series B

	LOOSE	IN PKG.
'32 Ford Vicky	4.00	8.00
Deora	5.00	12.00
Custom Mustang	5.00	12.00
Snake	5.00	10.00
Mongoose	5.00	10.00
S'cool Bus	6.00	15.00
Whip Creamer	4.00	8.00
Mutt Mobile	4.00	8.00

1996 Hot Wheels 5-Car Gift Pack

	LOOSE	IN PKG.
Cars of the 50's GP	6.00	12.00
Auto City GP	4.00	8.00
Corvette GP	6.00	12.00
Camaro GP	6.00	12.00
Porsche GP	4.00	8.00
Racing Trucks GP	4.00	8.00

1996 Hot Wheels Collectors Race Truck Series

Kenworth T-600	1.50	4.00
Nissan Truck	1.50	4.00
'56 Flashrider	2.00	5.00
Dodge Ram 1500 no tampo	5.00	15.00

1996 Hot Wheels Computer Car Series

	LOOSE	IN PKG.
'93 Camaro	4.00	8.00
Oscar Mayer Wiener Mobile	4.00	8.00
Rigor Motor	4.00	8.00
Power Pistons	4.00	8.00
Hydroplane	4.00	8.00
'96 Mustang Convertible	4.00	8.00

1996 Hot Wheels Crash and Smash Bikes

Cyber Force	3.00	6.00
Riptile	3.00	6.00
Street Sharks	3.00	6.00
Judge Dredd	4.00	8.00
Sonic The Hedgehog	4.00	8.00
Skullrider	3.00	6.00
Future Force	3.00	6.00

'94 JAGUAR XJ220

'94 RAMP TRUCK

'94 DRAGSTER

'94 STREET ROADER

1996 Hot Wheels Dark Rider Series II

	LOOSE	IN PKG.
Street Beast	1.50	4.00
Power Pistons	1.50	4.00
Thunderstreak	1.50	4.00
Big Chill	1.50	4.00

1996 Hot Wheels Fast Food Series

	LOOSE	IN PKG.
Pizzavette	1.50	4.00
Sweetstocker	5.00	12.00
Crunchchief	1.50	4.00
Pastapipe	1.50	4.00

1996 Hot Wheels Fire Squad Series

	LOOSE	IN PKG.
Ambulance	1.50	4.00
Flame Stopper	1.50	4.00
Fire-Eater	1.50	4.00
Rescue Ranger	1.50	4.00

1996 Hot Wheels First Editions

'96 Mustang Convertible	3.00	8.00
Chevy 1500	1.50	4.00
'70 Dodge Charger Daytona	3.00	8.00
Turbo Flame	1.50	4.00
Rail Rodder	1.50	4.00
Rocket Shot	1.50	4.00
VW Bus	30.00	75.00
Street Cleaver w/tampo	4.00	10.00
Radio Flyer Wagon	1.50	4.00
Air Attack	1.50	4.00
Twang Thang	1.50	4.00
Ferrari F50	1.50	4.00

1996 Hot Wheels Flame Thrower Series

Oshkosh Snow Plow	1.50	4.00
Hydroplane	1.50	4.00
Range Rover	2.00	5.00
'57 T-Bird	2.00	5.00

1996 Hot Wheels HW Classics

'65 Mustang Convertible	3.00	8.00
Mercedes 540K	1.50	4.00

	LOOSE	IN PKG.
'57 Flash Fire	1.50	4.00
'37 Bugatti	1.50	4.00
Street Beast	1.50	4.00
Fat Fendered '40	2.00	5.00
40's Woody	3.00	8.00
Bywayman	1.00	3.00
Range Rover	1.00	3.00
Baja Bug	1.00	3.00
Surf Patrol	1.00	3.00
Street Roader	1.00	3.00
'32 Ford Delivery	1.50	4.00

'94 MINI TRUCK

1996 Hot Wheels Mod Bod Series

	LOOSE	IN PKG.
School Bus	1.50	4.00
Hummer	1.50	4.00
VW Bug	1.50	4.00
'67 Camaro	2.00	5.00

1996 Hot Wheels Race Team Series II

	LOOSE	IN PKG.
Baja Bug	1.50	4.00
Bywayman	2.00	5.00
Ramp Truck	1.50	4.00
'57 Truck	1.50	4.00

1996 Hot Wheels Silver Series II

Dump Truck w/chr. Bed	4.00	10.00
40's Woodie	1.50	4.00
Wiener Mobile	1.50	4.00
'57 Chevy	2.50	6.00

1996 Hot Wheels Space Series

GM Lean Machine	1.50	4.00
Treadator	1.50	4.00
Radar Ranger	1.50	4.00
Alien	1.50	4.00

'94 ROLL PATROL

1996 Hot Wheels Speed Demons

Vampyra	1.50	4.00
Zombot	1.50	4.00
Rodzilla	1.50	4.00

1996 Hot Wheels Speed Fleet

GT Racer	1.00	3.00
VW Bug	1.00	3.00
Mazda Miata MX-5	1.00	3.00

'94 LUMINA STOCKER

'94 3-WINDOW

	LOOSE	IN PKG.
Limozeen	1.00	3.00
Lamborghini Diablo	1.00	3.00
Shadow Jet	1.00	3.00
Stealth	1.00	3.00
Splittin Image II	1.00	3.00
Mercedes 380SEL	1.00	3.00
Chevy Lumina	1.00	3.00
Cyber Cruiser	1.00	3.00
'93 Camaro	1.00	3.00
Purple Passion	4.00	10.00
Lexus SC400	1.00	3.00
Demo Man Lean Machine	2.50	6.00
Firebird Funny Car	1.00	3.00
Ferrari Testarossa	1.00	3.00
Lamborghini Countach	1.00	3.00
Sol-Aire CX4	1.00	3.00
Jaguar XJ220	1.00	3.00
BMW 850I	1.00	3.00
Ferrari F40	1.00	3.00
'93 HW Race Car	1.00	3.00
Nissan Custom Z	1.00	3.00
Dodge Viper	1.00	3.00
Pontiac Banshee	1.00	3.00
Custom Vette	1.00	3.00
Wiener Mobile	1.00	3.00
Treadator	1.00	3.00
Vector Avtech	1.00	3.00
'63 Corvette Split Window	1.50	4.00
Flashfire	1.00	3.00
Shock Factor	1.00	3.00
Limozeen	1.00	3.00
Ferrari 348	1.00	3.00
Lamborghini Diablo	1.00	3.00
Zender Fact 4	1.00	3.00
XT-3	1.00	3.00
Mini Truck	1.00	3.00
Toyota MR2	1.00	3.00
Turbo Streak	1.00	3.00
Alien	1.00	3.00
Audi	1.00	3.00
Silhouette Series II	1.00	3.00
Speed Shark	1.00	3.00
Ferrari 250	1.00	3.00
Toyota MR2 Rally	1.00	3.00
Porsche 930	1.00	3.00

1996 Hot Wheels Splatter Paint Series

	LOOSE	IN PKG.
Rescue Ranger	1.50	4.00
'80's Camaro	1.50	4.00
Sidesplitter	1.50	4.00
'55 Chevy	1.50	4.00

1996 Hot Wheels Sports Car Series

	LOOSE	IN PKG.
Shelby Cobra 427 (soccer)	1.50	4.00
Caddy (basketball)	1.50	4.00
Porsche 930 (baseball)	1.50	4.00
Custom Corvette (football)	1.50	4.00

1996 Hot Wheels Street Eater Series

	LOOSE	IN PKG.
Propper Chopper	1.50	4.00
Speed Machine	1.50	4.00
Roll Patrol	1.50	4.00
Silhoutte II	1.50	4.00

'94 RODZILLA

1996 Hot Wheels Treasure Hunt Series

COMPLETE SET	225.00	350.00
BOXED JC PENNEY SET (12)	250.00	400.00
JC PENNEY BOX/ CERTIFICATE	35.00	60.00
'40's Woodie	15.00	40.00
Auburn 852	12.00	35.00
Ferrari	12.00	30.00
Jaguar	12.00	30.00
'59 Caddy	12.00	35.00
Dodge Viper WH	25.00	60.00
Dodge Viper R Error	10.00	25.00
'57 Chevy	25.00	55.00
Ferrari 355	12.00	30.00
'58 Corvette	15.00	45.00
Lamborghini Countach	10.00	30.00
Dodge Ram 1500	12.00	35.00
'37 Bugatti	10.00	30.00

'94 SCHOOL BUS

1996 Hot Wheels Workhorses

Propper Chopper	1.50	4.00
Fuji Blimp	1.50	4.00
Peterbilt Dump Truck	1.50	4.00
School Bus	1.50	4.00
Recycling Truck	1.50	4.00
Ford Tractor	1.50	4.00
Tank Truck	1.50	4.00
Blimp	1.50	4.00
Cat Road Roller	1.50	4.00
Ford Stake Bed Truck	1.50	4.00
Good Humor Truck	1.50	4.00
Fire-Eater	1.50	4.00

'94 STEEL PASSION

'94 STEEL PASSION

1997 Hot Wheels 30th Anniversary '67 Muscle Cars

COMPLETE SET (3)		45.00
'67 Camaro	15.00	
'67 Custom Mustang	15.00	
'67 Pontiac GTO	15.00	

1997 Hot Wheels 30th Anniversary Pony Pack

COMPLETE SET (3)		40.00
'96 Mustang Coupe	10.00	
'67 Custom Mustang	15.00	
'65 Convertible Mustang	10.00	

1997 Hot Wheels 35th Anniversary Shelby Cobra

COMPLETE SET (2)		40.00
Viper	20.00	
Cobra Hardtop	20.00	

1997 Hot Wheels 40th Anniversary '57 Chevy

COMPLETE SET (4)		45.00
'57 Chevy	10.00	
'57 Chevy	10.00	
'57 Chevy	10.00	
'57 Chevy	10.00	

1997 Hot Wheels 40th Anniversary T-Bird

COMPLETE SET (2)		20.00
'57 T-Bird (convertible)	8.00	
'57 T-Bird (hardtop)	8.00	

1997 Hot Wheels 5-Car Packs

50's Cars GP	6.00	10.00
Action News Team	5.00	7.00
Auto City GP	5.00	8.00
Blimp/Support GP	5.00	8.00
Camaro GP	8.00	12.00
Chevy GP	5.00	8.00
Construction Crew GP	5.00	8.00
Corvette GP	8.00	12.00
Emergency GP	5.00	8.00
HW Race Team GP	5.00	8.00
I Love Trucks	5.00	7.00

Police 5-Car	5.00	7.00
Porsche GP	5.00	8.00
Race Team Series II	5.00	8.00
Rescue Squad	5.00	7.00
Road Repairs	5.00	7.00
Super Cars GP	5.00	8.00
Way Out Originals	4.00	6.00
World of Racing	4.00	6.00

1997 Hot Wheels
60th Anniversary European Classics

COMPLETE SET (2)		25.00
Mercedes 540K	10.00	
Talbot Lago	10.00	

1994 '57 CHEVY

1997 Hot Wheels Action Packs

Mars Rover dated front	10.00	25.00
Mars Rover no date	5.00	10.00
Home Improvement	8.00	15.00
Fire Fighter	5.00	8.00
Police Force	5.00	8.00
Construction	5.00	8.00
Undersea Adventure	5.00	8.00
Racing Team	5.00	8.00
Surf Patrol	5.00	8.00

1997 Hot Wheels
Biff! Bam! Boom! Series

Mini Truck	1.00	3.00
Limozeen	1.50	4.00
Range Rover	1.00	3.00
VW Bug	1.50	4.00

'95 FLAME STOPPER

1997 Hot Wheels
Blue Streak Series

	LOOSE	IN PKG.
'55 Chevy	1.00	3.00
Olds 442	1.00	3.00
Nissan Truck	5.00	15.00
Speed Blaster	1.00	3.00

1997 Hot Wheels
Caterpillar Action Machines

Front Shovel	1.00	3.00
Dump Truck	1.00	3.00
Bulldozer	1.00	3.00
Wheel Loader	1.00	3.00
Compactor	1.00	3.00

'95 PROPER CHOPPER

'96 LIMOZEEN

1997 Hot Wheels Collectible Sets

	LOOSE	IN PKG.
COMPLETE SET (5)		40.00
'67 Camaro	10.00	
'80's Camaro Z28	10.00	
'93 Camaro	10.00	
'95 Camaro Convertible	10.00	

1997 Hot Wheels Dealer's Choice Series

Silhouette II	1.00	3.00
Street Beast	1.00	3.00
'63 Corvette	2.00	5.00
Baja Bug	2.00	5.00

1997 Hot Wheels First Editions

Plymouth Barracuda	4.00	10.00
Firebird Funny Car	1.00	3.00
Lamborghini 25th Ann.	1.00	3.00
Excavator	8.00	20.00
Ford F-150 Truck	1.00	3.00
Way 2 Fast	1.00	3.00
'97 Corvette	1.00	3.00
Mercedes DTM Race Car	1.00	3.00
'59 Chevy Impala	1.00	3.00
BMW M Roadster	1.00	3.00
Scorchin' Scooter	3.00	8.00
Saltflat Racer	1.00	3.00

1997 Hot Wheels Heat Fleet Series

	LOOSE	IN PKG.
Police Cruiser	1.00	3.00
School Bus	1.00	3.00
Tank Truck	1.00	3.00
Ramblin' Wrecker	1.00	3.00

1997 Hot Wheels Phantom Racer Series

Power Rocket	1.50	4.00
Power Pistons	1.50	4.00
Power Pipes	1.50	4.00
Road Rocket	1.50	4.00

1997 Hot Wheels Quicksilver Series

	LOOSE	IN PKG.
Chevy Stocker	1.50	4.00
Silver Bullet (Aeroflash)	1.50	4.00
Ferrari 308	1.50	4.00
T-Bird Stock Car	1.50	4.00

1997 Hot Wheels Race Team Series III

	LOOSE	IN PKG.
Hummer	1.50	4.00
Chevy 1500	1.00	3.00
3-Window '34	2.00	5.00
'80's Corvette	1.00	3.00

1997 Hot Wheels Rockin' Rods Series

	LOOSE	IN PKG.
Twang Thang	1.00	3.00
Ferrari 355	1.00	3.00
Turbo Flame	1.00	3.00
Porsche 930	1.00	3.00

1997 Hot Wheels Speed Spray Series

COMPLETE SET (4)	LOOSE	IN PKG.
Hydroplane	1.00	3.00
Street Roader	1.00	3.00
XT-3	1.00	3.00
Funny Car	1.00	3.00

1997 Hot Wheels Spy Print Series

	LOOSE	IN PKG.
Stealth	1.00	2.00
Alien	1.00	2.00
Sol-Aire CX4	1.00	2.00
Custom Corvette	1.00	3.00

1997 Hot Wheels Street Beast Series

	LOOSE	IN PKG.
Unimog	1.00	3.00
Jaguar XJ220	1.00	3.00
Blown Camaro	1.50	4.00
Corvette Stingray	1.00	3.00

'96 BAJA BUG

'96 CITY POLICE

'96 STREET ROADER

'97 ROCKIN' RODS

1997 Hot Wheels Treasure Hunt Series

BOXED JC PENNEY SET (12)	225.00	300.00
'56 Flashsider	12.00	30.00
Silhouette II	10.00	25.00
Mercedes 500SL	10.00	25.00
Street Cleaver	12.00	30.00
GM Lean Machine	10.00	25.00
Hot Rod Wagon	15.00	45.00
Olds Aurora	12.00	30.00
Dog Fighter	10.00	25.00
Buick Wildcat	10.00	25.00
Blimp	10.00	25.00
Audi Avus	10.00	25.00
Rail Rodder	12.00	30.00

1997 Hot Wheels White Ice Series

	LOOSE	IN PKG.
Speed Machine	1.00	2.00
Shadow Jet	1.00	2.00
Splittin' Image II	1.00	2.00
Twin Mill II	1.00	2.00

1997 Hot Wheels X-V Racers

Mercedes Street	3.00	8.00
Mercedes Race	3.00	8.00
Ferrari Street	3.00	8.00
Ferrari Race	3.00	8.00
Laguna Lightning	3.00	8.00
Black Lightning	3.00	8.00
Live Wire	3.00	8.00
Thunderstreak	3.00	8.00
Big Thunder	3.00	8.00
Flat Out	3.00	8.00
Lightning Streak	3.00	8.00
Silver Storm	3.00	8.00
Quick Fire	3.00	8.00
Hot Rod	3.00	8.00
Hot Rod	3.00	8.00
Scortch Torch	3.00	8.00

1998 Hot Wheels Dash 4 Cash

Avus Quattro	1.00	3.00
Dodge Viper RT/10	1.00	3.00
Ferrari F40	1.00	3.00
Jaguar XJ 220	1.00	3.00

1998 Hot Wheels First Editions

Escort Rally	1.50	4.00
Slideout	4.00	12.00

Dodge Sidewinder	2.00	5.00
Dodge Caravan	2.00	5.00
Jaguar XK8	1.00	3.00
Jaguar D-Type	1.50	4.00
'32 Ford	2.50	6.00
'65 Impala Lowrider	1.50	4.00
'63 T-Bird	2.00	5.00
Dairy Delivery	2.50	6.00
Mercedes SLK	1.50	4.00
Lakester	2.00	5.00
Hot Seat	1.50	4.00
Cord	1.00	3.00
Pikes Peak Celica	1.50	4.00
IROC Firebird	1.50	4.00
'70 Roadrunner	2.50	6.00
Mustang Cobra	2.00	5.00
Panoz GTR-1	2.00	5.00
'40 Ford	2.00	5.00
Go Kart	2.00	5.00
Super Comp Dragster	2.50	6.00
Solar Eagle III	2.00	5.00
Tail Dragger	2.50	6.00
Tow Jam	2.50	6.00
Custom c3500	2.00	5.00
Custom c3500 w/thin tam.	3.00	8.00
Super Modified	2.00	5.00
Chaparral 2	1.50	4.00
Mustang Mach 1	1.50	4.00
Sweet 16 II	2.00	5.00
Callaway C-7	2.00	5.00
Chrysler Thunderbolt	1.50	4.00
Bad Mudder	1.50	4.00
At-A-Tude	1.50	4.00
Copperhead	1.50	4.00
Whatta Drag	1.00	3.00
Express Lane	1.50	4.00
Cat-A-Pult	1.50	4.00
Fathom This	2.00	5.00
Double Vision	1.50	4.00

'97 LAMBORGHINI DIABLO

1998 Hot Wheels First Editions Biohazard Series

Flame Stopper	.75	2.00
Hydroplane	.75	2.00
Recycling Truck	.75	2.00
Rescue Ranger	.75	2.00

1998 Hot Wheels Low 'N Cool Series

1997 '57 CHEVY

	LOOSE	IN PKG.
'59 Caddy	1.00	3.00
'59 Impala	1.00	3.00
Limozeen	1.00	3.00
Mini Truck	1.00	3.00

'97 FERRARI TESTAROSSA

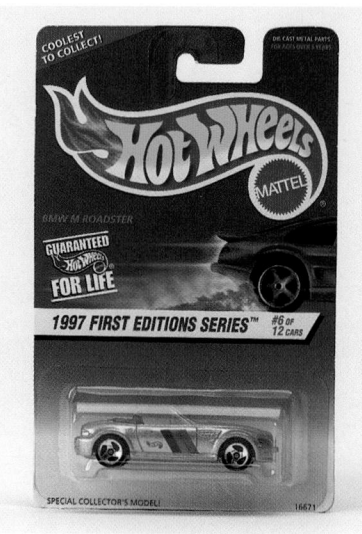

'97 BMW ROADSTER

1998 Hot Wheels Tattoo Machines

	LOOSE	IN PKG.
'57 T-Bird	.75	2.00
'93 Camaro	.75	2.00
Stutz Blackhawk	.75	2.00
Corvette Stingray	.75	2.00

1998 Hot Wheels Techno Bits

Shadow Jet II	.75	2.00
Power Pistons	.75	2.00
Shadow Jet	.75	2.00
Radar Ranger	.75	2.00

1998 Hot Wheels 30th Anniversary

	LOOSE	IN PKG.
COMP. COLL. SET (30)	120.00	150.00
1968 Deora	6.00	15.00
1969 '32 Ford Vicky	6.00	15.00
1970 Nomad	5.00	12.00
1971 Mutt Mobile	4.00	10.00
1972 Side Kick	4.00	10.00
1973 Sweet 16	4.00	10.00
1974 Rodger Dodger	3.00	8.00
1975 Large Charge	3.00	8.00
1976 Sting Ray	4.00	10.00
1977 '57 Chevy	4.00	10.00
1978 '57 T-Bird	4.00	10.00
1979 Auburn 852	3.00	8.00
1980 '40's Woodie	4.00	10.00
1981 Old Number 5	3.00	8.00
1982 Firebird Funny Car	3.00	8.00
1983 Shelby Cobra	5.00	12.00
1984 '65 Mustang	5.00	12.00
1985 XT-3	3.00	8.00
1986 Path Beater	3.00	8.00
1987 Sharkruiser	3.00	8.00
1988 Porsche 959	3.00	8.00
1989 '32 Ford Delivery	3.00	8.00
1990 Purple Passion	3.00	8.00
1991 '59 Caddy	4.00	10.00
1992 Goodyear Blimp	4.00	10.00
1993 Dodge Viper RT/10	4.00	10.00
1994 Rigor Motor	3.00	8.00
1995 Hydroplane	3.00	8.00
1996 VW Bus	12.00	30.00
1997 Scorchin' Scooter	6.00	15.00
Twin Mill w/pin, cert.	8.00	15.00

1998 Hot Wheels Treasure Hunts

	LOOSE	IN PKG.
BOXED JC PENNEY SET	200.00	275.00
Twang Thang	10.00	25.00
Scorchin' Scooter	15.00	40.00
Kenworth T600A	10.00	30.00
3 Window '34	12.00	30.00
Turbo Flame	10.00	20.00
Saltflat Racer	10.00	25.00
Street Beast	12.00	25.00
Road Rocket	10.00	25.00
Sol-Aire CX4	10.00	25.00
'57 Chevy	15.00	40.00
Stingray III	12.00	25.00
Way 2 Fast	10.00	25.00

1998 Hot Wheels Tropicool Series

	LOOSE	IN PKG.
Ice Cream Truck	1.00	3.00
Baja Bug	1.00	3.00
Classic Caddy	1.00	3.00
Corvette Convertible	1.00	3.00

1999 Hot Wheels Buggin' Out Series

	LOOSE	IN PKG.
Treadator	1.00	3.00
Shadow Jet	1.00	3.00

1999 Hot Wheels First Editions

'36 Cord	1.50	4.00
'99 Mustang w/T int.	1.50	4.00
'99 Mustang w/R int.	8.00	20.00
'38 Phantom	2.00	5.00

1999 Hot Wheels Treasure Hunts

	LOOSE	IN PKG.
Mercedes 540K	15.00	30.00
T-bird Stocker	18.00	30.00

Hot Wheels Consumer Editions

Albertson's Hiway Haul. (2)	3.00	8.00
Aquafresh 6 car set	20.00	40.00
Avon '93 Camaro	6.00	12.00
Avon '65/'96 Mustangs	7.50	15.00
Avon '63 Split/Custom Vette	7.50	15.00
Avon Park N' Plates Set (4)	20.00	35.00

'97 SHADOW JET II

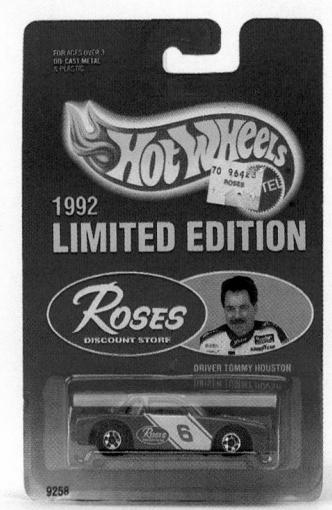

'92 ROSES RACE

'95 CHUCK E. CHEESE RACER

'95 C. REX RACER

Barbie 35th Camaro/7000	75.00	110.00
Barbie Hiway Hauler/5000	60.00	90.00
Blue Angels VW Bus	40.00	60.00
C.Rex Racer	6.00	12.00
C.Rex Mobile	7.50	15.00
Chicago Cubs 'Vettes (2)	75.00	125.00
Chuck E.Cheese Camaro	6.00	12.00
Chuck E. Cheese Custom Van	7.50	15.00
Chuck E. Che.'80's Corvette	6.00	12.00
Chuck E. Cheese '80's Firebird	7.50	15.00
Chuck E. Cheese Trailbuster	10.00	20.00
Coronet Buick Stocker	6.00	10.00
Dinty Moore Bywayman	4.00	8.00
Dinty Moore Hiway Hauler	4.00	8.00
Dodge Viper RT-10 BLA	10.00	20.00
Duracell '93 Camaro	30.00	50.00
Edelbrock '63 Corvette	12.00	20.00
Edelbrock '68 Camaro	15.00	25.00
FAO Schwarz '94 Gold Set	125.00	200.00
FAO Schwarz '95 Gold Set	125.00	200.00
FAO Schwarz '96 Gold Set	60.00	100.00
FAO Schwarz '95 His.of HW	60.00	100.00
FAO Schwarz '96 His.of HW	50.00	90.00
FAO Schwarz '97 His.of HW	50.00	75.00
FAO Schwarz Olympic Set	100.00	150.00
Feed the Children HH	10.00	18.00
Fisher Price '65 Mustang	12.00	25.00
Getty Camaro	10.00	18.00
Getty VW Bug	12.00	25.00
1994 Gulf Set (4)	15.00	25.00
HEB '95 Hiway Hauler	5.00	10.00
HEB '96 Hiway Hauler	5.00	10.00
Hills '58 Corvette	30.00	60.00
Hills '67 Camaro	45.00	70.00
Hills '67 GTO	20.00	40.00
Hills '70 Barracuda	20.00	35.00
Hills '70 Mustang	20.00	40.00
Hills '96 YIR (12) #/5000	40.00	75.00
Hills Cool N' Custom (8)	15.00	25.00
1994 Hormel Set (5)	25.00	40.00
1996 Hughes Fam.Mkt. (2)	4.00	8.00
JC Whitney '32 Ford Del.	50.00	100.00
JC Whitney '55 Chevy	20.00	40.00
JC Whitney '56 Flashsider	20.00	40.00
JC Whitney Baja Bug	20.00	40.00
JC Whitney Dairy Deliv.	20.00	40.00
JC Whitney F-150	20.00	35.00
JC Whitney Fat Fend.'40	25.00	45.00
JC Whitney Nomad	20.00	40.00
JC Whitney Roll Patrol	15.00	30.00
JC Whitney RV	20.00	35.00
JC Whitney Scorchin' Scoot.	25.00	50.00
JC Whitney VW Bus	90.00	160.00
Jewell T Hiway Hauler	5.00	10.00
Jiffy Lube '65 Impala	12.50	25.00
Jiffy Lube 67 GTO	15.00	30.00
Jiffy Lube Scorchin' Scooter	12.50	25.00
Jiffy Lube VW Bus	18.00	30.00

Kay-Bee Hot Rods (3 pk.)	30.00	50.00
Kell.Raisin Bran Dragster	7.50	15.00
K-Mart Pontiac 70th Ann.	30.00	50.00
K-Mart Thunder Truck	10.00	20.00
Kool-Aid Stocker R or BLU	6.00	12.00
Kool-Aid Nissan Truck	6.00	12.00
Kool-Aid Wacky Wrhse.Hau.	12.00	20.00
Lane Auto. Chevy Stocker	10.00	15.00
L.A.P.D. Squad car/10,000	40.00	75.00
L.A.P.D. Paddy Wagon	40.00	75.00
Lexmark '34 Ford	25.00	50.00
Lexmark '40 Ford	25.00	50.00
Lexmark Mercury	25.00	40.00
Lexmark Passion	25.00	50.00
Little Debbie Series I (3)	10.00	20.00
Little Debbie Series II (3)	10.00	20.00
Lucky's 1996 Hiway Hauler	5.00	10.00
Malt-O-Meal '32 Delivery	10.00	20.00
Malt-O-Meal 3 Wind. '34	10.00	20.00
Malt-O-Meal '56 Flashsider	10.00	20.00
Malt-O-Meal '57 Chevy	10.00	20.00
MSRA 40's Woodie	12.00	20.00
McDonald's Happy Meal Haul.	10.00	20.00
Osco/Sav-On Hiway Hauler	5.00	10.00
1992 Rose's LE car	8.00	15.00
Service Merch. 25th Ann.	100.00	175.00
Ser.Merch. Class.Amer.Cars	100.00	150.00
Shell 4 car set	10.00	20.00
Shop-Rite Hiway Hauler	5.00	10.00
Target Bla.Convertibles (8)	25.00	40.00
Target Designer Cars (8)	25.00	40.00
Target Motorin' Music (4)	35.00	60.00
Target Street Rods (4)	20.00	30.00
Target Then & Now (8)	25.00	40.00
Thunderbirds VW Bus	20.00	35.00
Tony's Pizza Lambourghini	5.00	10.00
U.S. Cam.Club '67 Camaro	15.00	25.00
U.S. Racing Team Hummer	15.00	25.00
Van De Kamps '67 Mustang	15.00	30.00
Van De Kamps Deora	15.00	25.00
Van de Kamps Fish-O-Saurus	20.00	35.00
Van De Kamps Hiway Hauler	15.00	25.00
Van De Kamps VW Bus	20.00	40.00
Von's Produce Hi.Hauler (2)	5.00	10.00
Woolworth's Hi.Hauler (2)	5.00	10.00
Yamahauler HH	12.00	25.00

'96 VAN DE KAMPS

1998 Hot Wheels Convention Zamac

	LOOSE	IN PKG.
COMPLETE SET (1-25)	2000.00	2500.00
'56 Flashsider	90.00	150.00
'57 Chevy	100.00	160.00
'59 Caddy	50.00	90.00
'67 Camaro	225.00	325.00
'70 Dodge Daytona Charger	60.00	100.00
'97 Corvette	60.00	100.00

ZAMAC '67 CAMARO

ZAMAC SHELBY COBRA

ZAMAC REDEMPTION

3-Window '34 Ford	75.00	135.00
40's Woodie	90.00	150.00
Auburn 852	40.00	80.00
Audi Avus	50.00	90.00
Camaro Race Car	50.00	90.00
Dodge Viper	90.00	150.00
Driven to the Max	40.00	80.00
Ferrari F-40	50.00	90.00
Jaguar XJ-220	50.00	90.00
Limozeen	40.00	80.00
Mazda MX-5 Miata	50.00	90.00
Mercedes 500SL	40.00	80.00
Porsche Carrera	40.00	80.00
Range Rover	40.00	80.00
Shelby Cobra	90.00	150.00
Street Beast	40.00	80.00
Swingfire	50.00	90.00
Tractor	60.00	100.00
VW Bug	200.00	300.00
Silhouette II Redemption	50.00	90.00

'75 TOY FAIR VAN

1975—99 Hot Wheels Toy Fair

Van	1200.00	1400.00
Passion	45.00	60.00
Camaro	100.00	125.00
Demon	100.00	125.00
Chevy Stocker	250.00	300.00
Power Piston	125.00	150.00
Deora	110.00	150.00
Twinmill	100.00	125.00
Ford GT-90	80.00	125.00

'92 TOY FAIR

'93 TOY FAIR

'94 TOY FAIR

'95 TOY FAIR

'96 TOY FAIR

'97 TOY FAIR

'98 TOY FAIR

'99 TOY FAIR

'76 P-911 GOLD SALES AWARD

Matchbox

'69 Mustang

Despite heavy competition from How Wheels, Matchbox collectors have a wide array of high quality products from which to choose

There's something to be said for foresight.

In the late 1940s, the good people at Lesney Products thought the idea of a small, die-cast car ("a complete toy," the box read) just might catch on.

It did, as Lesney beget Matchbox, whose sales reached $28 million by early 1969.

Ironically enough, it was arguably a lack of that same foresight that knocked Matchbox out of the spotlight. The Mattel toy company, armed with a huge advertising budget, launched its Hot Wheels line, a series of die-cast toy cars with frictionless wheels that kids took to like crazy, in 1969.

Matchbox was slow to react, and its sales promptly plummeted to $6 million later that same year. But still, to this day, the passion of Matchbox collectors persists admirably.

Matchbox Collectibles Inc., the direct-marketing arm of Matchbox (now owned by former nemesis Mattel), and a loyal legion of fans ensure that Matchbox cars are regularly bought and sold on the secondary market, in addition to the new items you can find at your neighborhood toy store. More than 2,000 Matchbox cars have been produced over the years, and some of the older ones have been valued higher than $1,000.

On the whole, though, Matchbox collecting can be a relatively affordable hobby. A thrifty shopper should be able to track down cars from the 1990s for less than five bucks each, with a few exceptions (the 1990 Corvette Grand Sport BLU HEINZ 57, for example, goes for a whopping $15 in mint condition). If one of your priorities is spending less per piece than you'd spend on a movie, sticking with cars from the last two decades would be a good idea.

If you venture further into Matchbox's past, however, you'll discover more high-dollar items. In tracking a few actual sales of items from 1956 to 1970, several cars went for more than $100, including the 1970 Model 39C Ford Tractor with the orange body, which sold for an even $200.

You'll find a few cars with prices well above $200 scattered throughout our price guide. The early Lesney cars, such as the 1948 driverless Diesel Road Roller Gw/R MW Y flywheel and the Caterpillar Bulldozer G with a blade and Tractor G without the blade, go for as much as $400 in they're still in their original package. But the biggest items were released in 1949. The Soap Box Racer GOL ($1,500) and the Rag and Bone Cart G ($1,200) are both very valuable due to scarcity and high demand.

One of the most unique and valuable Matchbox cars is the Vauxhall Victor in red (45a), which can fetch as much as $1,500, depending on condition. Then there's the four 1952 Lesney products, which range in value from $250 to $750, and a couple of items in the 1955 Matchbox line that will fetch sellers more than $200.

The very first Matchbox was the Aveling Barford Road Roller #1, a toy that owed its origin to the best-selling Dinky Model, in 1953. A driver was cast as part of the body, and variations to the center section and ends of the roof were made.

Matchbox's roots actually go back to 1947, when Rodney Smith and Leslie Smith (no relation) returned to London from stints in World War II to form Lesney Products, a castings business that they operated out of the same building that once housed a formerly condemned pub called The Rifleman. (The name "Lesney" is a combination of Leslie and Rodney.)

The Smiths were soon joined by Jack Odell, a former associate of Leslie, and spent several years in die-casts-for-hire mode, cranking out products such as the hook ceiling plate they made for General Electric Co. It wasn't until a year later that Lesney manufactured toy automobiles, starting with the Diesel Road Roller, the Cement Mixer and the Crawler Tractor. It was Odell who coined the term "Matchbox" in 1952 after he created a brass prototype of a small Road Roller and placed it in a matchbox-sized container so his daughter could take it with her to school.

Next came the "Matchbox 75," also referred to as the "1-75" series. Items in this core line of toys are approximately 1:64 in scale and comprise the first official Matchbox series issued by Lesney. Their wheel types — regular wheels, metal wheels and Superfast — divide them into three categories. The metal wheels are the earliest issues and are the most valuable. The issues of the cars with regular wheels were gray and silver, and black plastic was added later. The Matchbox 75 changes from year to year with new models and colors, but the Shovel Nose Tractor has consistently appeared in the line since 1976.

Superfast was Matchbox's answer to Hot Wheels. In 1969, Lesney began changing the wheels on the 1-75 series to allow the cars faster speeds when propelled (by kids, not adults, we presume) across hardwood floors and desktops. You won't find the name "Superfast" on any Matchbox cars today, but the same premise comprises the standard issue of most modern Matchbox cars.

Matchbox storage case.

The Matchbox 1999 line.

Matchbox unveiled some slightly larger vehicles in 1957 with the release of the Major Packs, a line that included vehicles such as combines, car transporters, double-articulated trailers and tankers. Although the toys used the same 1:64 scale as the 1-75 series, the vehicles were too large to fit in the Matchbox-size packaging if they were to remain true to scale. The Major Pack series was discontinued in 1966, but several of the more popular Major Pack issues, such as the M6-B Racing Car Transporter and the M8-B Guy Warrior Car Transporter, were converted to the King Size series, a 1:43 scale line of mostly construction and commercial vehicles.

Then came the Super Kings, which followed the Superfast revolution and included mostly the same vehicles as the King Size line but with the low-friction wheel and axle design found on the smaller models. As the Super Kings line became dominated by commercial equipment, the regular automobile toys became known as Speed Kings until 1978, when the lines were assimilated into one Super Kings series.

And finally, Matchbox came up with the Premiere Series (also known as the "World Class" series), which consisted of premium issues of the standard castings with better paint, printed details and rubber tires on chrome wheels.

Matchbox collecting has been around nearly as long as the cars themselves.

The man behind the original Matchbox Collectors Club was Fred Bronner, who launched the fledging MCC in 1966. Bronner, who had formed the Fred Bronner Corp. in 1956, handled the importing, marketing and sales of Lesney imported toys, including Matchbox, from his New York City office. In 1956, Bronner was given the exclusive rights to sell the Matchbox series in the United States. In 1963 Lesney bought out the Fred Bronner Corp., its inventory, and the New York facility located at 120 E. 23rd St.

By 1967, sales of Matchbox vehicles were booming. To keep up with increased demand, Lesney purchased a 20,000-foot manufacturing facility devoted solely to the production of its Matchbox line of die-cast toys.

By 1969, more than five million models were rolling out of the factory each week. The company was exporting its Matchbox toy line to 130 countries, while 40 percent of production ended up in U.S. toy shops. Lesney had 14 factories employing 6,500 people. Also in 1969, the chairman of the Smithsonian Institute selected an assortment of 21 Matchbox models to go on display inside the museum.

And Matchbox collectors certainly know a classic when they see one. The MB 38, Model "A" Ford Van continues to be one of the most popular Matchbox cars. In 1979 Lesney released the MB73E Model "A" Ford Saloon, which led to the release of the MB38 G Model "A" Ford Van in 1982. During 1987, 1988 and 1996, its use in a number of on-pack offers has made the acquisition of every issue a demanding task for collectors.

Most collectors categorize their vehicles by series, starting with the first, Regular Wheels, then breaking them down into series that include Yesteryears, King Size, Superfast, Convoy, Twin Packs, Sky Busters, Sea Kings, World Class, Premiere Collection, Originals, Promotional Vehicles, Play Sets and Track Sets.

The Models of Yesteryear began in 1956, when the N.H.P. Allchin Traction Engine in 1:80 scale was released, along with the first die-cast miniature of a steam-driven, road-going vehicle.

The bottom line is, collecting Matchbox toys should be fun. Whether you spend $1,500 or $5, whether you buy the 1949 Soap Box Racer or the 1998 Camaro Z-28, starting your collection and then adding to it over the years can be a satisfying and enjoyable experience.

1948 Lesney

	LOOSE
Diesel Road Roller G w/R MW Y flywheel, no driver	400.00
Diesel Road Roller G w/unpainted MW, no driver	250.00
Diesel Road Roller G w/unpainted MW driver	250.00
Caterpillar Bulldozer w/blade G	400.00
Caterpillar Bulldozer w/blade Y	175.00
Caterpillar Bulldozer w/blade OR	175.00
Caterpillar Tractor G, no blade	400.00
Caterpillar Tractor Y, no blade	175.00
Caterpillar Tractor OR, no blade	175.00
Cement Mixer	125.00

1949 Lesney

	LOOSE
Horse Drawn Milk Float OR	400.00
Horse Drawn Milk Float BLU	750.00
Rag and Bone Cart Y	750.00
Rag and Bone Cart G	1200.00
Ruston Bucyrus 10RB P/S Excavator	300.00
Soap Box Racer GOL	1500.00

1950 Lesney

	LOOSE
Jumbo the Elephant litho tin windup w/key	350.00
Prime Mover w/Trailer/Bulldozer OR w/OR trailer, G bulldozer	400.00
Prime Mover w/Trailer/Bulldozer OR w/BLU trailer, OR bulldozer	350.00
Prime Mover w/Trailer/Bulldozer OR w/BLU trailer, Y bulldozer w/R blade	300.00

1951 Lesney

	LOOSE
Muffin the Mule, cast metal	250.00

1952 Lesney

	LOOSE
Large Coronation Coach GOL coach, w/king/queen	750.00
Large Coronation Coach GOL coach w/queen	250.00
Large Coronation Coach GOLP queen only	350.00
Large Coronation Coach SILP queen only	450.00

1953 Lesney

	LOOSE
Small Coronation Coach SILP	80.00
Small Coronation Coach lt. GOLP	100.00
Small Coronation Coach GOL	125.00

'56 BEDFORD MILK VAN

1953 Matchbox

	LOOSE	IN PKG.
Diesel Road Roller dk. G	25.00	40.00
Diesel Road Roller LG	70.00	100.00
Dumper, G MW	90.00	125.00
Dumper, unpainted MW	30.00	50.00
Cement Mixer BLU w/OR MW	25.00	40.00
Cement Mixer BLU w/GR PW	30.00	50.00

1954 Lesney

	LOOSE	
Massey Harris Tractor, R w/BR wheels, BLA tires	300.00	.
Bread Bait Press	75.00	

1954 Matchbox

	LOOSE	IN PKG
Massey Harris Tractor w/fenders	40.00	60.00
London Bus R, BUY MATCHBOX MW	50.00	75.00

1955 Lesney

	LOOSE	
Conestoga Wagon, no barrels	125.00	
Conestoga Wagon, R barrels	125.00	

1955 Matchbox

	LOOSE	IN PKG.
Road Roller G w/T driver	60.00	90.00
6-Wheel Quarry Truck, MW	40.00	60.00
6-Wheel Quarry Truck, GR PW	150.00	225.00
Horse Drawn Milk Cart OR w/SIL bottles, MW	100.00	150.00
Horse Drawn Milk Cart OR w/WH bottles, MW	100.00	150.00
Horse Drawn Milk Cart OR w/OR bottles, MW	60.00	90.00
Horse Drawn Milk Cart OR w/GR PW	65.00	100.00
Caterpillar Tractor OR, no blade, w/OR driver	65.00	100.00
Caterpillar Tractor Y no blade, w/R driver	65.00	100.00
Caterpillar Tractor dk. Y, no blade, w/dk. Y driver	25.00	40.00
Dennis Fire Escape, no frt. bumper, no cast number	65.00	100.00
Mech. Horse and Trailer, R cab, GR trailer, MW	50.00	75.00
Road Tanker G w/MW	350.00	500.00
Road Tanker dk. Y w/MW	65.00	100.00
Road Tanker Y w/MW	50.00	75.00
Road Tanker R w/MW, ESSO	40.00	60.00
Road Tanker R w/MW, ESSO decal on side	50.00	75.00
Land Rover w/driver OL, MW	40.00	60.00
Bedford Wreck Truck T	40.00	60.00

1956 Matchbox

	LOOSE	IN PKG.
Daimler Ambulance	50.00	75.00
Prime Mover Tr. Tractor OR w/MW	35.00	60.00

'56 Ford Prefect

	LOOSE	IN PKG.
Prime Mover Tr. Tractor OR w/PW	150.00	225.00
Atlantic Trailer T w/MW	75.00	125.00
Bedford MATCHBOX REMOVAL Van MAR or BLU	135.00	200.00
Bedford MATCHBOX REMOVAL Van GR	50.00	75.00
Bedford MATCHBOX REMOVAL Van LG	50.00	75.00
Caterpillar D8 Bulldozer Y w/R blade	50.00	80.00
MG Midget Sports Car w/driver	65.00	100.00
Stake Truck MAR, GOL grill/fuel tanks, MW	65.00	100.00
Stake Truck MAR, SIL grill/fuel tanks, MW	35.00	50.00
Stake Truck MAR , MAR grill/fuel tanks	35.00	50.00
Stake Truck MAR, SIL grill/fuel tanks, GR PW	75.00	125.00
Stake Truck MAR, dk. R grill/fuel tanks, GR PW	75.00	125.00
Bedford Duple Long Distance Coach	50.00	75.00
Vauxhall Cresta sedan R w/WH or CRE roof, no windows	50.00	75.00
Berkeley Cavalier Tr. Trailer BLU	35.00	60.00
Berkeley Cavalier Tr. Trailer LG	50.00	75.00
Berkeley Cavalier Tr. Trailer met. G	150.00	225.00
Weatherhill Hydraulic Excavator Y	40.00	60.00
Bedford DUNLOP 12CWT Van	35.00	50.00
READY-MIX Concrete Truck, MW, GOL grill	50.00	75.00
READY-MIX Concrete Truck, MW, SIL grill	40.00	60.00
READY-MIX Concrete Truck, SIL PW	100.00	150.00
Bedford Low Loader, dk. G cab, T trailer	50.00	75.00
Bedford Compressor Truck	25.00	40.00
Bedford Milk Delivery Van	35.00	60.00
Ford Prefect sedan LB	75.00	125.00
Ford Prefect sedan GR/BR or OL/BR	50.00	75.00

1957 Matchbox

	LOOSE	IN PKG.
Dumper w/driver	40.00	60.00
Massey Harris Tractor R no fenders	50.00	75.00
London Bus, MW, BUY MATCHBOX SERIES	35.00	60.00
London Bus, GR PW, BUY MATCHBOX SERIES	50.00	75.00
Euclid Quarry Truck Y w/GR PW	150.00	225.00
Euclid Quarry Truck Y w/BLA PW	30.00	50.00
Dennis Fire Escape w/fr.bumper, #9 cast, MW	25.00	40.00
Dennis Fire Escape w/fr.bumper, #9 cast, GR PW	100.00	150.00
Atlantic Trailer T w/T towbar, GR PW	25.00	40.00

Atlantic Trailer OR w/BLA towbar, GR PW	75.00	125.00
Atlantic Trailer OR w/BLA towbar, BLA PW	25.00	40.00
Atlantic Trailer OR w/unpaint. towbar, BLA PW	25.00	40.00
Atlantic Trailer OR w/OR towbar, BLA PW	30.00	50.00
Ford Customline Station Wagon Y w/MW	30.00	50.00
Ford Customline Station Wagon Y w/GR PW	30.00	50.00
Jaguar XK140 Coupe CRE	30.00	50.00
Jaguar XK140 Coupe R	100.00	150.00
Ford Zodiac Mk II sedan LB, no windows, MW	25.00	40.00
Ford Zodiac Mk II sedan dk. G, no windows, MW	25.00	40.00
Ford Zodiac Mk II sedan dk. G, no windows, GR PW	30.00	50.00
Ford Zodiac Mk II sedan SIL/OR, no windows, GR PW	30.00	50.00
Ford Zodiac Mk II sedan T/OR, no windows, GR PW	30.00	50.00
Ford Zodiac Mk II sedan, T/OR w/G windows, GR PW	50.00	75.00
Ford Zodiac Mk II sedan, T/OR w/G windows, SIL PW	30.00	50.00
Volkswagen Van BLU MATCHBOX EXPRESS, MW	50.00	75.00
Volkswagen Van BLU MATCHBOX EXPRESS, GR PW	75.00	100.00
Volkswagen Van BLU MATCHBOX EXPRESS, SIL PW	90.00	125.00
Volkswagen Van BLU MATCHBOX EXPRESS, BLA PW	100.00	150.00
Marshall Horse Box Truck, R cab, BR horse box, MW	40.00	60.00
Marshall Horse Box Truck, R cab, BR horse box, GR PW	40.00	60.00
Marshall Horse Box Truck, R cab, BR horse box, SIL PW	65.00	100.00
Marshall Horse Box Truck, R cab, BR horse box, BLA PW	100.00	150.00
Austin A50 sedan BLU/G, MW	40.00	60.00
Austin A50 sedan BLU/G, GR PW	40.00	60.00
Coca-Cola Lorry, no base, uneven cases	100.00	150.00
Coca-Cola Lorry, no base, even cases	75.00	125.00
Refuse Truck GR/BR, w/MW	75.00	125.00
Refuse Truck dk. GR w/MW	25.00	40.00
Refuse Truck dk. GR w/GR PW	50.00	75.00
Refuse Truck SIL w/GR PW	65.00	100.00
Ford Zodiac Convertible Pl, T interior/base, MW	75.00	125.00
Ford Zodiac Convertible Pl, LB interior/base, MW	35.00	50.00

	LOOSE	IN PKG.
Ford Zodiac Convertible PI, LB interior/base, GR PW	50.00	75.00
Ford Zodiac Convertible PI, LB interior/base, SIL PW	60.00	90.00
Bedford Tipper Truck R w/T dumper, MW	30.00	40.00
Bedford Tipper Truck R w/T dumper, GR PW	30.00	40.00
Bedford Tipper Truck R w/BLA PW	25.00	35.00
D-Type Jaguar G, 41 decal, MW	40.00	60.00
D-Type Jaguar G, 41 decal, GR PW	40.00	60.00
Bedford EVENING NEWS Van, Y/OR, MW	40.00	60.00
Bedford EVENING NEWS Van, Y/OR, GR PW	40.00	60.00
Bedford EVENING NEWS Van, Y/OR, BLA PW	40.00	60.00

1958 Matchbox

	LOOSE	IN PKG.
Road Roller G w/R MW	40.00	60.00
Mechanical Horse & Trailer, R cab, T trailer, MW	50.00	75.00
Mechanical Horse & Trailer, R cab, T trailer, GR PW	50.00	75.00
Road Tanker ESSO R, GOL trim, MW	30.00	50.00
Road Tanker ESSO R, SIL trim, MW	25.00	40.00
Road Tanker ESSO R, GR PW	25.00	40.00
Road Tanker ESSO R, SIL PW	125.00	200.00
Road Tanker ESSO R, BLA PW	65.00	100.00
Bedford Wreck Truck T, MW	50.00	75.00
Bedford Wreck Truck T, GR PW	50.00	75.00
Daimler Ambulance, MW	25.00	40.00
Daimler Ambulance, GR PW	25.00	40.00
Daimler Ambulance, SIL PW	75.00	125.00
Caterpillar Dozer Y, no blade braces, Y w/Y blade	50.00	75.00
MGA Sports Car WH, MW, GOL grille	65.00	100.00
MGA Sports Car WH, MW, SIL grille	50.00	75.00
MGA Sports Car WH, GR PW	65.00	100.00
MGA Sports Car WH, SIL PW	100.00	150.00
Long Distance Coach LG LONDON TO GLA..	35.00	60.00
Long Distance Coach G LONDON TO GLA..	65.00	100.00
Vauxhall Cresta sedan CRE, no windows, MW	30.00	50.00
Vauxhall Cresta sedan CRE, no windows, GR PW	50.00	75.00
Vauxhall Cresta sedan CRE, G windows, GR PW	35.00	60.00
Vauxhall Cresta sedan CRE/LB, G windows, GR PW	250.00	400.00

Vauxhall Cresta sedan GR/BLU, G windows, GR PW	35.00	60.00
Vauxhall Cresta sedan BRON/BLU, G windows, GR PW	50.00	75.00
Vauxhall Cresta sedan GR/PI , G windows, GR PW	35.00	60.00
Vauxhall Cresta sedan GR/PI, G windows, SIL PW	35.00	60.00
Vauxhall Cresta sedan GOL, G windows, GR PW	35.00	60.00
Vauxhall Cresta sedan GOL, G windows, SIL PW	35.00	60.00
Vauxhall Cresta sedan COP, G windows, GR PW	35.00	60.00
Vauxhall Cresta sedan COP, G windows, SIL PW	35.00	60.00
Vauxhall Cresta sedan COP, G windows, BLA PW	25.00	40.00
Hillman Minx sedan G w/MW	150.00	225.00
Hillman Minx sedan BLU/GR w/GR roof, MW	50.00	75.00
Hillman Minx sedan BLU/GR w/GR roof, GR PW	50.00	75.00
Hillman Minx sedan BLU w/CRE roof, GR PW	50.00	75.00
Rolls Royce Silver Cloud BLU, MW	30.00	50.00
Rolls Royce Silver Cloud, GR PW	35.00	60.00
Rolls Royce Silver Cloud, SIL PW	35.00	60.00
Vauxhall Victor sedan Y w/no windows, MW	25.00	40.00
Vauxhall Victor sedan Y w/no windows, GR PW	25.00	40.00
Vauxhall Victor sedan Y w/G windows, GR PW	25.00	40.00
Vauxhall Victor sedan Y w/clear windows, GR PW	25.00	40.00
Vauxhall Victor sedan Y w/G windows, SIL PW	30.00	50.00
Vauxhall Victor sedan Y w/G windows, BLA PW	20.00	35.00
Morris Minor 1000 G w/MW	40.00	60.00
Morris Minor 1000 G w/GR PW	50.00	75.00
Morris Minor 1000 BLU w/GR PW	65.00	100.00
Trojan 1-Ton BROOKE BOND TEA Van R, MW	25.00	40.00
Trojan 1-Ton BROOKE BOND TEA Van R, GR PW	30.00	50.00
Meteor Sports Boat/Trailer BLU, T deck, MW	30.00	50.00
Meteor Sports Boat/Trailer BLU, T deck, GR PW	50.00	75.00
Meteor Sports Boat/Trailer BLU, T deck, SIL PW	65.00	100.00
M3 Army Halftrack Personnel Carrier, MW front/rollers	30.00	50.00
M3 Army Halftrack Personnel Carrier, GR PW fr., met.rollers	35.00	60.00

M3 Army Halftrack Personnel Carrier, GR PW front/rollers	50.00	75.00
M3 Army Halftrack Personnel Carrier, GR PW fr., SIL plast.rollers	40.00	60.00
M3 Army Halftrack Personnel Carrier, BLA PW fr./rollers	25.00	40.00
Commer Pickup dk. T w/MW	35.00	60.00
Commer Pickup lt. T w/MW	50.00	75.00
Commer Pickup lt. T w/GR PW	30.00	50.00
Commer Pickup dk. T w/GR PW	35.00	60.00
Commer Pickup dk. T w/SIL PW	65.00	100.00
Commer Pickup R/WH w/SIL PW	200.00	300.00
Commer Pickup R/GR w/SIL PW	65.00	100.00
Commer Pickup R/GR w/GR PW	50.00	75.00
Commer Pickup R/GR w/BLA PW	50.00	75.00
Flatbed Transporter, PORTLAND CEMENT, MW	30.00	50.00
Flatbed Transporter, PORTLAND CEMENT, GR PW	30.00	50.00
Flatbed Transporter, PORTLAND CEMENT, SIL PW	65.00	100.00
Flatbed Transporter, PORTLAND CEMENT, BLA PW	100.00	150.00
Maserati 4CL T/1948 Racer R w/BLA PW	50.00	75.00
Maserati 4CL T/1948 Racer R w/BLA plast.tires/spok.wheels	75.00	125.00
Maserati 4CL T/1948 Racer Y w/BLA tires/spoked wheels	50.00	75.00
Aston Martin DB2 Saloon met. LG w/MW	35.00	60.00
Aston Martin DB2 Saloon met. LG w/GR PW	30.00	50.00
Aston Martin DB2 Saloon R w/GR PW	100.00	150.00
Aston Martin DB2 Saloon R w/BLA PW	100.00	150.00
Army Saracen Personnel Carrier, BLA PW	20.00	35.00
DUKW Army Amphibian, MW	50.00	75.00
DUKW Army Amphibian, GR PW	35.00	60.00
DUKW Army Amphibian, BLA PW	35.00	60.00
London Trolley Bus R, BLA rods, MW	125.00	200.00
London Trolley Bus R, R rods, MW	35.00	60.00
London Trolley Bus R, R rods, GR PW	25.00	40.00
Wolseley 1500 sedan Y/G w/GOL grille	50.00	75.00
Wolseley 1500 sedan Y/G w/SIL grille	30.00	50.00
Wolseley 1500 sedan G w/SIL grille	35.00	60.00
Wolseley 1500 sedan GR w/SIL grille	75.00	125.00
BEA Coach, British European Airways decals, GR PW	25.00	40.00
BEA Coach, BEA decals, GR PW	30.00	50.00

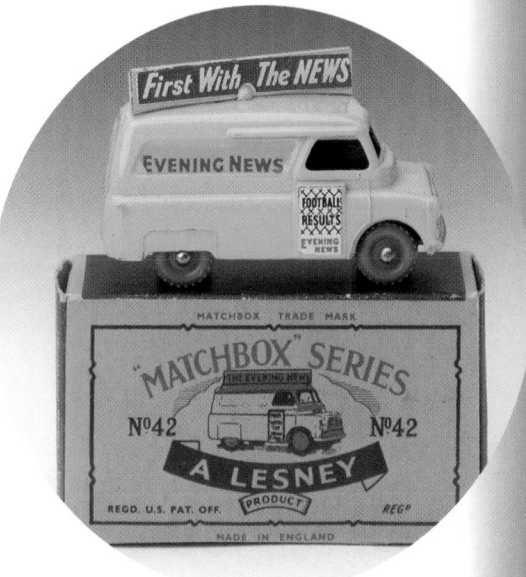

'57 BEDFORD EVENING NEWS VAN

BEA Coach, BEA decals, SIL PW	65.00	100.00
BEA Coach, BEA decals, BLA PW	65.00	100.00
Ford Thames Singer Van LG w/GR PW	30.00	50.00
Ford Thames Singer Van LG w/SIL PW	65.00	100.00
Ford Thames Singer Van G w/GR PW	65.00	100.00
Ford Thames Singer Van G w/SIL PW	75.00	125.00
Morris J2 BUILDERS SUPPLY Pickup LB, rear wind., GR PW, R/BLA decals	25.00	40.00
Morris J2 BUILDERS SUPPLY Pickup LB, rear wind., SIL PW, R/BLA decals	30.00	50.00
Morris J2 BUILDERS SUPPLY Pickup LB, rear wind., GR PW, R/WH decals	35.00	60.00
Morris J2 BUILDERS SUPPLY Pickup LB, rear window, SIL PW, R/WH decals	30.00	50.00
Morris J2 BUILDERS SUPPLY Pickup LB, rear wind., BLA PW, R/WH decals	25.00	40.00
Morris J2 BUILDERS SUPPLY Pickup LB, no rear win., BLA PW, R/WH decals	25.00	40.00

'58 ALBION CHIEFTAIN

1959 Matchbox

	LOOSE	IN PKG.
Caterpillar Tractor Y w/metal rollers	35.00	60.00
Merryweather Marquis Fire Engine R, T ladder, GR PW	25.00	40.00
Merryweather Marquis Fire Engine R, GOL ladder, GR PW	25.00	40.00
Merryweather Marquis Fire Engine R, GOL ladder, BLA PW	18.00	30.00
Merryweather Marquis Fire Engine R, SIL ladder, BLA PW	15.00	25.00
Merryweather Marquis Fire Engine R, T ladder, BLA PW	15.00	25.00
Land Rover OL, w/o driver, no roof, GR PW	50.00	75.00
Land Rover OL, w/o driver, no roof, BLA PW	25.00	40.00
Atlantic Super Prime Mover Truck Tractor OR, GR PW	250.00	400.00
Atlantic Super Prime Mover Truck Tractor OR, BLA PW	25.00	40.00
ERF 686 Truck EVEREADY FOR LIFE, BLU, GR PW	30.00	50.00
ERF 686 Truck EVEREADY FOR LIFE, BLU, SIL PW	60.00	90.00
ERF 686 Truck EVEREADY FOR LIFE, BLU, BLA PW	30.00	50.00
Weatherhill Hydraulic Excavator, GR PW	30.00	50.00

Weatherhill Hydraulic Excavator, BLA PW	20.00	35.00
Bedford Low Loader LG cab w/MW	30.00	50.00
Bedford Low Loader LG cab w/GR PW	50.00	75.00
Bedford Low Loader G cab w/GR PW	65.00	100.00
Thames Trader Compressor Truck Y, GR PW	125.00	175.00
Thames Trader Compressor Truck Y, BLA PW	25.00	40.00
Ferret Scout Car OL w/BLA PW	20.00	30.00
General Service Lorry OL w/BLA PW	30.00	50.00
Ford 3-Ton 4x4 Army Ambulance OL w/BLA PW	35.00	60.00
Scammell Breakdown Truck OL, BLA PW, G hook	25.00	40.00
Scammell Breakdown Truck OL, BLA PW, SIL hook	25.00	40.00
Scammell Breakdown Truck OL BLA PW, GR hook	25.00	40.00
3.4 Litre Jaguar met. BLU, GR PW	30.00	50.00
3.4 Litre Jaguar BLU, GR PW	40.00	60.00
Citroen DS19 Y, GR PW	40.00	60.00
Citroen DS19 Y, SIL PW	75.00	125.00
Saladin Armoured Car OL, BLA PW	25.00	40.00
Austin Mk 2 Radio Truck OL, BLA PW	25.00	40.00
Commer 30 CWT NESTLE'S Van MAR, GR PW	50.00	75.00
Commer 30 CWT NESTLE'S Van R, GR PW	40.00	60.00
Ford Thames Estate Car Y/LB, no windows, GR PW	25.00	40.00
Ford Thames Estate Car Y/LB, clear windows, GR PW	30.00	50.00
Ford Thames Estate Car Y/LB, G windows, GR PW	25.00	40.00
Ford Thames Estate Car Y/LB, clear windows, SIL PW	25.00	40.00
Ford Thames Estate Car Y/LB, G windows, SIL PW	25.00	40.00
Ford Thames Estate Car Y/LB, G windows, BLA PW	25.00	40.00
Austin 200-Gallon Water Truck OL, BLA PW	30.00	50.00
Fordson Power Major Farm Tractor BLU, GR fr.wheels, GR tires/OR rear whe.	30.00	50.00
Fordson Power Major Farm Tractor BLU, BLA fr.wheels, BLA tires/OR rear whe.	25.00	40.00
Fordson Power Major Farm Tractor BLU, GR tires/OR whe.	30.00	50.00
Fordson Power Major Farm Tractor BLU, GR tires/Y wheels	50.00	75.00
Fordson Power Major Farm Tractor BLU, BLA tires/Y wheels	65.00	100.00
Fordson Power Major Farm Tractor BLU, BLA tires/OR wheels	30.00	50.00

'58 LONG DISTANCE COACH

Sugar Container Truck TATE/LYLE BLA PW	25.00	40.00
Ford Thames Trade Wreck Truck, GR PW	30.00	50.00
Ford Thames Trader Wreck Truck, BLA PW	30.00	50.00
Caterpillar Bulldozer Y w/blade braces, MW	25.00	40.00
Caterpillar Bulldozer Y w/blade braces, SIL PW	65.00	100.00
Caterpillar Bulldozer Y w/blade braces, BLA PW	25.00	35.00
Aston Martin Racing Car G, GR driver, 52 decal	40.00	60.00
Aston Martin Racing Car G, GR driver, 41 decal	40.00	60.00
Aston Martin Racing Car G, GR driver 5 decal	40.00	60.00
Aston Martin Racing Car G, R driver, 19 decal	30.00	50.00
Aston Martin Racing Car G, WH driver, 19 decal	30.00	50.00
Aston Martin Racing Car G, WH driver, 3 decal	40.00	60.00
Aston Martin Racing Car G, WH driver, 53 decal	40.00	60.00
Commer Milk Delivery Truck, SIL PW	30.00	50.00
Commer Milk Delivery Truck, GR PW	50.00	75.00
Commer Milk Delivery Truck, BLA PW	30.00	50.00
READY MIX Concrete Truck OR, OR mixer, GR PW	30.00	50.00
READY MIX Concrete Truck OR, OR mixer, SIL PW	100.00	150.00
READY MIX Concrete Truck OR, OR mixer, BLA PW	15.00	25.00
Austin A55 Cambridge, two-tone G GR PW	30.00	50.00
Austin A55 Cambridge, two-tone G SIL PW	30.00	50.00
Austin A55 Cambridge, two-tone G BLA PW	30.00	50.00
Magirus Deutz 6-Wheel Crane Truck SIL, SIL PW	30.00	50.00
Magirus Deutz 6-Wheel Crane Truck SIL, GR PW	30.00	50.00
Magirus Deutz 6-Wheel Crane Truck SIL, BLA PW	25.00	40.00
Lambretta TV175 Scooter/Sideca G, BLA PW	50.00	75.00
Leyland Royal Tiger Coach BLU, GR PW	30.00	50.00
Leyland Royal Tiger Coach BLU, SIL PW	20.00	35.00
Leyland Royal Tiger Coach BLU, BLA PW	15.00	25.00
Sports Boat-Trailer w/outboard motor, GR PW	50.00	75.00
Sports Boat-Trailer w/outboard motor, BLA PW	25.00	40.00

	LOOSE	IN PKG.
Chevrolet Impala BLU w/LB roof, GR PW	30.00	50.00
Chevrolet Impala BLU w/LB roof, SIL PW	30.00	50.00
Chevrolet Impala BLU w/LB roof, BLA PW	30.00	50.00

1962 Matchbox

	LOOSE	IN PKG.
Aveling Barford Road Roller G, R PW	15.00	25.00
Bedford Lomas Ambulance, GR PW	75.00	125.00
Bedford Lomas Ambulance, SIL PW	50.00	75.00
Bedford Lomas Ambulance, BLA PW	20.00	30.00
Jaguar XKE R, clear windows, GR PW	30.00	50.00
Jaguar XKE R, G windows, GR PW	25.00	40.00
Jaguar XKE R, clear windows, BLA PW	30.00	50.00
Jaguar XKE BRON, clear windows, BLA PW	30.00	50.00
Volkswagen Caravette Camper LG, GR PW	35.00	50.00
Volkswagen Caravette Camper LG, BLA PW	35.00	50.00
Pontiac Convertible PUR	65.00	100.00
Pontiac Convertible Y	35.00	50.00
Aveling Barford Tractor Shovel Y w/ Y shovel/base/driver	30.00	50.00
Aveling Barford Tractor Shovel Y Y shovel, R base/driver	25.00	40.00
Aveling Barford Tractor Shovel Y R shovel, Y base/driver	20.00	35.00
Aveling Barford Tractor Shovel Y R shovel/base/driver	30.00	50.00
Drott Excavator R, w/SIL motor/base, MW	30.00	50.00
Drott Excavator R w/SIL motor/base, SIL MW	65.00	100.00
Drott Excavator R, SIL motor/base, BLA MW	20.00	35.00
Drott Excavator OR, SIL motor/base, BLA MW	20.00	35.00
Drott Excavator OR w/OR motor/base, BLA MW	30.00	50.00
Jaguar 3.8 Litre Saloon R, GR PW	20.00	35.00
Jaguar 3.8 Litre Saloon R, SIL PW	25.00	40.00
Jaguar 3.8 Litre Saloon met. R, SIL PW	25.00	40.00
Jaguar 3.8 Litre Saloon R, BLA PW	18.00	30.00
Harley Davidson Motorcycle-Sidecar, BRON w/BLA tires	125.00	175.00
Ferrari F1 Racing Car R, WH dri.	30.00	50.00
Ferrari F1 Racing Car R, GR dri.	30.00	50.00

1963 Matchbox

	LOOSE	IN PKG.
Dennis Refuse Truck BLU w/GR container, no porthole in rear	30.00	50.00
Dennis Refuse Truck BLU w/GR container, porthole in rear	12.00	20.00
Hoveringham Tipper R cab, OR tipper	12.00	20.00
Ford Zephyr 6 Mk III sedan, GR PW	20.00	35.00
Ford Zephyr 6 Mk III sedan, SIL PW	18.00	30.00
Ford Zephyr 6 Mk III sedan, BLA PW	50.00	75.00
Vauxhall Victor Estate Car Y, G interior, GR PW	20.00	35.00
Vauxhall Victor Estate Car Y, G interior, SIL PW	25.00	40.00
Vauxhall Victor Estate Car Y, G interior, BLA PW	18.00	30.00
Vauxhall Victor Estate Car Y, R interior, SIL PW	18.00	30.00
Vauxhall Victor Estate Car Y, R interior, BLA PW	18.00	30.00
Commer Ice Cream Canteen BLU, GR PW	100.00	150.00
Commer Ice Cream Canteen BLU, BLA PW	20.00	30.00
Commer Ice Cream Canteen met. BLU, BLA PW	75.00	125.00
Commer Ice Cream Canteen CRE w/roof/side decals, BLA PW	50.00	75.00
Commer Ice Cream Canteen CRE /oval roof decal, plain side decals, BLA PW	30.00	50.00
Mercedes Benz MAR, GR PW	18.00	30.00
Mercedes Benz R, GR PW	18.00	30.00
Mercedes Benz MAR, SIL PW	20.00	35.00
Mercedes Benz MAR, BLA PW	25.00	40.00
Mercedes Benz R, BLA PW	50.00	75.00
Ford Fairlane Police Car dk. BLU, BLA PW	65.00	100.00
Ford Fairlane Police Car LB, GR PW	65.00	100.00
Ford Fairlane Police Car LB, SIL PW	65.00	100.00
Ford Fairlane Police Car LB, BLA PW	20.00	35.00
Ford Fairlane Fire Chief Car R, GR PW	65.00	100.00
Ford Fairlane Fire Chief Car R, SIL PW	100.00	150.00
Ford Fairlane Fire Chief Car R, BLA PW	25.00	40.00
TV Service Van w/ladder/antenna TV sets, GR PW, RENTASET decals	125.00	175.00
TV Service Van w/ladder/antenna TV sets, GR PW, RADIO RENTALS decals	150.00	200.00

TV Service Van w/ladder/antenna TV sets, BLA PW, RENTASET decals	30.00	50.00
TV Service Van w/ladder/antenna TV sets, BLA PW, RADIO RENTALS decals	50.00	75.00

1964 Matchbox

	LOOSE	IN PKG.
Euclid Quarry Truck Y	15.00	25.00
Caterpillar Tractor Y w/BLA PW	20.00	30.00
Scammell Mountaineer Snowplow, GR PW	75.00	100.00
Scammell Mountaineer Snowplow, BLA PW	20.00	35.00
Caterpillar Crawler Bulldozer, SIL PW	65.00	100.00
Caterpillar Crawler Bulldozer, BLA PW	20.00	35.00
Pontiac Grand Prix, BLA PW	20.00	35.00
Bedford Petrol Tanker w/tilt cab, Y cab, BP, GR PW	125.00	175.00
Bedford Petrol Tanker w/tilt cab, Y cab, BP, BLA PW	20.00	30.00
Bedford Petrol Tanker w/tilt cab, dk. BLU cab, ARAL, BLA PW	100.00	150.00
Mark 10 Jaguar, GR PW	100.00	150.00
Mark 10 Jaguar, BLA PW	20.00	30.00
Lincoln Continental BLU, BLA PW	15.00	25.00
Lincoln Continental G, BLA PW	15.00	25.00
Snow Trac Tractor, WH treads, SNOW TRAC decals	20.00	30.00
Snow Trac Tractor, WH treads, plain sides	12.00	20.00
Snow Trac Tractor, WH treads, SNOW TRAC cast into sides	12.00	20.00
Snow Trac Tractor, GR treads, SNOW TRAC cast into sides	35.00	60.00
Rolls Royce Phantom V T, GR PW	65.00	100.00
Rolls Royce Phantom V T, BLA PW	18.00	30.00
Rolls Royce Phantom V GR, BLA PW	25.00	40.00
John Deere Tractor, GR PW	18.00	30.00
John Deere Tractor, BLA PW	12.00	20.00
John Deere Trailer w/3 barrels, GR PW	15.00	25.00
John Deere Trailer w/3 barrels, BLA PW	15.00	25.00
Airport Foamite Crash Tender, SIL nozzle	10.00	15.00
Airport Foamite Crash Tender, GOL nozzle	20.00	35.00
Jeep Gladiator Pickup Truck, G interior	30.00	50.00
Jeep Gladiator Pickup Truck, WH interior	20.00	35.00

'58 COKE TRUCK

1965 Matchbox

'58 DAIMLER AMBULANCE

	LOOSE	IN PKG.
London Bus, LONGLIFE decals	18.00	30.00
London Bus, VISCO STATIC decals or stickers	12.00	20.00
London Bus, BARON OF BEEF	150.00	200.00
Taylor Jumbo Crane, Y weight box	12.00	20.00
Taylor Jumbo Crane, R weight box	15.00	25.00
Safari Land Rover G w/BR luggage on roof	15.00	25.00
Safari Land Rover BLU w/BR luggage on roof	12.00	20.00
Safari Land Rover BLU w/T lug.	12.00	20.00
Safari Land Rover GOL w/T lug.	65.00	100.00
Dodge Wreck Truck, BP, BLA PW, Y cab, G body	15.00	25.00
Chevrolet Impala Taxi Cab OR, GR PW, WH interior	200.00	350.00
Chevrolet Impala Taxi Cab OR, BLA PW, WH or R interior	20.00	30.00
Chevrolet Impala Taxi Cab Y, BLA PW, WH or R interior	15.00	25.00
Trailer Caravan Y	12.00	20.00
Trailer Caravan Pl	15.00	25.00
8-Wheel Crane Truck dk. G, BLA PW	12.00	20.00
Ford GT WH w/R removable wheels, 6 decal	75.00	125.00
Ford GT WH, Y wheels, 6 decal	10.00	15.00
Ford GT WH, Y wheels, 9 decals	10.00	15.00
Ford GT Y, Y wheels	35.00	60.00
Ford GT WH, Y wheels, 6 label	10.00	15.00
Ford GT WH, Y wheels, 9 label	10.00	15.00
Studebaker Lark Wagonaire w/hunter, 1/2 dogs	25.00	40.00
Ford Corsair w/boat/rack on roof, GR PW	25.00	40.00
Ford Corsair w/boat/rack on roof, BLA PW	10.00	15.00
BRM Racing Car BLU, BLA tires, 5 decal/label	10.00	15.00
BRM Racing Car BLU, BLA tires, 3 decal	30.00	50.00
BRM Racing Car R, BLA tires, 5 decal or label	25.00	40.00
Cadillac S/S Ambulance, w/regular wheels	15.00	25.00
Fiat 1500 LB w/lug. on roof	12.00	20.00
Fiat 1500 R w/lug. on roof	75.00	100.00
Mercedes Benz Coach LB	50.00	75.00
Mercedes Benz Coach OR	12.00	20.00
Hatra Tractor Shovel OR, OR PW, GR tires	18.00	30.00
Hatra Tractor Shovel OR, OR PW, BLA tires	12.00	20.00

Hatra Tractor Shovel OR, R PW, BLA tires	10.00	15.00
Hatra Tractor Shovel OR, Y wheels, BLA tires	10.00	15.00
Hatra Tractor Shovel Y, R PW, BLA tires	10.00	15.00
Hatra Tractor Shovel Y, Y PW, BLA tires	10.00	15.00
Ferrari Berlinetta LB, w/spoked or CHR wheel hubs	50.00	75.00
Ferrari Berlinetta G, spoked or CHR wheel hubs	15.00	25.00
Ferrari Berlinetta G, chrome hubs	12.00	20.00

1966 Matchbox

	LOOSE	IN PKG.
Ford Refuse Truck, BLA PW	10.00	15.00
Ford Mustang Fastback WH	12.00	20.00
Ford Mustang Fastback OR	75.00	125.00
Boat and Trailer, dull BLU deck	15.00	25.00
Boat and Trailer, bright BLU deck	10.00	15.00
Leyland Pipe Truck w/6 pipes, BLA PW, SIL grill	8.00	12.00
Leyland Pipe Truck w/6 pipes, BLA PW, white grill	12.00	20.00
Lotus Racing Car OR	18.00	30.00
Lotus Racing Car G	15.00	25.00
Mercedes Benz 230SL Conv.CRE w/regular wheels	8.00	12.00
Mercedes Benz 230SL Conv.WH w/regular wheels	12.00	20.00
Fire Pumper, DENVER decals	12.00	20.00
Fire Pumper, shield labels	10.00	15.00
Fire Pumper, no labels	12.00	20.00
Opel Diplomat GOL, GR motor	12.00	20.00
Opel Diplomat GOL, CHR motor	12.00	20.00
Dodge Cattle Truck, metal base	10.00	15.00
Dodge Cattle Truck, plastic base	10.00	15.00
Dodge Dump Truck	12.00	20.00
Ford Galaxie Police Car, BLU dome light	25.00	40.00
Ford Galaxie Police Car, R dome light	20.00	35.00
Land Rover Fire Truck, GR PW	135.00	200.00
Land Rover Fire Truck, BLA PW	12.00	20.00
Ford Galaxie Fire Chief Car	12.00	20.00
Leyland Site Office Truck	10.00	15.00
Alvis Stalwart BP EXPLORATION, Y PW	25.00	40.00
Alvis Stalwart BP EXPLORATION, G PW	12.00	20.00
MG 1100 w/driver/dog	15.00	25.00
Atkinson Grit Spreader	12.00	20.00
Standard Jeep CJ5	12.00	20.00
Daimler London Bus CRE, ESSO EXTRA PETROL	15.00	25.00

Daimler London Bus G, ESSO EXTRA PETROL	12.00	20.00
Daimler London Bus R, ESSO EXTRA PETROL	8.00	12.00

1967 Matchbox

	LOOSE	IN PKG.
Dodge Stake Truck, BLU/G stakes	50.00	75.00
Dodge Stake Truck, G stakes	8.00	12.00
Rolls Royce Silver Shadow R, CHR hubs	10.00	15.00
Volkswagen Camper SIL raised 6-window roof	15.00	25.00
Honda Motorcycle/Trailer OR no decals	20.00	30.00
Honda Motorcycle/Trailer OR HONDA decals	25.00	40.00
Honda Motorcycle/Trailer Y HONDA decals	12.00	20.00
Ford Tractor	8.00	12.00
Hay Trailer	6.00	10.00
GMC Refrigerator Truck	10.00	15.00
Mercedes Benz Unimog T LB chassis	12.00	20.00
Mercedes Benz Unimog BLU R chassis	12.00	20.00
Claas Combine Harvester	6.00	10.00
Greyhound Bus, clear windows	50.00	75.00
Greyhound Bus, BR windows	10.00	15.00
Volkswagen 1600TL R CHR hubs, no roof rack	12.00	20.00
Volkswagen 1600TL R CHR hubs, MAR roof rack	15.00	25.00
Volkswagen 1600TL PUR CHR hubs, no roof rack	125.00	175.00

1968 Matchbox

	LOOSE	IN PKG.
Mercedes Benz Lorry G, BLA PW, OR canopy	8.00	12.00
Mercedes Benz Lorry G, BLA PW, Y canopy	8.00	12.00
Mercedes Trailer G, BLA PW, OR canopy	8.00	12.00
Mercedes Trailer G, BLA PW, Y canopy	8.00	12.00
Mercedes Benz Binz Ambulance	10.00	15.00
Ford Pickup, WH grill	10.00	15.00
Ford Pickup, SIL grill	12.00	20.00
Iso Grifo sportscar w/CHR hubs	8.00	12.00
Volkswagen 1500 Saloon WH with 137 on doors	8.00	12.00
Foden Concrete Truck	12.00	20.00
Ford Cortina GT LB, no roof rack	12.00	20.00
Ford Cortina GT LB, w/roof rack	15.00	25.00
GMC Tipper Truck	12.00	20.00
Mack Dump Truck	15.00	25.00

	LOOSE	IN PKG.
Leyland Petrol Tanker G, BP labels, SIL grill	10.00	15.00
Leyland Petrol Tanker G, BP labels, WH grill	10.00	15.00
Leyland Petrol Tanker BLU, ARAL labels, SIL grill	50.00	75.00
Volkswagen Camper SIL, no windows on roof	15.00	25.00
Pony Trailer w/2 horses	10.00	15.00
Mercedes Benz 300SE G	12.00	20.00
Mercedea Benz 300SE BLU	12.00	20.00
DAF Tipper Container Truck BLU, Y container, GR cover	18.00	30.00
DAF Tipper Container Truck SIL, Y container, GR cover	10.00	15.00
Ford Zodiac Mk IV sedan SIL/BLU	8.00	12.00
Mercury Parklane Police Car, R dome light	35.00	60.00
Mercury Parkland Police Car, BLU dome light	6.00	10.00
DAF Girder Truck	8.00	12.00
Mercury Cougar LG, CHR hubs	6.00	10.00
Dodge Crane Truck, R hook	15.00	25.00
Dodge Crane Truck, Y hook	15.00	25.00
Ford Heavy Wreck Truck, ESSO, BR windows	40.00	60.00
Ford Heavy Wreck Truck, ESSO, G windows	12.00	20.00
Mercury Commuter Station Wagon, CHR hubs	10.00	15.00

'58 MARSHALL HOUSE

1969 Matchbox

	LOOSE	IN PKG.
Mercedes Benz Lorry GOL, OR canopy	12.00	20.00
Mercedes Benz Lorry GOL, Y canopy	12.00	20.00
Mercedes Benz Lorry R, Y canopy, TRANSCONT..	6.00	10.00
Mercedes Benz Lorry OL, T canopy, USA48350	8.00	12.00
Mercedes Benz Lorry OL drab, T canopy, USA48350	30.00	50.00
Mercedes Benz Lorry OL, T canopy, "4TS 702K"	6.00	10.00
Mercedes Benz Lorry BLU, OR/Y canopy, IMS	12.00	20.00
Mercedes Trailer GOL, OR canopy	12.00	20.00
Mercedes Trailer GOL, Y canopy	12.00	20.00
Mercedes Trailer R, Y canopy, TRANSCONT..	6.00	10.00
Mercedes Trailer OL, T canopy, USA48350	8.00	12.00
Mercedes Trailer drab OL, T canopy, USA48350	30.00	50.00

Mercedes Trailer OL, T canopy, 4TS 702K	6.00	10.00
Mercedes Trailer BLU, OR/Y canopy, IMS	12.00	20.00
Lotus Europa BLU, no Superfast on base	50.00	75.00
Lotus Europa BLU, Superfast on base	8.00	12.00
Lotus Europa PUR	8.00	12.00
Lotus Europa BLA	10.00	15.00
Mercedes Benz Scaffold Truck, BLA PW	12.00	20.00
Mercedes Benz Scaffold Truck	12.00	20.00
Iso Grifo sportscar dk. BLU	12.00	20.00
Iso Grifo sportscar BLU	12.00	20.00
Iso Grifo sportscar LB	6.00	10.00
Iso Grifo sportscar powder BLU	8.00	12.00
Case Bulldozer, G treads	8.00	12.00
Case Bulldozer, BLA treads	10.00	15.00
AEC Ergomatic Horse Box, BLA PW	12.00	20.00
Field Car G hubs	200.00	300.00
Field Car R hubs, unpainted base	6.00	10.00
Field Car R hubs, BLA base	8.00	12.00
Lamborghini Marzal R	10.00	15.00
Lamborghini Marzal PI	10.00	15.00
Lamborghini Marzal Y	25.00	40.00
Lamborghini Marzal CP	10.00	15.00
Lincoln Continental G/GOL	15.00	25.00
Lamborghini Miura Y, WH int.	50.00	75.00
Lamborghini Miura Y, R int.	10.00	15.00
Lamborghini Miura GOL, WH int.	50.00	75.00
Merryweather Fire Engine MAR	8.00	12.00
Merryweather Fire Engine R	10.00	15.00
Iron Fairy Crane	12.00	20.00
Ford Kennel Truck w/4 dogs	15.00	25.00
AEC Ergomatic 8-Wheel Tipper, WH grill , DOUGLAS	15.00	25.00
AEC Ergomatic 8-Wheel Tipper, SIL grill, DOUGLAS	10.00	15.00
AEC Ergomatic 8-Wheel Tipper, SIL grill, POINTER	8.00	12.00
Rolls Royce Silver Shadow Convertible Coupe BLU	12.00	20.00
Rolls Royce Silver Shadow Convertible Coupe GOL	12.00	20.00
Rolls Royce Silver Shadow Convertible Coupe LI/GOL	12.00	20.00

'59 EVER READY TRUCK

1970 Matchbox

	LOOSE	IN PKG.
Mercedes Benz Binz Ambulance CRE, SFW, rear hatch opens	10.00	15.00
Mercedes Benz Binz Ambulance WH, SFW, hatch doesn't open	6.00	10.00
Mercedes Benz Binz Ambulance OL, SFW, hatch doesn't open	6.00	10.00
Dodge Stake Truck, SFW	12.00	20.00

Ford Pickup, SFW	12.00	20.00
Ford Refuse Truck, SFW	12.00	20.00
Ford Mustang Fastback WH, R interior, SFW	20.00	35.00
Ford Mustang Fastback R, R interior, SFW	25.00	40.00
Ford Mustang Fastback R, CRE interior, SFW	20.00	35.00
Ford Mustang Wildcat Dragster WILDCAT labels	10.00	15.00
Ford Mustang Wildcat Dragster, RAT ROD labels	15.00	25.00
Ford Mustang Wildcat Dragster, no labels	10.00	15.00
Leyland Pipe Truck w/6 pipes, SFW	12.00	20.00
Safari Land Rover GOL, luggage on roof, SFW	15.00	25.00
Setra Coach GOL, T roof	12.00	20.00
Setra Coach GOL, WH roof	8.00	12.00
Setra Coach Y, WH roof	6.00	10.00
Setra Coach R, WH roof	6.00	10.00
Dodge Wreck Truck BP SFW	15.00	25.00
Volkswagen 1500 Saloon CRE, SFW	12.00	20.00
Volkswagen 1500 Saloon R, SFW	15.00	25.00
AEC Ergomatic Horse Box SFW	15.00	25.00
Field Car Y, SFW	10.00	15.00
Field Car OL, SFW	5.00	8.00
Field Car drab OL, SFW	30.00	50.00
Field Car OR, SFW	4.00	6.00
Field Car R, SFW	4.00	6.00
Lotus Racing Car, SFW	20.00	35.00
Road Dragster R	10.00	15.00
Road Dragster PUR	12.00	20.00
Road Dragster met. R	12.00	20.00
Foden Concrete Truck, SFW	15.00	25.00
Pontiac Grand Prix PUR SFW	25.00	40.00
Freeman Inter-City Commuter Coach PUR	10.00	15.00
Freeman Inter-City Commuter Coach GOL	10.00	15.00
Freeman Inter-City Commuter Coach MAR	10.00	15.00
Volkswagen Camper BLU w/opening roof, OR interior/roof	10.00	15.00
Volkswagen Camper OR w/opening roof, OR interior/roof	75.00	125.00
Volkswagen Camper OR w/opening roof, WH interior, OR roof	10.00	15.00
Volkswagen Camper OL w/opening roof, no interior	6.00	10.00
Volkswagen Camper WH w/opening roof, PIZZA VAN	8.00	12.00

Rolls Royce Silver Shadow R, SFW	10.00	15.00
Rolls Royce Silver Shadow GOL, SFW	10.00	15.00
Ford Cortina GT LB, SFW	25.00	40.00
Ford Cortina GT BLU, SFW	12.00	20.00
GMC Tipper Truck w/SFW	12.00	20.00
Mercedes Benz 230SL Convertible CRE, SFW, R interior	12.00	20.00
Mercedes Benz 230SL Convertible Y, SFW, R interior	12.00	20.00
Mercedes Benz 230SL Convertible Y, SFW, BLA interior	10.00	15.00
Mack Dump Truck GOL, SFW	15.00	25.00
Mack Dump Truck OL, SFW	25.00	40.00
Mack Dump Truck dk. OL, SFW	8.00	12.00
Fire Pumper SFW, no water gun	15.00	25.00
Fire Pumper SFW, water gun cast	8.00	12.00
Racing Mini OR	10.00	15.00
Racing Mini met. OR	10.00	15.00
8-Wheel Crane Truck R, SFW, OR boom	125.00	175.00
8-Wheel Crane Truck R, SFW, GOL boom	15.00	25.00
Leyland Petrol Tanker, SFW, BLU cab, WH tank, ARAL	30.00	50.00
Leyland Petrol Tanker, SFW, G cab, WH tank, BP	12.00	20.00
Leyland Petrol Tanker, SFW, R cab, WH tank, National..	200.00	300.00
Leyland Petrol Tanker, SFW, PUR cab, GR tank, National..	135.00	200.00
Lamborghini Miura Y, SFW	30.00	50.00
Lamborghini Miura met. OR, SFW	12.00	20.00
Lamborghini Miura GOL, SFW	10.00	15.00
Opel Diplomat, SFW	12.00	20.00
Hot Rod Draguar	12.00	20.00
Dodge Cattle Truck SFW, GR box	8.00	12.00
Dodge Cattle Truck SFW, SIL/GR box	15.00	25.00
Honda Motorcycle/Trailer SFW, Y trailer, BLU motorcycle	10.00	15.00
Honda Motorcycle/Trailer SFW, Y, PUR motorcycle	12.00	20.00
Honda Motorcycle/Trailer SFW, Y trailer, PI motorcycle	12.00	20.00
Honda Motorcycle/Trailer SFW, OR trailer, BLU-G motorcycle	5.00	8.00
Honda Motorcycle/Trailer SFW, Y trailer, BLU-G motorcycle	5.00	8.00
Ford GT, SFW, WH	10.00	15.00
Ford GT, SFW, met. OR	10.00	15.00
Iron Fairy Crane SFW, R, Y boom	50.00	75.00

Iron Fairy Crane	65.00	100.00
SFW, R, LI boom		
Iron Fairy Crane	20.00	35.00
SFW, OR-R w/Y or LI boom		
Pony Trailer w/2 horses	12.00	20.00
SFW, Y		
Pony Trailer w/2 horses	5.00	8.00
SFW, OR		
Pony Trailer w/2 horses	6.00	10.00
SFW, CRE		
Pony Trailer w/2 horses	4.00	6.00
SFW, WH w/BLU-GR tailgate, POLIZEI		
Pony Trailer w/2 horses	2.50	4.00
SFW, WH w/LI tailgate		
Pony Trailer w/2 horses	2.50	4.00
SFW, G w/WH roof, POLIZEI		
Pony Trailer w/2 horses	4.00	6.00
SFW, WH w/R roof		
GMC Refrigerator Truck	25.00	40.00
SFW, R w/BLU/G container		
GMC Refrigerator Truck	15.00	25.00
SFW, Y w/R container		
Ford Group 6 w/SFW, dr. G	65.00	100.00
Ford Group 6, SFW, met. G	10.00	15.00
Ford Group 6 PUR, SFW	6.00	10.00
Mercedes Benz 300SE met. BLU	30.00	50.00
SFW		
Mercedes Benz 300SE met. OR	15.00	25.00
SFW		
Mercedes Benz 300SE GOL	6.00	10.00
SFW		
Mercedes Benz 300S OL	50.00	75.00
SFW, w/STAFF labels		
Mercedes Benz 300SE SIL/GR	15.00	25.00
SFW		
DAF Tipper Container Truck	15.00	25.00
w/SFW		
Dodge Dump Truck	12.00	20.00
SFW, BLU cab, Y dumper		
Dodge Dump Truck	12.00	20.00
SFW, met. BLU cab, Y dumper		
Mercedes Benz Unimog	12.00	20.00
SFW, BLU		
Mercedes Benz Unimog	12.00	20.00
SFW, met. lt. BLU		
Mercedes Benz Unimog	50.00	75.00
SFW, OL w/star label		
Mercedes Benz Unimog	5.00	8.00
SFW, OL w/"A" label		
Ford Kennel Truck w/4 dogs	12.00	20.00
SFW		
AEC Ergomatic 8-Wheel Tipper	12.00	20.00
SFW		
Dodge Charger Mk III concept car	5.00	8.00
SFW, met. MAG, met. G base		
Dodge Charger Mk III concept car	5.00	8.00
SFW, met. R w/met. G base		

'59 FORDSON TRACTOR

'59 HYDRAULIC EXCAVATOR

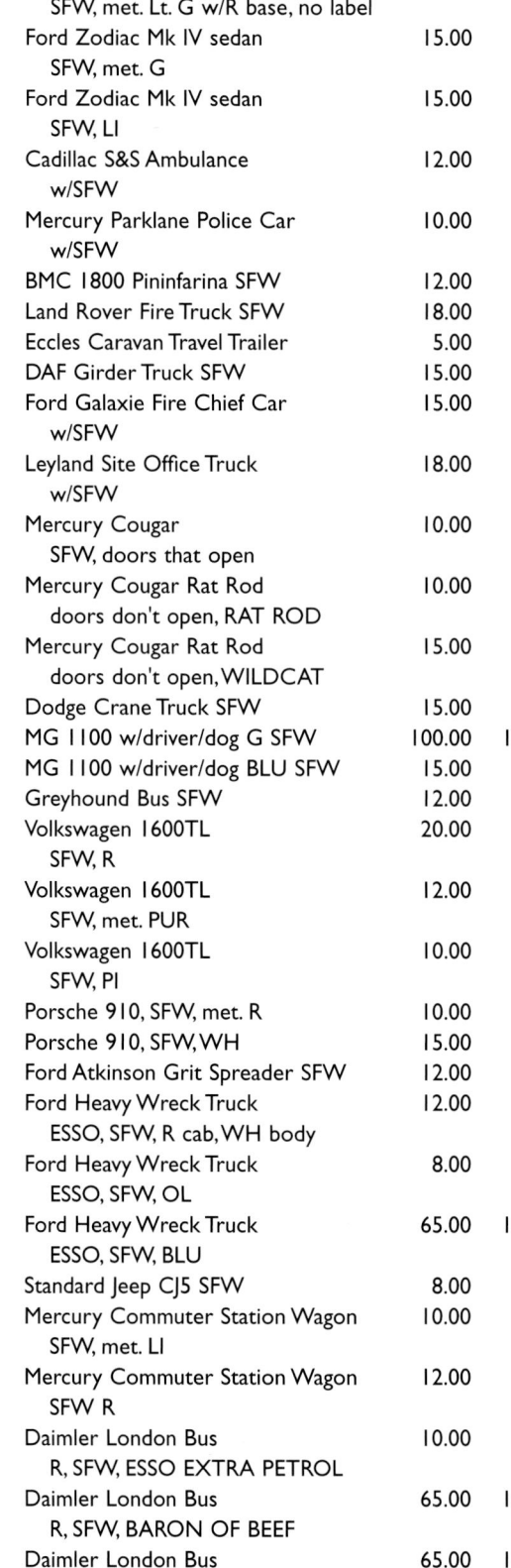

Dodge Charger Mk III concept car SFW, met. Lt. G w/R base, no label	10.00	15.00
Ford Zodiac Mk IV sedan SFW, met. G	15.00	25.00
Ford Zodiac Mk IV sedan SFW, LI	15.00	25.00
Cadillac S&S Ambulance w/SFW	12.00	20.00
Mercury Parklane Police Car w/SFW	10.00	15.00
BMC 1800 Pininfarina SFW	12.00	20.00
Land Rover Fire Truck SFW	18.00	30.00
Eccles Caravan Travel Trailer	5.00	8.00
DAF Girder Truck SFW	15.00	25.00
Ford Galaxie Fire Chief Car w/SFW	15.00	25.00
Leyland Site Office Truck w/SFW	18.00	30.00
Mercury Cougar SFW, doors that open	10.00	15.00
Mercury Cougar Rat Rod doors don't open, RAT ROD	10.00	15.00
Mercury Cougar Rat Rod doors don't open, WILDCAT	15.00	25.00
Dodge Crane Truck SFW	15.00	25.00
MG 1100 w/driver/dog G SFW	100.00	150.00
MG 1100 w/driver/dog BLU SFW	15.00	25.00
Greyhound Bus SFW	12.00	20.00
Volkswagen 1600TL SFW, R	20.00	35.00
Volkswagen 1600TL SFW, met. PUR	12.00	20.00
Volkswagen 1600TL SFW, PI	10.00	15.00
Porsche 910, SFW, met. R	10.00	15.00
Porsche 910, SFW, WH	15.00	25.00
Ford Atkinson Grit Spreader SFW	12.00	20.00
Ford Heavy Wreck Truck ESSO, SFW, R cab, WH body	12.00	20.00
Ford Heavy Wreck Truck ESSO, SFW, OL	8.00	12.00
Ford Heavy Wreck Truck ESSO, SFW, BLU	65.00	100.00
Standard Jeep CJ5 SFW	8.00	12.00
Mercury Commuter Station Wagon SFW, met. LI	10.00	15.00
Mercury Commuter Station Wagon SFW R	12.00	20.00
Daimler London Bus R, SFW, ESSO EXTRA PETROL	10.00	15.00
Daimler London Bus R, SFW, BARON OF BEEF	65.00	100.00
Daimler London Bus R, SFW, INN ON THE PARK	65.00	100.00
Daimler London Bus R, SFW, THE MINIATURE VEHICLE/N.A.M.C.	65.00	100.00
Ferrari Berlinetta, SFW, met. G	50.00	75.00
Ferrari Berlinetta, SFW, R	15.00	25.00

1971 Matchbox

	LOOSE	IN PKG.
Mod Rod R PW, WILDCAT label	12.00	20.00
Mod Rod BLA PW, WILDCAT label	8.00	12.00
Mod Rod BLA PW, flower label	10.00	15.00
Mod Rod BLA PW, spotted cat label	8.00	12.00
Mod Rod BLA PW, scorpion label	12.00	20.00
Mod Rod BLA PW, CHR body, stripes	12.00	20.00
Jeep Hot Rod, PI	12.00	20.00
Jeep Hot Rod, R	12.00	20.00
Jeep Hot Rod, OL	10.00	15.00
Jeep Hot Rod, OL drab	25.00	40.00
Gruesome Twosome, GOL Y windows	30.00	50.00
Gruesome Twosome, GOL PUR windows	12.00	20.00
Gruesome Twosome, R PUR windows	6.00	10.00
Hairy Hustler, met. OR PUR windows, 5 labels	50.00	75.00
Hairy Hustler, met. OR Y windows, 5 labels	10.00	15.00
Hairy Hustler, met OR Y windows, scorpion label	12.00	20.00
Hairy Hustler, WH Y windows, no labels	25.00	40.00
Hairy Hustler, WH Y windows, checkers & stripes tampo	12.00	20.00
Hairy Hustler, Y Y windows, flames tampo	25.00	40.00
AMX Javelin, LI SIL hood scoop, doors open	6.00	10.00
AMX Javelin, LI BLA hood scoop, doors open	3.00	5.00
AMX Javelin, met. BLU BLA hood scoop, doors open	3.00	5.00
AMX Javelin, met. BLU BLA hood scoop, doors don't open	3.00	5.00
AMX Javelin, met. G BLA hood scoop, doors open	3.00	5.00
AMX Javelin, met. BLU BLA hood scoop, doors don't open	3.00	5.00
AMX Javelin, R BLA hood scoop, doors don't open	12.00	20.00
Baja Dune Buggy, met. Lt. G w/flower label	6.00	10.00
Baja Dune Buggy, met. Lt. G police shield label	12.00	20.00
Baja Dune Buggy, met. G flower label	8.00	12.00
Baja Dune Buggy, met. G sunburst label	10.00	15.00

Fork Lift Truck	6.00	10.00
no steering wheel, Lansing Bagnall labels, Y forks		
Fork Lift Truck	8.00	12.00
cast steering wheel, HI LIFT labels, w/roof, BLA forks		
Fork Lift Truck	10.00	15.00
cast st.wheel, HI LIFT labels, no roof, BLA forks		
The Londoner London Bus	6.00	10.00
R SWINGING LONDON label, BLA/GR base		
The Londoner London Bus	12.00	20.00
R SWINGING LONDON label, unpainted base		
The Londoner London Bus	200.00	300.00
GOL CHR SWINGING LONDON label		
The Londoner London Bus	200.00	300.00
SIL CHR SWINGING LONDON label		
The Londoner London Bus	65.00	100.00
R PRESTON GUILD MERCHANT 1972		
The Londoner London Bus	65.00	100.00
R LONDON KENSINGTON HILTON		
The Londoner London Bus	65.00	100.00
R TYPHOO TEA		
The Londoner London Bus	65.00	100.00
R IMPEL 73		
The Londoner London Bus	6.00	10.00
R BERGER PAINTS		
The Londoner London Bus	135.00	200.00
R ICP INTERCHEMICALS/ PLASTICS		
The Londoner London Bus	135.00	200.00
R BORREGARD PAPER		
The Londoner London Bus	135.00	200.00
R SELLOTAPE SELBSTKLEBEBANDER		
The Londoner London Bus	65.00	100.00
R SELLOTAPE PACKAGING SYSTEMS		
The Londoner London Bus	135.00	200.00
R SELLOTAPE ELECTRICAL TAPE		
The Londoner London Bus	135.00	200.00
R SELLOTAPE INTERNATIONAL OPERATIONS		
The Londoner London Bus	65.00	100.00
R CHAMBOURCY YOGURT		
The Londoner London Bus	25.00	40.00
R ESSO EXTRA PETROL		
The Londoner London Bus	65.00	100.00
Y/CRE BERGER PAINTS		
The Londoner London Bus	50.00	75.00
Y/CRE IMPEL 76		
The Londoner London Bus	50.00	75.00
R SELFRIDGES		

The Londoner London Bus R AVIEMORE CENTRE/SANTA CLAUS LAND	50.00	75.00
The Londoner London Bus R AMCEL	65.00	100.00
The Londoner London Bus R BARON OF BEEF	65.00	100.00
The Londoner London Bus Y/R SWINGING LONDON	100.00	150.00
The Londoner London Bus R AIM BUILDING FUND 1976	25.00	40.00
The Londoner London Bus R, no labels	6.00	10.00
The Londoner London Bus R/WH BERGER PAINTS	100.00	150.00
The Londoner London Bus WH/BLU BERGER PAINTS	135.00	200.00
The Londoner London Bus Y/BLU BERGER PAINTS	135.00	200.00
The Londoner London Bus met. R LUFTHANSA	135.00	200.00
The Londoner London Bus R ARMY & NAVY	30.00	50.00
The Londoner London Bus R EDUSCHO KAFFEE	135.00	200.00
The Londoner London Bus OR JACOB'S BISCUIT MAKERS	30.00	50.00
The Londoner London Bus R JACOB'S BISCUIT MAKERS	30.00	50.00
The Londoner London Bus R ILFORD Hp5 FILM	100.00	150.00
The Londoner London Bus R MUSEUM OF LONDON	100.00	150.00
The Londoner London Bus R SILVER JUBILEE	30.00	50.00
The Londoner London Bus met. GR SILVER JUBILEE	10.00	15.00
The Londoner London Bus met. GR BERGER PAINTS	50.00	75.00
The Londoner London Bus BLU DEUTSCHLANDS AUTOPARTNER	25.00	40.00
The Londoner London Bus BLU MATCHBOX 1953-1978	25.00	40.00
The Londoner London Bus OR MATCHBOX 1953-1978	50.00	75.00
The Londoner London Bus R MATCHBOX 1953-1978	6.00	10.00
The Londoner London Bus R BUSCH GARDENS	30.00	50.00
The Londoner London Bus R THE BISTO BUS	10.00	15.00
Mod Tractor	8.00	12.00
Big Banger, R unpainted base, BLU windows	10.00	15.00
Big Banger, R unpainted base, Y windows	10.00	15.00
Maserati Bora, R	10.00	15.00

'59 SERVICE TRUCK

Maserati Bora, GOL	10.00	15.00
Soopa Coopa, BLU	10.00	15.00
Soopa Coopa, PI	10.00	15.00
unpainted base, flower label		
Soopa Coopa, PI	20.00	35.00
R base, flower label		
Soopa Coopa, OR	65.00	100.00
JAFFA MOBILE label		
Siva Spider, R, SIL trim	12.00	20.00
Siva Spider, R, BLA trim	12.00	20.00
Siva Spider, dr. BLU, BLA trim	12.00	20.00
Siva Spider, lt. BLU, BLA trim	12.00	20.00
Tyre Fryer, BLU	10.00	15.00
Tyre Fryer, OR, JAFFA MOBILE"	75.00	125.00
Dragon Wheels	12.00	20.00
Boss Mustang, Y	5.00	8.00
Boss Mustang, dk. GR	6.00	10.00
Stretcha Fetcha Ambulance, WH	10.00	15.00
Stretcha Fetcha Ambulance, R	25.00	40.00
UNFALL RETTUNG label		
Stretcha Fetcha Ambulance	10.00	15.00
GR, VIPER VAN		
Pi-Eyed Piper, BLU	10.00	15.00
Pi-Eyed Piper	65.00	100.00
BLU/R, BIG BANGER decals, BLU		
windows		
Citroen SM, met. OR	12.00	20.00
OR interior		
Citroen SM, met. OR	6.00	10.00
CRE interior		
Citroen SM, met. OR	6.00	10.00
Y interior		
Citroen SM, met. OR	6.00	10.00
tan interior		
Citroen SM, met. FLU	12.00	20.00
no markings		
Citroen SM, met. BLU	8.00	12.00
8 tampo		
Citroen SM, met. BLU	25.00	40.00
w/roof rack		
Tanzara, OR, CHR interior	8.00	12.00
Tanzara, WH, CHR interior	12.00	20.00
Tanzara, WH, R interior	12.00	20.00
Woosh-N-Push	10.00	15.00
Hovercraft SRN6	3.00	5.00
Mercury Commuter Station Wagon	10.00	15.00
raised roof, met. LI		
Mercury Commuter Station Wagon	12.00	20.00
raised roof, R		
Toe Joe Wreck Truck, met. LI	3.00	5.00
G booms, R hooks		
Toe Joe Wreck Truck, met. LI	12.00	20.00
G booms, BLA hooks		
Toe Joe Wreck Truck, met. LI	50.00	75.00
WH booms, BLA hooks		
Toe Joe Wreck Truck, Y	12.00	20.00
G booms, BLA hooks		
Toe Joe Wreck Truck, Y	3.00	5.00
R booms, BLA hooks		

'60 PICKFORD REMOVAL VAN

	LOOSE	IN PKG.
Toe Joe Wreck Truck, Y-OR R booms, BLA hooks	3.00	5.00
Toe Joe Wreck Truck, Y-OR HITCHHIKER label	65.00	100.00
Toe Joe Wreck Truck, R G boom, BLA hooks	65.00	100.00
Toe Joe Wreck Truck, R R boom, BLA hooks	65.00	100.00
Toe Joe Wreck Truck, R R boom, R hooks	65.00	100.00

1973 Matchbox

	LOOSE	IN PKG.
Monteverdi Hai, OR unpainted base, ivory interior	6.00	10.00
Monteverdi Hai, OR SIL base, ivory interior	6.00	10.00
Monteverdi Hai, OR unpainted base, Y interior	6.00	10.00
Monteverdi Hai, OR BLA base, 3 labels	6.00	10.00
Monteverdi Hai, OR BLA base, 6 labels	10.00	15.00
Mercedes Benz 350SL Convertible OR, BLA roof	5.00	8.00
Mercedes Benz 350SL Convertible Y, BLA roof	5.00	8.00
Mercedes Benz 350SL Convertible SIL, BLA roof	12.00	20.00
Mercedes Benz 350SL Convertible met. OR, BLA roof	6.00	10.00
Mercedes Benz 350SL Convertible met. OR, WH roof	5.00	8.00
Mercedes Benz 350SL Convertible MAR, WH roof	5.00	8.00
Mercedes Benz 350SL Convertible R, WH roof	6.00	10.00
Mercedes Benz 350SL Convertible BLU, no roof	5.00	8.00
Mercedes Benz 350SL Convertible PUR, no roof	6.00	10.00
Mercedes Benz 350SL Convertible WH, no roof, translucent R interior	5.00	8.00
Mercedes Benz 350SL Convertible GR, no roof, translucent WH interior	25.00	40.00
Mercedes Benz 350SL Convertible T, no roof, translucent WH interior	25.00	40.00
Mercedes Benz 350SL Convertible R, no roof, translucent WH interior	25.00	40.00
Mustang Piston Popper(Rolamatic) met. BLU, SUPERFAST, cast on base	50.00	75.00
Mustang Piston Popper(Rolamatic) met. BLU, ROLAMATIC cast on base	3.00	5.00
Mustang Piston Popper(Rolamatic) WH	135.00	200.00
Mustang Piston Popper Y(Rolamatic) HOT POPPER	6.00	10.00
Rallye Royale	6.00	10.00

Rod Roller, Y met. R rear wheels	12.00	20.00
Rod Roller, Y R rear wheels	10.00	15.00
Rod Roller, Y BLA rear wheels	6.00	10.00
Rod Roller, OR-Y	8.00	12.00
Team Matchbox Formula 1 Racer Y, WH driver, 8 label	175.00	250.00
Team Matchbox Formula 1 Racer Y, WH driver, 4 label	175.00	250.00
Team Matchbox Formula 1 Racer met. BLU, WH driver, 5 label	30.00	50.00
Team Matchbox Formula 1 Racer met. G, WH driver, 5 label	30.00	50.00
Team Matchbox Formula 1 Racer R, WH driver, 8 label	8.00	12.00
Team Matchbox Formula 1 Racer R, WH driver, 44 label	5.00	8.00
Team Matchbox Formula 1 Racer R, Y driver, 44 label	10.00	15.00
Team Matchbox Formula 1 Racer OR, T driver, 44 label, w/trailer	30.00	50.00
Team Matchbox Formula 1 Racer OR, Y driver, 44 label	30.00	50.00
Lamborghini Countach opening rear cowl, Y w/CHR interior	5.00	8.00
Lamborghini Countach opening rear cowl, R, SIL interior	5.00	8.00

Lamborghini Countach
   opening rear cowl, R, GR interior, BLA
   base
	6.00	10.00

Lamborghini Countach
   opening rear cowl, R, GR interior,
   unpainted base
	5.00	8.00

Lamborghini Countach opening rear cowl, R, Y interior	5.00	8.00
Lamborghini Countach opening rear cowl, R, WH interior	5.00	8.00
Lamborghini Countach opening rear cowl, R, T inerior	5.00	8.00
Lamborghini Countach opening rear cowl, Y, lt. GR interior	30.00	50.00
Datsun 126X, Y OR base, no tampo	6.00	10.00
Datsun 126X, Y unpainted base, no tampo	10.00	15.00
Datsun 126X, Y OR base, OR/R flame tampo	10.00	15.00
Datsun 126X, Y OR base, BLA/R flame tampo	10.00	15.00
Stingeroo Cycle, PUR PUR handlebars	10.00	15.00
Stingeroo Cycle, PUR BLU-GR handlebars	12.00	20.00
Clipper, concept car opening cockpit, met. MAG	6.00	10.00

Clipper, concept car opening cockpit, hot Pl	35.00	60.00
Chop Suey Motorcycle, MAG OR handlebars	12.00	20.00
Chop Suey Motorcycle, MAG R handlebars	10.00	15.00
Chop Suey Motorcycle, MAG BLA handlebars	12.00	20.00
Chop Suey Motorcycle, MAG dk. R handlebars	10.00	15.00
Articulated Truck removable trailer, OR-Y cab/trailer, lt. BLU trailer base	4.00	6.00
Articulated Truck removable trailer, Y cab, lt. BLU trailer, Y trailer base	4.00	6.00
Articulated Truck rem. dk. BLU trailer, Y cab, Y tr.base w/tow hk.	50.00	75.00
Articulated Truck removable trailer, R cab, BLU trailer, BLU trailer base	25.00	40.00
Articulated Truck removable trailer, R cab, SIL trailer, R trailer base	8.00	12.00
Wildlife Truck(Rolamatic) lion under transparent canopy, Y, Y canopy	6.00	10.00
Wildlife Truck(Rolamatic) lion under transparent canopy, Y, BLU canopy	4.00	6.00
Wildlife Truck(Rolamatic) lion under transparent canopy, Y, clear canopy	4.00	6.00
Wildlife Truck(Rolamatic) lion under transparent canopy, Y, GR canopy	4.00	6.00
Wildlife Truck(Rolamatic) lion under transparent canopy, WH, BLU canopy	4.00	6.00
Wildlife Truck(Rolamatic) lion under transparent canopy, WH, clear canopy	4.00	6.00
Wildlife Truck(Rolamatic) lion under transparent canopy, WH, GR canopy	4.00	6.00
Freeway Gas Tanker, BURMAH	5.00	8.00
Freeway Gas Tanker, CHEVRON	5.00	8.00
Freeway Gas Tanker, SHELL	5.00	8.00
Freeway Gas Tanker, EXXON Y/WH	5.00	8.00
Freeway Gas Tanker, EXXON R/WH	30.00	50.00
Freeway Gas Tanker, BP, Y	25.00	40.00
Freeway Gas Tanker, BP, WH/Y	5.00	8.00
Saab Sonnet, BLU	10.00	15.00
Saab Sonnet, WH	135.00	200.00

'60 COKE DELIVERY TRUCK

	LOOSE	IN PKG.
Hot Rocker Mercury Capri	10.00	15.00
Turbo Fury, 69 label	12.00	20.00
Turbo Fury, 86 label	12.00	20.00
Jumbo Jet Motorcycle	12.00	20.00
Maxi Taxi Mercury Capri	6.00	10.00

1974 Matchbox

	LOOSE	IN PKG.
Badger Exploration Truck	4.00	6.00
Rolamatic radar, met. OR-R		
Badger Exploration Truck	4.00	6.00
Rolamatic radar, OL		
Badger Exploration Truck	25.00	40.00
Rolamatic radar, OL drab		
Stoat Armored Truck, met. GOL	8.00	12.00
Stoat Armored Truck	5.00	8.00
OL, BLA hubs		
Stoat Armored Truck	30.00	50.00
OL drab, CHR hubs		
Beach Hopper(Rolamatic)	12.00	20.00
High-Tailer Team Matchbox Racer	8.00	12.00
Renault 17TL, 9 label on hood	5.00	8.00
Renault 17TL, 6 label on hood	5.00	8.00
Renault 17TL, FIRE label on hood	10.00	15.00
Weasel Armored Vehicle, met. G	5.00	8.00
Weasel Armored Vehicle, OL drab	30.00	50.00
Weasel Armored Vehicle, OL	5.00	8.00
Weasel Armored Vehicle, met. LG	5.00	8.00

1975 Matchbox

	LOOSE	IN PKG.
Pontiac Firebird, met. BLU	5.00	8.00
dual CHR hood scoops		
Seafire Boat, WH deck	5.00	8.00
BLU hull		
Seafire Boat, R deck	4.00	6.00
WH hull		
Seafire Boat, R deck	12.00	20.00
BLU hull		
Seafire Boat, WH deck	50.00	75.00
BR hull w/trailer		
Seafire Boat, R deck	12.00	20.00
Y hull w/trailer		
Seafire Boat, BLA deck	12.00	20.00
Y hull w/trailer		
DeTomaso Pantera, WH	3.00	5.00
BLU base, 8 hood label		
DeTomaso Pantera, WH	3.00	5.00
unpainted base, 8 hood label		
DeTomaso Pantera, WH	6.00	10.00
BLU base, 9 hood label		
DeTomaso Pantera, WH	6.00	10.00
BLU base, sunburst hood label		
DeTomaso Pantera, WH	25.00	40.00
lt. PUR base, 8 hood label		
DeTomaso Pantera, BLU	3.00	5.00
BLA base		
Big Bull Bulldozer, OR rollers	4.00	6.00

Big Bull Bulldozer, Y rollers	4.00	6.00
Big Bull Bulldozer, BLA rollers	5.00	8.00
Mini HaHa Mini Cooper	10.00	15.00
Hondarora Motorcycle, R SIL handlebars/seat	6.00	10.00
Hondarora Motorcycle, R BLA handlebars/seat	4.00	6.00
Hondarora Motorcycle, R BLA handlebars, WH seat	50.00	75.00
Hondarora Motorcycle, OR BLA handlebars/seat	8.00	12.00
Hondarora Motorcycle, OL drab BLA handlebars/seat	30.00	50.00
Hondarora Motorcycle, OL BLA handlebars/seat	4.00	6.00
Hondarora Motorcycle, met. R BLA handlebars/seat	30.00	50.00
Hondarora Motorcycle, met. G BLA handlebars/seat	4.00	6.00
Hondarora Motorcycle, Y no driver	3.00	5.00
Hondarora Motorcycle, Y T driver	3.00	5.00
Hondarora Motorcycle, Y BR driver	3.00	5.00
Hondarora Motorcycle, Y G driver	30.00	50.00
Range Rover Police Patrol (Rolamatic) WH, POLICE labels, frosted windows	8.00	12.00
Range Rover Police Patrol (Rolamatic) OL drab, AMBULANCE	25.00	40.00
Range Rover Police Patrol (Rolamatic) OL drab, POLICE	25.00	40.00
Range Rover Police Patrol (Rolamatic), lt. OL, AMBULANCE	4.00	6.00
Range Rover Police Patrol (Rolamatic) lt. OL, POLICE	4.00	6.00
Range Rover Police Patrol (Rolamatic) OR, SITE ENGINEER	12.00	20.00
Range Rover Police Patrol (Rolamatic) OR, POLICE	8.00	12.00
Range Rover Police Patrol (Rolamatic) WH, COUNTY SHERIFF	8.00	12.00
Range Rover Police Patrol (Rolamatic) BLU, PARIS DAKAR 81	25.00	40.00
Range Rover Police Patrol (Rolamatic) met. T, PARIS DAKAR 83	5.00	8.00
Range Rover Police Patrol (Rolamatic) T, PARIS DAKAR 83	5.00	8.00
Blaze Buster Fire Engine, R WH ladder, SIL interior	125.00	175.00
Blaze Buster Fire Engine, R BLA ladder, SIL interior	12.00	20.00
Blaze Buster Fire Engine, R Y ladder, SIL interior	6.00	10.00
Blaze Buster Fire Engine, R Y ladder, WH interior	3.00	5.00

'60 SUGAR CONTAINER TRUCK

Blaze Buster Fire Engine, R OR-Y ladder, FIRE labels	3.00	5.00
Blaze Buster Fire Engine, R OR-Y ladder, No. 32 labels	8.00	12.00
Atlas Dump Truck, BLU OR dumper	6.00	10.00
Atlas Dump Truck, R met. SIL dumper	6.00	10.00
Atlas Dump Truck, BLU Y dumper	8.00	12.00
Vantastic, OR exposed engine, unpainted base	8.00	12.00
Vantastic, OR exposed engine, WH base	4.00	6.00
Vantastic, OR no exposed engine, WH base, 34 on hood	4.00	6.00
Vantastic, OR no exposed engine, WH base, sunburst label	15.00	25.00
Vantastic, OR no exposed engine, WH tab base, 34 label	12.00	20.00
Vantastic, OR no exposed engine, WH tab base, 3 label	50.00	75.00
Fandango, WH, 6 label	10.00	15.00
Fandango, WH, 35 label	8.00	12.00
Fandango, R, 35 label	8.00	12.00
Fandango, R, sunburst label	8.00	12.00
Fandango, R, 35 label BLA base, BLU fan	25.00	40.00
Formula 5000, R, 5000 label	6.00	10.00
Formula 5000, OR, 5000 label	6.00	10.00
Formula 5000, R TEXACO on hood	8.00	12.00
Hellraiser	10.00	15.00
Cosmobile, met. BLU upper Y lower, Y windows	8.00	12.00
Cosmobile, met. R upper T lower, Y windows	12.00	20.00
Cosmobile, met. G upper BLA lower, PUR windows	15.00	25.00
Cosmobile, met. G upper BLA lower, Y windows	15.00	25.00

1976 Matchbox

	LOOSE	IN PKG.
Dodge Challenger, R hood grills, no scoop, SIL interior	3.00	6.00
Dodge Challenger, R hood grills, no scoop, WH interior	3.00	6.00
Dodge Challenger R hood grills, no scoop, R interior	5.00	10.00
Dodge Challenger, BLU hood grilles, no scoop, R interior	3.00	6.00
Hovercraft	5.00	10.00
Volkswagen Rabbit, met. G rack/surfboards, Y interior	4.00	8.00

'61 CATERPILLAR

Volkswagen Rabbit, Y rack/surfb., ADAC labels, roof light/antenna	15.00	30.00
Volkswagen Rabbit, met. G rack/surfboards, R interior	6.00	12.00
Volkswagen Rabbit, Y rack/surfboards, R interior	3.00	6.00
Volkswagen Rabbit, R rack/surfboards, Y interior	2.50	5.00
Volkswagen Rabbit, met. SIL rack/surfboards, R interior	3.00	6.00
Volkswagen Rabbit, met. SIL rack/surfboards, T interior	10.00	20.00
Volkswagen Rabbit, met. SIL rack/surfboards, BLU interior	40.00	80.00
Volkswagen Rabbit, BLA rack/surfboards, R stripe tampo, no rack	2.50	5.00
Volkswagen Rabbit, BLA rack/surfboards, R/OR stripe, 9 tampo, no rack	5.00	10.00
Bedford Car Transporter	4.00	8.00
Badger Cement Truck, Rolamatic	2.50	5.00
Site Dumper, Y Y dumper, BLA interior	2.50	5.00
Site Dumper, Y R dumper, BLA interior	3.00	6.00
Site Dumper, OR-R OR-R dumper, WH interior	20.00	40.00
Site Dumper, OR-R met. GR dumper, WH interior	4.00	8.00
Shovel Nose Tractor/Tractor Shovel lt. Y, R shovel, CHR hubs	5.00	10.00
Shovel Nose Tractor/Tractor Shovel Y, R shovel, BLA hubs	7.50	15.00
Shovel Nose Tractor/Tractor Shovel LI, Y shovel	75.00	150.00
Shovel Nose Tractor/Tractor Shovel dk. Y, R shovel	4.00	8.00
Shovel Nose Tractor/Tractor Shovel dk. Y, MAR shovel	2.50	5.00
Shovel Nose Tractor/Tractor Shovel dk. Y, BLA shovel	3.00	6.00
Shovel Nose Tractor/Tractor Shovel dk. OR, R shovel	20.00	40.00
Shovel Nose Tractor/Tractor Shovel dk. OR, BLA shovel	5.00	10.00
Shovel Nose Tractor/Tractor Shovel lt. OR, BLA shovel	5.00	10.00
Shovel Nose Tractor/Tractor Shovel PUR, BLA shovel, Macau cast	4.00	8.00
Shovel Nose Tractor/Tractor Shovel dk. Y, R shovel, Macau cast	2.50	5.00
Shovel Nose Tractor/Tractor Shovel Y, BLA shovel, THOMAE MUCOSOLVAN, Macau	10.00	20.00
Shovel Nose Tractor/Tractor Shovel lt. OR, BLA shovel, THOMAE MUCOSOLVAN, Macau	15.00	30.00

Shovel Nose Tractor/Tractor Shovel BLU, R shovel, Macau cast	4.00	8.00
Shovel Nose Tractor/Tractor Shovel Y, BLA shovel, THOMAE MUCOSOLVAN, Thailand	20.00	40.00
Shovel Nose Tractor/Tractor Shovel BLU, BLA shovel, SPASMO MUCOSOLVAN	6.00	12.00
Swamp Rat airboat, OL T hull, SWAMP RAT labels	3.00	6.00
Swamp Rat airboat, OL T hull, camouflage, T driver	2.50	5.00
Swamp Rat airboat, OL T hull, camouflage, BLA driver	6.00	12.00
Atlas Skip Truck, R, Y skip	3.00	6.00
Atlas Skip Truck, R, BLU skip	50.00	100.00
Atlas Skip Truck, OR, R skip	50.00	100.00
Atlas Skip Truck, OR, Y skip	40.00	75.00
Atlas Skip Truck, BLU, Y skip	2.50	5.00
Jeep(with or without top), OL star label, no gun or roof cast	7.50	15.00
Jeep(with or without top), OL drab 21*11 label, no gun or roof cast	30.00	60.00
Jeep(with or without top), OL 21*11 label, no gun or roof cast	5.00	10.00
Jeep(with or without top), OL 21*11 label, gun cast	4.00	8.00
Jeep(with or without top), G	65.00	125.00
Jeep(with or without top), Y	4.00	8.00
Jeep(with or without top), BLU WH roof, U.S. MAIL tampo	4.00	8.00
Jeep(with or without top), lt. BLU WH roof, U.S. MAIL tampo	5.00	10.00
BMW 3.0 CSL, OR	4.00	8.00
BMW 3.0 CSL, WH Y dome light, POLIZEI label	20.00	40.00
BMW 3.0 CSL, WH BLU dome light, POLIZEI label	20.00	40.00
BMW 3.0 CSL, WH, G tampo	40.00	75.00
BMW 3.0 CSL, WH BMW/MANHALTER label	25.00	50.00
BMW 3.0 CSL, R, BMW label	30.00	60.00
Crane Truck, Y	4.00	8.00
Crane Truck, R	25.00	50.00
Police Launch Boat WH deck, BLU hull, no tab, lt. BLU figures	3.00	6.00
Police Launch Boat WH deck, BLU hull, tab, lt. BLU figures	20.00	40.00
Police Launch Boat WH deck, R hull, OR-Y figures	4.00	8.00
Police Launch Boat WH deck, R hull, lt. BLU figures	7.50	15.00
Police Launch Boat BLA deck, dk. GR hull/figures	3.00	6.00
Police Launch Boat WH deck, BLU hull, R figures	4.00	8.00

Police Launch Boat	4.00	8.00
WH deck/hull/figures		
Personnel Carrier	4.00	8.00
Faun Earth Mover Dump Truck	2.50	5.00
OR-Y, OR-Y dumper, no markings, England cast		
Faun Earth Mover Dump Truck	2.50	5.00
Y, Y dumper, no markings, England cast		
Faun Earth Mover Dump Truck	3.00	6.00
Y, Y dumper, CAT tampos, England cast		
Faun Earth Mover Dump Truck	2.00	4.00
Y, met. SIL dumper, OR stripes, Macau cast		
Faun Earth Mover Dump Truck	2.00	4.00
Y, met. SIL dumper, OR stripes, China cast		
Faun Earth Mover Dump Truck	2.50	5.00
BLU, Y dump, OR stripes/tools tampo, China cast		
Faun Earth Mover Dump Truck	2.50	5.00
OR-Y, OR-Y dumper, OR stripes, China cast		
Faun Earth Mover Dump Truck	2.00	4.00
OR-Y, R dumper, no markings, China cast		
Faun Earth Mover Dump Truck	2.00	4.00
OR, OR dumper		
Faun Earth Mover Dump Truck	2.00	4.00
OR, BLA dumper		
Fire Chief Car	5.00	10.00
Self-Propelled Gun, Rolamatic	4.00	8.00
Dodge Cattle Truck w/cattle	4.00	8.00

1977 Matchbox

	LOOSE	IN PKG.
Snorkel Fire Engine w/closed cab	5.00	10.00
Caravan Travel Trailer	3.00	6.00
Police Motorcyclist, Honda CB750	20.00	35.00
rider, CRE, POLIZEI label, wire wheels		
Police Motorcyclist, Honda CB750	7.50	15.00
rider, WH, POLIZEI label, wire wheels		
Police Motorcyclist, Honda CB750	7.50	15.00
w/rider, white w/POLIZEI label, mag wheels		
Police Motorcyclist, Honda CB750	2.50	5.00
rider, WH, POLICE label, wire wheels		
Police Motorcyclist, Honda CB750	2.50	5.00
rider, WH, POLICE label, mag wheels, WH seat		
Police Motorcyclist, Honda CB750	7.50	15.00
rider, WH, POLICE label, mag wheel, G seat		
Police Motorcyclist, Honda CB750	5.00	10.00
rider, WH, POLICE label, mag wheels, BLA seat		
Police Motorcyclist, Honda CB750	6.00	12.00
rider, BLA, L.A.P.D. label		

'62 JAGUAR 3.8

Police Motorcyclist, Honda CB750 WH, 4 label, mag wheels, R seat, no rider	5.00	10.00
Police Motorcyclist, Honda CB750 rider, WH, Japanese lettering tampo	5.00	10.00
Bedford Horse Box w/2 horses R, T box, G windows	10.00	20.00
Bedford Horse Box w/2 horses R, lt. BR box, G windows	5.00	10.00
Bedford Horse Box w/2 horses OR, G windows	3.00	6.00
Bedford Horse Box w/2 horses OR, clear windows	5.00	10.00
Bedford Horse Box w/2 horses OR, PUR windows	4.00	8.00
Bedford Horse Box w/2 horses met. G	4.00	8.00
Bedford Horse Box w/2 horses Y, lt. BR box	4.00	8.00
Bedford Horse Box w/2 horses dk. OR, T box	4.00	8.00
Bedford Horse Box w/2 horses dk. OR, lt. BR box	3.00	6.00
Bedford Horse Box w/2 horses BLU, Y box, LI wheels, R hubs	4.00	8.00
Bedford Horse Box w/2 horses BLU, Y box, LI wheels, BLU hubs	10.00	20.00
Bedford Horse Box w/2 horses R, dk. T box, MANAUS cast on base	15.00	30.00
Bedford Horse Box w/2 horses WH, WH box, CIRCUS CIRCUS tampo	3.00	6.00
Mercedes Benz Container Truck R, T container, SEA/LAND labels	3.00	6.00
Mercedes Benz Container Truck R, T container, N.Y.K. labels	3.00	6.00
Mercedes Benz Container Truck R, T container, O.C.L. labels	5.00	10.00
Mercedes Benz Container Truck Y, Y container, DEUTSCHE BUNDESPOST	15.00	30.00
Mercedes Benz Container Truck R, T container, CONFERN labels	15.00	30.00
Mercedes Benz Container Truck R, WH container, MATCHBOX labels	5.00	10.00
Mercedes Benz Container Truck R, WH container, MAYFLOWER labels	4.00	8.00
Mercedes Benz Container Truck R, WH container, CONFERN over MAYFLOWER	10.00	20.00
Mercedes Benz Container Truck G, G container, CONFERN over MAYFLOWER	40.00	75.00
Sambron Jack Lift, Y, no tampo	3.00	6.00
Sambron Jack Lift, LI R/WH stripes	2.00	4.00
Sambron Jack Lift, WH R stripes	2.00	4.00

'62 JAGUAR XKE

Sambron Jack Lift, G	2.00	4.00
R/WH stripes		
Sambron Jack Lift, OR-Y	2.00	4.00
R stripes		
Jeep CJ6	3.00	6.00
Holden Pickup, MAR	6.00	12.00
Y motorcycles, 500 labels		
Holden Pickup, R	4.00	8.00
Y motorcycles, 500 labels		
Holden Pickup, R	10.00	20.00
Y motorcycles, star label		
Holden Pickup, R	6.00	12.00
OL motorcycles, sunburst label		
Holden Pickup, CRE	4.00	8.00
SUPERBIKE label		
Holden Pickup, WH	6.00	12.00
SUPERBIKE label		
Holden Pickup, CRE	6.00	12.00
HONDA label		
Holden Pickup, met. BLU	15.00	30.00
PARIS DAKAR labels		
Airport Coach, met. BLU	3.00	6.00
AMERICAN AIRLINES, no tab on base		
Airport Coach, met. BLU	10.00	20.00
AMERICAN AIRLINES, tab on base		
Airport Coach, met. BLU	3.00	6.00
BRITISH AIRWAYS, no tab on base		
Airport Coach, met.BLU	10.00	20.00
BRITISH AIRWAYS, tab on base		
Airport Coach, met. BLU	3.00	6.00
LUFTHANSA, no tab on base		
Airport Coach, met. BLU	10.00	20.00
LUFTHANSA, tab on base		
Airport Coach, R, QANTAS	6.00	12.00
Airport Coach, R, TWA	6.00	12.00
England cast on base		
Airport Coach, R, TWA	15.00	30.00
Manaus cast on base		
Airport Coach, OR, SCHULBUS	15.00	30.00
Airport Coach, met. BLU, BRITISH	5.00	10.00
Airport Coach, WH, ALITALIA	5.00	10.00
England cast on base		
Airport Coach, WH, ALITALIA	3.00	6.00
Macau cast on base		
Airport Coach, WH, LUFTHANSA	15.00	30.00
Airport Coach, OR, LUFTHANSA	2.50	5.00
Airport Coach, OR, PAN AM	2.50	5.00
Airport Coach, WH, STORK SB	5.00	10.00
Airport Coach, R, VIRGIN ATLANTIC	3.00	6.00
Airport Coach, met. BLU, AUSTRALIAN	4.00	8.00
Airport Coach, met. BLU, GIROBANK	4.00	8.00
Airport Coach, WH, BLU roof, KLM	4.00	8.00
Airport Coach, WH, G roof, ALITALIA	3.00	6.00
Ford Transit, OR, no tab on base	5.00	10.00
Ford Transit, OR, tab on base	15.00	30.00
Seasprite Helicopter, WH	2.00	4.00
small windows		

1978 Matchbox

	LOOSE	IN PKG.
Porsche 911 Turbo met BR unpainted base	7.50	15.00
Porsche 911 Turbo met. BR BLA base	4.00	8.00
Porsche 911 Turbo SIL	4.00	8.00
Porsche 911 Turbo GR, R interior	4.00	8.00
Porsche 911 Turbo met. G	4.00	8.00
Porsche 911 Turbo R, clear windows	2.50	5.00
Porsche 911 Turbo R opaque windows	4.00	8.00
Porsche 911 Turbo BLA	2.00	4.00
Porsche 911 Turbo WH	4.00	8.00
Porsche 911 Turbo dk BLU WRANGLER 47	4.00	8.00
Porsche 911 Turbo dk. BLU, PORSCHE	2.00	4.00
Porsche 911 Turbo LB	2.00	4.00
Porsche 911 Turbo Y	2.00	4.00
Porsche 911 Turbo lt. Y	2.00	4.00
U.S. Mail Jeep, U.S. MAIL	3.00	6.00
U.S. Mail Jeep, GLIDING CLUB	5.00	10.00
U.S. Mail Jeep	7.50	15.00
Ford Escort RX2000 WH T interior, DUNLOP labels	2.00	4.00
Ford Escort RX2000 WH R interior, DUNLOP labels	40.00	75.00
Ford Escort RX2000 WH T interior, PHANTOM labels	3.00	6.00
Ford Escort RX2000 BLU T interior, PHANTOM labels	3.00	6.00
Ford Escort RX2000 G T interior, DUNLOP labels	2.50	5.00
Ford Escort RX2000 G T interior, seagull labels	2.50	5.00
Ford Escort RX2000 G WH interior, seagull labels	2.50	5.00
Ford Escort RX2000 G R interior, seagull labels	40.00	75.00
Renault 5TL Y, T interior, LeCAR	3.00	6.00
Renault 5TL Y, R interior, LeCAR	5.00	10.00
Renault 5TL BLU, no markings	5.00	10.00
Renault 5TL GR, T interior no markings	5.00	10.00
Renault 5TL GR, R interior A5 tampos	7.50	15.00
Renault 5TL GR, R interior no markings	3.00	6.00
Renault 5TL GR, R interior, LeCAR	4.00	8.00
Renault 5TL WH, RENAULT	5.00	10.00
Renault 5TL WH, ROLOTIL, BLA base	2.50	5.00
Renault 5TL WH, ROLOIL, R base	7.50	15.00
Renault 5TL R, TURBO	7.50	15.00
Diesel Shunter Locomotive G	4.00	8.00
Diesel Shunter Locomotive Y R undercarriage	3.00	6.00
Diesel Shunter Locomotive Y met. R undercarriage	15.00	30.00

Flat Car w/container	3.00	6.00
T container, NYK		
Flat Car w/container	5.00	10.00
T container, UNITED STATES LINES		
Flat Car w/container	3.00	6.00
T container, SEA/LAND		
Flat Car w/container	5.00	10.00
T container, OCL		
Flat Car w/container	7.50	15.00
lt. BR container, NYK		
Flat Car w/container	6.00	12.00
lt. BR container, SEA/LAND		
Flat Car w/container	12.50	25.00
BLU container, UNITED STATES LINES		
Flat Car w/container	12.50	25.00
BLU container, SEA/LAND labels		
Flat Car w/container	15.00	30.00
OR container, OCL labels		
Flat Car w/container	12.50	25.00
R container, NYK		
Flat Car w/container	4.00	8.00
WH container, no labels		
Flat Car w/container	4.00	8.00
Y container, no labels		
Toyota Celica GT BLU	2.50	5.00
small rear wheels, 78 tampos		
Toyota Celica GT Y	20.00	35.00
small rear wheels, YELLOW FEVER		
Field Gun dk. G	5.00	10.00
Field Gun G	15.00	30.00
Chevrolet Ambulance WH	3.00	6.00
various markings, no tab on base		
Chevrolet Ambulance WH	12.50	25.00
AMBULANCE/cross labels, tab on base		
Chevrolet Ambulance GR	12.50	25.00
PARIS DAKAR 81		
Chevrolet Ambulance R	4.00	8.00
NOTARZT tampos		
Chevrolet Ambulance WH	4.00	8.00
PACIFIC AMBULANCE tampo		
Chevrolet Ambulance R	2.00	4.00
GOL/WH trim, FIRE RESCUE		
Steam Locomotive R,	2.50	5.00
England cast, 4345 labels		
Steam Locomotive R, Eng. cast, NP labels	5.00	10.00
Steam Locomotive met. R	65.00	125.00
England cast, 4345 labels		
Steam Locomotive G	5.00	10.00
England cast, 4345 labels		
Steam Locomotive G	4.00	8.00
England cast, NP labels		
Steam Locomotive G	5.00	10.00
BRITISH RAILWAYS, Macau cast		
Steam Locomotive R	2.00	4.00
4345 labels, Macau cast		
Steam Locomotive G	2.50	5.00
4345 labels, Macau cast		

'62 PONTIAC CONVERTIBLE

Steam Locomotive G	4.00	8.00
WEST SOMERSET RAILWAY, England cast		
Steam Locomotive R	4.00	8.00
WH NORTH YORKSHIRE.., Macau		
Steam Locomotive R	7.50	15.00
WH/BLA NORTH YORKS.., England cast		
Steam Locomotive Y	3.00	6.00
123/efg tampo, China cast		
Steam Locomotive BLU	4.00	8.00
HUTCHINSON, Macau cast		
Steam Locomotive G	7.50	15.00
WH emblem tampo, Macau cast		
Steam Locomotive dk. G	4.00	8.00
GWR tampo, Macau cast		
Steam Locomotive BLA	5.00	10.00
BRITISH RAILWAYS, England cast		
Steam Locomotive BLU/R accents	3.00	6.00
Macau cast		
Steam Locomotive Y	2.00	4.00
123/456 tampo, China cast		
Steam Locomotive G	2.00	4.00
BRITISH RAILWAYS, China cast		
Steam Locomotive R	2.50	5.00
4345 tampo, China cast		
Steam Locomotive G	20.00	40.00
Kelloggs Rooster head, China cast		
Steam Locomotive WH, no markings	5.00	10.00
GRAFFIC TRAFFIC, China cast		
Railway Passenger Coach R	3.00	6.00
431 432" labels, England cast		
Railway Passenger Coach R	40.00	75.00
NYK labels, England cast		
Railway Passenger Coach R	5.00	10.00
GWR labels, England cast		
Railway Passenger Coach R	5.00	10.00
5810-6102 labels, England cast		
Railway Passenger Coach G	5.00	10.00
431 432 labels, England cast		
Railway Passenger Coach G	4.00	8.00
5310-6102, England cast		
Railway Passenger Coach R	2.00	4.00
431 432, Macau cast		
Railway Passenger Coach R	2.00	4.00
431 432, China cast		
Railway Passenger Coach LG/Y/R	5.00	10.00
China cast		
Railway Passenger Coach G	2.00	4.00
BRITISH RAILWAYS, China cast		
Railway Passenger Coach R	7.50	15.00
KELLOGG'S 431 432, China cast		
Railway Passenger Coach WH	5.00	10.00
Graffic Traffic China cast		
Ford Tractor BLU	2.50	5.00
Ford Tractor G	3.00	6.00
Ford Tractor dk. BLU	25.00	50.00
Ford Tractor Y	2.50	5.00

'63 COMMERCIAL ICE CREAM TRUCK

Combine Harvester R	3.00	6.00
Combine Harvester Y	3.00	6.00
Combine Harvester lime G/BLU	5.00	10.00
Ford Wreck Truck R, BR windows	3.00	6.00
Ford Wreck Truck R, BLU windows	5.00	10.00
Ford Wreck Truck Y	3.00	6.00
Ford Wreck Truck OR/R	75.00	150.00
Freeway Gas Tanker Trailer CASTROL label	40.00	75.00
Freeway Gas Tanker Trailer BURMAH label	4.00	8.00
Freeway Gas Tanker Trailer OCTANE label	4.00	8.00
Freeway Gas Tanker Trailer French flag label	40.00	75.00
Freeway Gas Tanker Trailer Canadian flag label	50.00	100.00
Freeway Gas Tanker Trailer ARAL label	12.50	25.00
Freeway Gas Tanker Trailer CHEVRON label	4.00	8.00
Freeway Gas Tanker Trailer SHELL label	4.00	8.00
Freeway Gas Tanker Trailer EXXON label, WH cab	5.00	10.00
Freeway Gas Tanker Trailer EXXON label, R cab	25.00	50.00
Freeway Gas Tanker Trailer BP label, Y base	20.00	40.00
Freeway Gas Tanker Trailer BP label, BLA base, G tra.base	5.00	10.00
Datsum 260Z 2+2 MAR, doors open	2.50	5.00
Datsum 260Z 2+2 PUR, doors open	5.00	10.00
Datsum 260Z 2+2 MAG, doors open	4.00	8.00
Datsum 260Z 2+2 BLU, doors open	4.00	8.00
Datsum 260Z 2+2 GR, doors open	2.00	4.00
Datsum 260Z 2+2 BLA doors cast shut	2.00	4.00
Datsum 260Z 2+2 GR doors cast shut, England cast	4.00	8.00
Datsum 260Z 2+2 GR doors cast shut, China cast	40.00	75.00
Armored Truck R WELLS FARGO, clear windows	15.00	30.00
Armored Truck R WELLS FARGO, blue windows	3.00	6.00
Armored Truck G, DRESDNER BANK	20.00	40.00
Armored Truck army G DRESDNER BANK	25.00	50.00
Mercury Cougar Villager Sta.Wag. G	3.00	6.00
Mercury Cougar Villager Sta.Wag BLU	4.00	8.00

'63 COMMERCIAL MILK DELIVERY TRUCK

1979 Matchbox

	LOOSE	IN PKG.
'57 Chevy met. MAG	5.00	10.00
'57 Chevy R, CHERRY BOMB tampos	4.00	8.00
'57 Chevy BLA w/R hood flame tampos	2.00	4.00

'57 Chevy PI w/R hood flame tampos	5.00	10.00
'57 Chevy pale G, R hood flame tampos	4.00	8.00
'57 Chevy OR, R hood, flame tampos	4.00	8.00
'57 Chevy met R w/R hood flame tampos	4.00	8.00
'57 Chevy met. PUR, R hood flame tampos	4.00	8.00
'57 Chevy, R/R hood HEINZ 57 CHEVY tampos	12.50	25.00
'57 Chevy met. PUR MILKY WAY tampos	12.50	25.00
'57 Chevy BLA, dk. R hood flame tampos	2.00	4.00
'57 Chevy R/R hood, CHR windows SIL stripe tampos(World Class)	4.00	8.00
'57 Chevy R, YEL flame outlines SIL trim, CHR interior	3.00	6.00
'57 Chevy WH, PI/BLU accents CHR interior/grill	2.00	4.00
Plymouth Gran Fury Police WH POLICE tampos w/shield	2.00	4.00
Plymouth Gran Fury Police WH METRO tampos	2.50	5.00
Plymouth Gran Fury Police WH BLU POLICE tampos	2.00	4.00
Plymouth Gran Fury Police WH POLICE SFPD tampos, dk. BLU windows	2.50	5.00
Plymouth Gran Fury Police WH POLICE SFPD tampos, G windows	25.00	50.00
Citroen CX Station Wagon BLU BLU windows	5.00	10.00
Citroen CX Station Wagon BLU clear windows	2.50	5.00
Citroen CX Station Wagon dk. BLU R interior, clear windows	50.00	100.00
Citroen CX Station Wagon Y	3.00	6.00
Pontiac Firebird Trans Am	3.00	6.00
Toyota Celica XX CRE made in Japan/J-21 on base	7.50	15.00
Toyota Celica XX R made in Japan/J-21 on base	7.50	15.00
Mitsubishi Galant Eterna R made in Japan/J-22 on base	7.50	15.00
Mitsubishi Galant Eterna Y made in Japan/J-22 on base	7.50	15.00
Mustang GT350	7.50	15.00
Lincoln Continental Mark V R WH roof	3.00	6.00
Mazda Savannah RX-7 WH no spoiler	3.00	6.00
Mazda Savannah RX-7 BLA GOL stripes, no spoiler	3.00	6.00
Mazda Savannah RX-7 GOL no spoiler, GOL striped hood/roof	2.50	5.00

'63 FODEN READYMIX TRUCK

Mazda Savannah RX-7 BLA	15.00	30.00
no spoil., RX7/MAZDA tampos, Manaus cast		
Mazda Savannah RX-7 BLU	7.50	15.00
no spoiler, England cast		
Rolls Royce Silver Shadow II	2.50	5.00
met. SIL/GR		
Rolls Royce Silver Shadow II R	2.50	5.00
Rolls Royce Silver Shadow II T	2.50	5.00
Pannier Tank Locomotive	3.00	6.00
Ford Cortina 1600 GL met. G	3.00	6.00
doors open		
Ford Cortina 1600 GL met. R	3.00	6.00
doors open		
Ford Cortina 1600 GL T,	3.00	6.00
doors open		
Ford Cortina 1600 GL R	7.50	15.00
doors shut, opaque WH windows		
Ford Cortina 1600 GL GOL	12.50	25.00
Ford Cortina 1600 GL lt. OR	10.00	20.00
Ford Cortina 1600 GL met. OR	10.00	20.00
Ford Cortina 1600 GL R	50.00	100.00
WH/OR flame tampos		
Mercedes Benz 450SEL BLU	2.50	5.00
T interior		
Mercedes Benz 450SEL BLU	3.00	6.00
R interior		
Caterpillar Bulldozer Y, plastic roof	3.00	6.00
Y blade, T canopy		
Caterpillar Bulldozer Y, plastic roof	3.00	6.00
Y blade, BLA canopy, England cast		
Caterpillar Bulldozer Y w/plastic roof	2.00	4.00
Y blade, BLA canopy, Macau cast		
Caterpillar Bulldozer Y, plastic roof	2.00	4.00
Y blade, BLA canopy, Thailand cast		
Caterpillar Bulldozer Y, plastic roof	5.00	10.00
BLA blade, BLA canopy		
Caterpillar Bulldozer Y w/plastic roof	5.00	10.00
BLA blade, T canopy		
Caterpillar Bulldozer Y, plastic roof	7.50	15.00
no blade, BLA canopy		
Caterpillar Bulldozer R, plastic roof	5.00	10.00
Y blade, BLU canopy		
Caterpillar Bulldozer OR, plastic roof	5.00	10.00
OR blade, BLA canopy, LOSINGER		
Caterpillar Bulldozer R, plastic roof	5.00	10.00
lime G blade, BLU canopy		
Caterpillar Bulldozer Y, plastic roof	2.00	4.00
Y blade, R canopy		
Chevy Van OR, clear windows	15.00	30.00
BLU/R stripes		
Chevy Van OR, BLU windows	3.00	6.00
BLU/R stripes		
Chevy Van OR, BLU windows	3.00	6.00
BLU/WH stripes		
Chevy Van OR, BLU windows	3.00	6.00
R/BLA stripes		

Chevy Van OR, OR windows R/BLA stripes	3.00	6.00
Chevy Van OR, R windows R/BLA stripes	3.00	6.00
Chevy Van OR, G windows R/BLA stripes	4.00	8.00
Chevy Van dk. OR, BLU windows R/BLA stripes	7.50	15.00
Chevy Van OR, BLU windows R/BLA stipes	5.00	10.00
Chevy Van OR, BLU windows MATCHBOX COLLECTORS CLUB	15.00	30.00
Chevy Van WH BLU windows USA 1 tampos	5.00	10.00
Chevy Van WH, BLU windows ADIDAS tampo	15.00	30.00
Chevy Van G, BLU windows CHEVY, Y stripes	5.00	10.00
Chevy Van GR, BLU windows CHEVY, BR stripes	5.00	10.00
Chevy Van met. GR, BLU windows VANPIRE tampos	2.50	5.00
Chevy Van Y, MATCHBOX COL..	10.00	20.00
Chevy Van Y, PEPSI CHALLENGE	3.00	6.00
Chevy Van WH/MAR, DR. PEPPER	5.00	10.00
Chevy Van Y, STP SON OF A GUN	30.00	60.00
Chevy Van BLA GOODWRENCH RACING TEAM..	3.00	6.00
Chevy Van OR/Y KODAK FILM 4 RACING	4.00	8.00
Chevy Van WH, 25/G accent tampo	3.00	6.00
Chevy Van GOODRICH 5 TIME NATIONAL CHAMPION DALE EARNHARDT	3.00	6.00
Chevy Van Y, PENNZOIL 30	4.00	8.00
Chevy Van BLU/OR 43 STP OIL TREATMENT	3.00	6.00
Chevy Van BLA PONTIAC EXCITEMENT 2	3.00	6.00
Chevy Van BLA/G MELLO YELLO 42 tampos	3.00	6.00
Chevy Van OR/W PUROLATOR 10 tampos	4.00	8.00
Chevy Van WH, PUR/LG graphics	2.00	4.00
Bomag Road Roller Y, R interior England cast	3.00	6.00
Bomag Road Roller OR, BLU stripes	2.50	5.00
Bomag Road Roller Y/R stripes bridge/road tampos	2.50	5.00
Ford Model A CRE, spare tire cast dk. G fenders	5.00	10.00

1980 Matchbox

	LOOSE	IN PKG.
Ambulance Citroen CX WH, AMBULANCE tampos	2.50	5.00
Ambulance Citroen CX WH, MARINE DIVISION POLICE tampos	3.00	6.00

Cosmic Blues WH	5.00	10.00
BLU accents, England cast		
Cosmic Blues WH	2.50	5.00
BLU accents, Macau cast		
Cosmic Blues WH	2.50	5.00
BLU accents, China cast		
Cosmic Blues BLU	2.00	4.00
WH accents, China cast		
Cosmic Blues OR/Y	.75	2.00
MAG/BLA accents(1993)		
Cosmic Blues BLA	2.50	5.00
OR/WH fluorescent flames(1996)		
Refuse Truck R	10.00	20.00
Y container, no COLLECTOMATIC on container		
Refuse Truck R	3.00	6.00
Y container, COLLECTOMATIC on container		
Refuse Truck MAG	2.50	5.00
Y container		
Refuse Truck BLU	2.50	5.00
OR container, METRO labels		
Refuse Truck WH	2.00	4.00
BLU container, METRO labels		
Refuse Truck WH	5.00	10.00
BLU container, Chinese lettering		
Refuse Truck WH	2.50	5.00
BLU container, no labels		
Refuse Truck GR	1.50	3.00
Y container, STATE CITY tampos		
Refuse Truck OR	1.50	3.00
GR container, REFUSE DISPOSAL tampos		
Refuse Truck G	1.50	3.00
Y container, REFUSE DISPOSAL tampos		
Refuse Truck R	3.00	6.00
Y container, REFUSE DISPOSAL tampos		
Refuse Truck Y	2.00	4.00
WH container, DISPOSAL UNIT tampos		
Refuse Truck OR	1.50	3.00
WH container, no markings		
Refuse Truck OR/R	1.50	3.00
lt. GR container, BLA recycle logos		
Ford Camper Pickup Truck	20.00	40.00
Y windows, 35 on base		
Ford Camper Pickup Truck	3.00	6.00
no camper windows		
Articulated Trailer	3.00	6.00
BLU container, Y trailer base		
Articulated Trailer	4.00	8.00
met. GR container, R trailer base		
Harley Davidson Motorcycle	3.00	6.00
Motor Home T	3.00	6.00
Mercedes Benz Taxi/Polizei	2.50	5.00
T/CRE TAXI sign on roof		

'63 FORD ZEPHYR

Mercedes Benz Taxi/Polizei	3.00	6.00
WH, BLU roof light		
Mercedes Benz Taxi/Polizei	4.00	8.00
WH/G, POLIZEI tampo, BLU roof light		
Mercedes Benz Taxi/Polizei	3.00	6.00
WH/G, roof light		
Porsche 928 T	3.00	6.00
Porsche 928 BLU	3.00	6.00
Porsche 928 BLA	5.00	10.00
BR interior, PORSCHE/stripe tampos		
Porsche 928 BLA	3.00	6.00
R interior, PORSCHE/stripe tampos		
Corvette T-Roof R	20.00	40.00
WH accents, no CORVETTE cast		
Corvette T-Roof R	3.00	6.00
WH accents, CORVETTE cast fr./rear		
Corvette T-Roof BLA	2.50	5.00
clear windows, G/OR stripes		
Corvette T-Roof BLA	5.00	10.00
opaque windows, G/OR stripes		
Corvette T-Roof BLA	2.50	5.00
clear windows, Y/OR stripes		
Corvette T-Roof BLA	2.50	5.00
GR interior, THE FORCE tampo		
Corvette T-Roof BLA	15.00	30.00
R interior, THE FORCE tampo, Manaus cast		
Corvette T-Roof G	5.00	10.00
BRUT/FABERGE tampos		
Corvette T-Roof metallic R	5.00	10.00
TURBO VETTE tampos, LW		
Corvette T-Roof BLA	3.00	6.00
TURBO VETTE tampos		
Corvette T-Roof	3.00	6.00
baseball team logos(29 variations)		
Dodge Challenger	7.50	15.00
Ford Model A CRE, no spare	3.00	6.00
dk. G fenders, G windows		
Ford Model A LG	3.00	6.00
no spare, G fender, G windows		
Ford Model A LG, no spare	3.00	6.00
G fenders, no windows		
Ford Model A T, no spare	2.50	5.00
BR fenders, Y windows		
Ford Model A T, no spare	2.50	5.00
BR fenders, clear windows		
Ford Model A R, no spare	2.50	5.00
BLA fenders, clear windows		
Ford Model A BLA, no spare	2.50	5.00
BLA fenders, flame tampos		
Ford Model A PUR, no spare	2.50	5.00
Y fenders, flame tampos		
Ford Model A Y, no spare	6.00	12.00
R fenders, PAVA tampo		
Ford Model A R, no spare	10.00	20.00
G fenders		

'63 REFUSE TRUCK

Ford Model A OR/Y	6.00	12.00
no spare, WH fend., GT/yel.jac.		
Ford Model A LB	6.00	12.00

1981 Matchbox

	LOOSE	IN PKG.
S-2 Jet BLA/Y	3.00	6.00
S-2 Jet LB/WH	2.50	5.00
S-2 Jet LB, WH base, GR wing	3.00	6.00
S-2 Jet BLU/WH, Macau	7.50	15.00
S-2 Jet. BLU/WH, China	2.50	5.00
S-2 Jet OL/BLA	3.00	6.00
Mazda Savanna RX7 GR	7.50	15.00
Japan cast, stripe/RX7 tampo		
Mazda Savanna RX7 Y	7.50	15.00
Japan cast, stripe/RX7 tampo		
Nissan Fairlady Z R	7.50	15.00
Nissan Fairlady Z SIL	7.50	15.00
Swing Wing Jet R/WH	2.50	5.00
Swing Wing Jet R/WH/GR	2.50	5.00
Swing Wing Jet BLA/GR	3.00	6.00
Leyland Articulated Truck	3.00	6.00
BLU cab, GR trailer		
Leyland Articulated Truck	3.00	6.00
BLU cab, GR trailer, INTERNATIONAL		
Leyland Articulated Truck	4.00	8.00
R cab, GR trailer		
Leyland Articulated Truck	4.00	8.00
BLU cab, Y tr., INTER.., England cast		
Leyland Articulated Truck	3.00	6.00
BLU cab, Y tr., INTER.., Macau		
Leyland Articulated Truck	20.00	40.00
BLU cab/trailer, PAUL'S		
Atlas Excavator OR/BLA	5.00	10.00
Atlas Excavator OR/GR	5.00	10.00
Atlas Excavator Y/BLA	2.50	5.00
Atlas Excavator Y/BLA, Macau	2.00	4.00
Atlas Excavator Y, Macau	6.00	12.00
Atlas Excavator Y/BLA, R scoop	1.50	3.00
Atlas Excavator R/ WH	2.00	4.00
Chevy Pro Stocker WH	7.50	15.00
Chevy Pro Stocker WH	5.00	10.00
34 tampo, GR base		
Chevy Pro Stocker WH	7.50	15.00
34 tampo, R base		
Chevy Pro Stocker WH	5.00	10.00
34 tampo, unpainted base		
Chevy Pro Stocker OR, 4	2.50	5.00
Chevy Pro Stocker WH	2.50	5.00
PEPSI 14 tampo, R interior		
Chevy Pro Stocker WH	30.00	60.00
PEPSI 14 tampo, BLA interior		
Chevy Pro Stocker WH	3.00	6.00
SUPERSTAR 217 tampos		
Chevy Pro Stocker BLA	4.00	8.00
HALLEY'S COMET tampos		

'63 POLICE PATROL

'64 JAGUAR MARK TEN

Chevy Pro Stocker WH/OR	4.00	8.00
21, 355 CID tampo		
Chevy Pro Stocker WH	3.00	6.00
7-UP tampo, R interior		
Chevy Pro Stocker WH	30.00	60.00
7-UP tampo, BLA interior		
Chevy Pro Stocker BLU/WH	3.00	6.00
70 BAILEY EXCAVATING tampo		
Volvo Zoo Truck R/BLU	5.00	10.00
Volvo Zoo Truck R	5.00	10.00
GR cage, T or BR lions		
Volvo Zoo Truck R	7.50	15.00
GR cage, WH lions		
Volvo Zoo Truck OR/GR	10.00	20.00
BMW M1 GR, 52	2.50	5.00
BMW M1 GR, 52 , smoke win.	2.50	5.00
BMW M1 GR, 52, Y win.	5.00	10.00
BMW M1, GR, 52, G win.	30.00	60.00
Ferrari 308 GTB R	2.50	5.00
Ferrari 308 GTB OR/R	2.50	5.00
Ferrari 308 GTB OR/R	2.50	5.00
FERRARI logo		
Ferrari 308 GTB OR/R#}Y windows,	3.00	6.00
FERRARI logo		
Ferrari 308 GTB OR/R	5.00	10.00
GR base, clear win. , FERRARI		
Ferrari 308 GTB OR/R	2.00	4.00
GR base, clear win., FERRARI, Macau		
Ferrari 308 GTB R/BLU	2.00	4.00
PIONEER tampos		
Ferrari 308 GTB Y/R	2.00	4.00
FERRARI 308 GTB tampos		
Ferrari 308 GTB OR/BLU	5.00	10.00
RAT RACING TEAM tampos		
Ferrari 308 GTB R	40.00	75.00
DATA EAST/SECRET SERVICE		
Ferrari 308 GTB R	2.50	5.00
CHR windows, World Class		
Ferrari 308 GTB R	2.50	5.00
FERRARI logo on hood		
Ferrari 308 GTB R	2.50	5.00
FERRARI, Thailand cast		
Ferrari 308 GTB WH	4.00	8.00
G windows, GT, Macau		
Ferrari 308 GTB Y, Macau	2.00	4.00
Orange Peel Dodge Charger	3.00	6.00
Mazda Savannah RX7 LG	3.00	6.00
Mazda Savannah RX7 BLU	3.00	6.00
Mazda Savannah RX7 BLU	6.00	12.00
R/WH stripes		
Toyota Celica XX R	4.00	8.00
Toyota Celica XX R	4.00	8.00
SUNBURNER tampo		
Nissan Fairlady Z BLA	3.00	6.00
Nissan Fairlady Z BLA, Z tam.	5.00	10.00
Nissan Fairlady Z WH	7.50	15.00
Mitsubishi Galant Eterna LG	3.00	6.00
Mitsubishi Galant Eterna G	3.00	6.00

	LOOSE	IN PKG.
Mitsubishi Galant Eterna LG CRE/R HOT POINTS tampo	4.00	8.00
Mitsubishi Galant Eterna LG WH/R HOT POINTS tampo	4.00	8.00

1982 Matchbox

	LOOSE	IN PKG.
Revin' Rebel Dodge Challenger OR, BLU roof REVIN' REBEL tampos	2.50	6.00
Revin' Rebel Dodge Challenger OR, BLU roof	5.00	12.00
Revin Rebel Dodge Challenger OR, WH roof REVIN REBEL tampos	4.00	10.00
Jeep Eagle/4x4 Golden Eagle Off-Road Jeep/Jeep Wrangler T GOLDEN EAGLE tampo	1.50	4.00
Jeep Eagle/4x4 Golden Eagle Off-Road Jeep/Jeep Wrangler, R GOLDEN EAGLE tampo, metal base	1.50	4.00
Jeep Eagle/4x4 Golden Eagle Off-Road Jeep/Jeep Wrangler, R GOLDEN EAGLE tampo, plastic base	1.50	4.00
Jeep Eagle/4x4 Golden Eagle Off-Road Jeep/Jeep Wrangler, OL plastic gun, no roll bar	3.00	8.00
Jeep Eagle/4x4 Golden EagleE {Off-Road Jeep/Jeep Wrangler 50th ANNIVERSARY JEEP tampo	6.00	15.00
Jeep Eagle/4x4 Golden Eagle Off-Road Jeep/Jeep Wrangler, PI WH interior, Dream Machines (1993)	2.00	5.00
Jeep Eagle/4x4 Golden Eagle Off-Road Jeep/Jeep Wrangler, BLU PI/Y accents(1993)	1.50	4.00
Jeep Eagle/4x4 Golden Eagle Off-Road Jeep/Jeep Wrangler, PUR BAD TO THE BONE on hood, teal BLU interior(1995)	1.25	3.00
Jeep Eagle/4x4 Golden Eagle Off-Road Jeep/Jeep Wrangler, GR BAD TO THE BONE on hood, BLA interior(1996)	1.25	3.00
Volkswagen Rompin Rabbit 4x4, WH, ROMPIN RABBIT tampos	2.50	6.00
Volkswagen Rompin Rabbit 4x4, Y, RUFF RABBIT tampos	2.50	6.00
Rover 3500 Police, R (European model)	2.50	6.00
Rover 3500 Police, WH (European model) POLICE tampo roof lights, England cast	2.50	6.00
Rover 3500 Police, WH (European model) POLICE tampo roof lights, China cast	2.00	5.00

Rover 3500 Police, WH (European model) POLICE tampo roof lights, Manaus cast	12.00	30.00
Rover 3500 Police, WH (European model), no markings roof lights, England cast(Graffic traffic)	1.50	4.00
Fiat Abarth, WH R interior, MATCHBOX tampo	1.50	4.00
Fiat Abarth, WH BLA interior, MATCHBOX tampo	40.00	100.00
Fiat Abarth, WH, ALITALIA tampo	1.50	4.00
Fiat Abarth, WH R/OR/Y stripe tampo, Macau cast	4.00	10.00
Fiat Abarth, WH MATCHBOX 11 tampo, Manaus cast	15.00	40.00
Mustang Cobra	3.00	8.00
Pontiac Firebird S/E, R, no markings	1.50	4.00
Pontiac Firebird S/E, BLA FIREBIRD tampo	1.50	4.00
Pontiac Firebird S/E, BLA HALLEY'S COMET tampo	3.00	8.00
Pontiac Firebird S/E, BLU stripes	2.00	5.00
Pontiac Firebird S/E, R MAACO labels	2.50	6.00
Pontiac Firebird S/E, BLU stripes, Laser Wheels	1.50	4.00
Pontiac Firebird S/E powder BLU, WH stripes	5.00	12.00
Pontiac Firebird S/E, PUR FIREBIRD tampo	1.50	4.00
4x4 Mini-Pickup, Dunes Racer OR, roll bar/rally lights	1.50	4.00
4x4 Mini-Pickup, Dunes Racer Y, roll bar/rally lights	1.50	4.00
4x4 Mini-Pickup, Dunes Racer WH, roll bar/rally lights, BOB JANE T-MART tampo	6.00	15.00
4x4 Mini-Pickup, Dunes Racer WH, roll bar/rally lights, 63 tampo	1.50	4.00
Leyland Tanker(European model) R cab, ELF/R stripe tampo	2.50	6.00
Leyland Tanker(European model) Y cab, SHELL, WH tank, Y base	3.00	8.00
Leyland Tanker(European model) R cab, SHELL, WH tank, R base	20.00	50.00
Leyland Tanker(European model) BLA cab tank, GAS tampo	2.00	5.00
Pontiac Trans Am, metallic T	2.00	5.00
Pontiac Trans Am, metallic GOL	2.00	5.00
Pontiac Trans Am, WH	1.50	4.00
London Bus, R, large windows BERGER PAINTS labels	5.00	12.00
London Bus, R, large windows LAKER SKYTRAIN labels	4.00	10.00
London Bus, large windows WH upper, lt. BLU lower MATCHBOXC No.1/Montepna	8.00	20.00

London Bus, R, large windows MATCHBOX No. I/Montepna, England cast	30.00	75.00
London Bus, dr. G, large windows CHESTERFIELD CENTENARY labels	6.00	15.00
London Bus, R, large windows MATCHBOX LONDON BUS, England cast	3.00	8.00
London Bus, R, large windows MATCHBOX LONDON BUS, Macau cast	1.50	4.00
London Bus, R, large windows NICE TO MEET YOU! JAPAN 1984, England cast	3.00	8.00
London Bus, R, large windows Japanese writing on labels, England cast	5.00	12.00
London Bus, R, large windows YORK FESTIVAL & MYSTERY PLAYS, England cast	4.00	10.00
London Bus, dk. BLU, large windows NESTLE MILKYBAR, England cast	3.00	8.00
London Bus, R, large windows NESTLE MILKYBAR, Macau cast	4.00	10.00
London Bus, dk. G, large windows ROWNTREE FRUIT GUMS, Macau cast	4.00	10.00
London Bus, R, large windows ROWNTREE FRUIT GUMS, England cast	4.00	10.00
London Bus, dk. BLU, large windows KEDDIES No. I IN ESSEX, England cast	20.00	50.00
London Bus, MAR, large windows RAPPORT, England cast	4.00	10.00
London Bus, large windows WH upper, BLA lower TORVALE FISHER ENGINEERING CO., Macau	4.00	10.00
London Bus, large windows WH upper, OR lower W H SMITH TRAVEL, Macau cast	4.00	10.00
London Bus, R, large windows YOU'LL LOVE NEW YORK	1.50	4.00
London Bus, large windows SPACE FOR YOUTH 1985/ STAFFORDSHIRE POLICE, Macau cast	4.00	10.00
London Bus, BLU, large windows CITYRAMA, Macau cast	4.00	10.00
London Bus, R, large windows no labels, England cast	2.00	5.00
London Bus, R, large windows no labels, China cast	3.00	8.00
London Bus, R, large windows NURENBURG 1986, Macau cast	30.00	75.00
London Bus, R, large windows FIRST M.I.C.A. CONVENTION, Macau cast	80.00	200.00
London Bus, R, large windows FIRST M.I.C.A. CONVENTION, England cast	80.00	200.00

'64 LINCOLN CONTINENTAL

'64 PONTIAC GRAND PRIX

London Bus, large windows M.I.C.A. MATCHBOX INTL COLLECTORS ASSOCIATION	5.00	12.00
London Bus, R, large windows AROUND LONDON TOUR BUS, China cast	1.50	4.00
London Bus, BLU, large windows NATIONAL TRAMWAY MUSEUM, China cast	4.00	10.00
London Bus, large windows WH upper, R lower MIDLAND BUS TRANSPORT MUSEUM, China cast	4.00	10.00
London Bus, R, large windows BAND-AID PLASTERS PLAYBUS, China cast	4.00	10.00
London Bus, BLU, large windows NATIONAL GIROBANK, China cast	4.00	10.00
London Bus, R, large windows MATCHBOX-NIAGARA FALLS, China cast	3.00	8.00
London Bus, R, large windows FERIA DEL JUGUETE VALENCIA, 12 FEBRERO 1987	60.00	150.00
London Bus, large windows T upper, BLU lowerWEST MIDLANDS TRAVEL, China cast	4.00	10.00
London Bus, WH, large windows DENNEY-HAPPY 1000TH BIRTHDAY, DUBLIN	4.00	10.00
London Bus, R, large windows 123abc, MY FIRST MATCHBOX-NURENBURG 1990	5.00	12.00
London Bus, R, large windows 123abc, Matchbox Preschool	3.00	8.00
London Bus, Y, large windows IT'S THE REAL THING-COKE, China cast	4.00	10.00
London Bus, MAR, large windows CORNING GLASS CENTER, China cast	1.50	4.00
London Bus, CHR, large windows CELEBRATING A DECADE OF MATCHBOX CONVENTIONS	12.50	25.00
London Bus, R, large windows MARKFIELD PROJECT SUPPORT APPEAL 92, China cast	3.00	8.00
London Bus, R, large windows LONDON WIDE TOUR BUS, China cast	1.50	4.00
London Bus, WH, large windows no labels, China cast, Graffic Traffic	1.50	4.00
Peterbilt Cement Truck, met. G OR barrel, BIG PETE tampos	1.50	4.00
Peterbilt Cement Truck, BLU Y barrel, KWIK SET CEMENT tampos	1.50	4.00
Peterbilt Cement Truck, Y OR barrel, DIRTY DUMPER tampos	20.00	50.00

Peterbilt Cement Truck, Y GR barrel, PACE CONSTRUCTION tampos	1.50	4.00
Peterbilt Cement Truck, R LI barrel	2.50	6.00
Peterbilt Cement Truck, PI WH barrel, READYMIX tampo	4.00	10.00
Peterbilt Cement Truck, R OR barrel, Manaus cast	15.00	40.00
Peterbilt Cement Truck, Y R barrel, PACE CONSTRUCTION tampos	1.50	4.00
Peterbilt Cement Truck, OR BLA barrel	1.50	4.00
Peterbilt Cement Truck, R BLA barrel, WH barrel base(1996)	1.25	3.00
4x4 Jeep, Desert Dawg, WH R roof, DESERT DAWG tampo, England cast	1.50	4.00
4x4 Jeep, Desert Dawg, COP R roof, England cast	1.50	4.00
4x4 Jeep, Desert Dawg, BLA WH roof, LAREDO tampo, Macau cast	1.50	4.00
4x4 Jeep, Desert Dawg, BLA WH roof LAREDO tampo, Hong Kong cast	8.00	20.00
4x4 Jeep, Desert Dawg, BLA WH roof, LAREDO tampo, Thailand cast	1.50	4.00
4x4 Jeep, Desert Dawg, dk. T R roof, GOLDEN EAGLE, England	8.00	20.00
4x4 Jeep, Desert Dawg, R WH roof, GOLDEN EAGLE, Macau cast	4.00	10.00
4x4 Jeep, Desert Dawg, OL T roof, camouflage tampo, Macau cast	1.50	4.00
4x4 Jeep, Desert Dawg, Y LI roof, Macau cast	4.00	10.00
4x4 Jeep, Desert Dawg, BLA R roof, LAREDO tampo, Macau cast	4.00	10.00
4x4 Jeep, Desert Dawg, T T roof, BR camouflage	1.50	4.00
4x4 Jeep, Desert Dawg, Y BLA roof, PI/BLU accents	1.50	4.00
4x4 Jeep, Desert Dawg, OL OL canopy, WH star, V-9872-3(1996)	1.25	3.00
Toyota Mini Pickup Camper, SIL WH stepped roof, BIG FOOT tampos	1.50	4.00
Toyota Mini Pickup Camper, SIL WH flat roof, BIG FOOT tampos	1.50	4.00
Toyota Mini Pickup Camper, SIL BLA roll bar, BIG FOOT tampos	15.00	40.00
Toyota Mini Pickup Camper, R WH flat roof, ASPEN SKI HOLIDAYS, metal base	1.50	4.00
Toyota Mini Pickup Camper, R WH flat roof, ASPEN SKI HOLIDAYS, plastic base	1.50	4.00

Toyota Mini Pickup Camper, WH	4.00	10.00
WH flat roof, SLD PUMP SERVICE tampo		
Audi Quattro, WH	1.50	4.00
AUDI 20 tampo, England cast		
Audi Quattro, WH	1.50	4.00
AUDI 20 tampo, Macau cast		
Audi Quattro, WH	12.00	30.00
AUDI 20 tampo, Manaus cast		
Audi Quattro, WH	1.50	4.00
DUCKHAMS/PIRELLI tampo		
Audi Quattro, PUR	1.50	4.00
QUATTRO 0000 tampo		
Audi Quattro, BLU	4.00	10.00
Quattro 0000 tampo		
Audi Quattro, met. dk. GR	1.50	4.00
pictogram/AUDI 2584584		
Peterbilt Tipper	1.50	4.00
Datsun 280ZX, BLA, WH interior	1.50	4.00
Datsun 280ZX, BLA, R interior	1.50	4.00
Toyota Celica GT, Y	2.00	5.00
oversized rear wheels, YELLOW FEVER tampo		
Formula Racing Car, met. T	1.50	4.00
England cast		
Formula Racing Car, met. T	1.50	4.00
Macau cast		
Formula Racing Car, met. T	15.00	30.00
Manaus cast		
Formula Racing Car, met. R	20.00	40.00
Manaus cast		
Peterbilt Quarry Truck, Y	2.00	5.00
GR dumper, DIRTY DUMPER, England cast		
Peterbilt Quarry Truck, Y	1.50	4.00
GR dumper, DIRTY DUMPER, Macau cast		
Peterbilt Quarry Truck, Y	1.50	4.00
GR dumper, PACE, Macau cast		
Peterbilt Quarry Truck, Y	1.50	4.00
GR dumper, PACE, Thailand cast		
Peterbilt Quarry Truck, OR	4.00	10.00
GR dumper, LOSINGER, Macau cast		
Peterbilt Quarry Truck, WH	20.00	40.00
GR dumper, CEMENT COMPANY, Manaus		
Peterbilt Quarry Truck, Y	4.00	10.00
R dumper, PACE, INTERCOM CITY, China cast		
Peterbilt Quarry Truck, Y	1.50	4.00
R dumper, PACE CONSTRUCTION		
Mazda Savannah RX-7, BLA	1.50	4.00
spoiner, GOL stripe accents, Macau cast		
Mazda Savannah RX-7, WH	1.50	4.00
spoiler, 7/stripe accents, Macau cast		
Mazda Savannah RX-7, BLA	12.50	25.00
spoiler, RX7/MAZDA tampos, Manaus cast		

'64 SCAMMELL SNOW PLOW

Trans Am T-Roof, Pontiac, BLA firebird hood design, TURBO tampos, England cast	2.00	5.00
Trans Am T-Roof, Pontiac, BLA firebird hood design, TRANS AM tampos, Macau cast	1.50	4.00
Trans Am T-Roof, BLA tiger stripes, Macau cast	6.00	12.00
Trans Am T-Roof, met. SIL firebird hood design, Macau cast	1.50	4.00
Trans Am T-Roof, R 3 ROOSTER RACING TEAM tampo, Macau cast	5.00	12.00
Sunburner Maserati Bora, BLA Y/R flame tampos, England cast	3.00	8.00
Sunburner Maserati Bora, BLA Y/R flame tampos, Macau cast	1.50	4.00
Sunburner Maserati Bora, BLA Y/R flame tampos, Hong Kong cast	1.50	4.00
Matra Rancho, lt. BLU(European model)	2.50	6.00
Matra Rancho, dk. BLU (European model), SURF RESCUE tampos	2.50	6.00
Matra Rancho, dk. BLU (European model), no markings	4.00	10.00
Matra Rancho, BLA (European model), SURF RESCUE tampos	2.00	5.00
Matra Rancho, OR (European model), SURF 2 tampos	1.50	4.00
Matra Rancho, Y (European model), MARINE RESCUE tampos	1.50	4.00
Matra Rancho, WH (European model), no markings, Griffic Traffic(stickers included w/set)	3.00	8.00
Ford Model A Truck, BLU CHAMPION	1.50	4.00
Ford Model A Truck, BLU KELLOGGS labels	4.00	10.00
Ford Model A Truck, BLU MATCHBOX ON THE MOVE IN '84	40.00	100.00
Ford Model A Truck, WH, PEPSI	3.00	8.00
Ford Model A Truck, WH 2MATCHBOX USA	12.50	25.00
Ford Model A Truck, WH BEN FRANKLIN	250.00	500.00
Ford Model A Truck, BLU MATCHBOX SPEEDSHOP, nonchrome-lettered wheels	1.50	4.00
Ford Model A Truck, BLU MATCHBOX SPEEDSHOP, chrome-lettered wheels	30.00	60.00
Ford Model A Truck, BLA 2nd M.I.C.A. CONVENTION	100.00	200.00

Ford Model A Truck, BLU KELLOGGS RICE KRISPIES	5.00	12.00
Ford Model A Truck, Y MATCHBOX SERIES MODEL A FORD VAN	1.50	4.00
Ford Model A Truck, BLU MATCHBOX 40TH ANNIVERSARY 1990	3.00	8.00
Toyota Celica Supra, WH	1.50	4.00
Toyota Celica Supra, R TWIN CAM 24 tampos	3.00	8.00
Toyota Celica Supra, WH SUPRAA tampos	1.50	4.00
Toyota Celica Supra, WH R/BLU/Y tampos	4.00	10.00
Corvette T-Roof, WH stripes, England cast	1.50	4.00
Corvette T-Roof, WH stripes, Macau cast	1.50	4.00
Corvette T-Roof, BLU flame tampos, no rear SFW	1.50	4.00
Corvette T-Roof, BLU flame tampos, rear SFW	20.00	40.00
Corvette T-Roof, Y CORVETTE tampo	1.50	4.00
Corvette T-Roof, BLU stripes, Manaus cast	20.00	40.00
Corvette T-Roof, OR CHR windshield, World Class	2.00	5.00
Corvette T-Roof, R VETTE/CHEVY logo, China cast	1.50	4.00
Corvette T-Roof, met. BLU CHR windshield, World Class	2.00	5.00
Corvette T-Roof, BLA CHR windshield, World Class	3.00	8.00
Corvette T-Roof, R WH stripe, Y VETTE	1.50	4.00
Corvette T-Roof, met. BLU R/WH accents	1.50	4.00
Corvette T-Roof, met. dk. GR from 40th Anniversary set	1.50	4.00
Kenworth Conventional Aerodyne R, stripes, England cast	1.50	4.00
Kenworth Conventional Aerodyne BLA, stripes, England cast	1.50	4.00
Kenworth Conventional Aerodyne met. GR, R/BLU stripes, Macau cast	1.50	4.00
Kenworth Conventional Aerodyne BLU, Macau cast	1.50	4.00
1957 T-Bird, R	3.00	8.00
1957 T-Bird, CRE/R 2-tone	2.50	6.00
1957 T-Bird, BLA	1.50	4.00
Peterbilt Conventional, BLA	1.50	4.00
Peterbilt Conventional, WH NASA tampos	1.50	4.00
4x4 Chevy Van, met. lt. G RIDIN HIGH tampos	2.00	5.00
4x4 Chevy Van, met. dk. G BLA horseshoes, WH 4x4 on hood	2.00	5.00

4x4 Chevy Van, met. dk. G	4.00	10.00
WH horseshoes, BLA 4x4 on hood		
4x4 Chevy Van, met. G	5.00	12.00
BLA horseshoes, WH 4x4 on hood		
4x4 Chevy Van, WH	1.50	4.00
MATCHBOX RACING tampos		
4x4 Chevy Van, WH	5.00	12.00
TOKYO GIANTS tampos		
4x4 Chevy Van, WH	4.00	10.00
CASTROL RACING TEAM tampos		
4x4 Chevy Van, WH	1.50	4.00
MATCHBOX MOTORSPORTS tampos		
4x4 Chevy Van, WH	3.00	8.00
no markings, Graffic Traffic(stickers included w/set)		
4x4 Chevy Van, fluorescent Y	1.50	4.00
R/BLU graphics		
4x4 Chevy Van, BLA	1.50	4.00
PI/lt. G graphics		
Kenworth COE Aerodyne, WH	1.50	4.00
BR/BLU stripes, England cast		
Kenworth COE Aerodyne, WH	1.50	4.00
BR/BLU stripes, Macau cast		
Kenworth COE Aerodyne, met. SIL	1.50	4.00
PUR/OR tampos		
Kenworth COE Aerodyne, white	15.00	40.00
w/CHEF BOYARDEE labels		
Kenworth COE Aerodyne, R	1.50	4.00
Y/OR/WH stripes		
Hot Chocolate Volkswagen Beetle	2.00	5.00
BLA, met. BR sides		
Hot Chocolate Volkswagen Beetle	1.50	4.00
met. BLU		
Jaguar SS100, R	3.00	8.00
partially painted hood, England cast		
Jaguar SS100, R	1.50	4.00
R hood, England cast		
Jaguar SS100, R	1.50	4.00
R hood, Macau cast		
Jaguar SS100, BLU, Macau cast	1.50	4.00
Jaguar SS100, BLU, GR hood	1.50	4.00
Jaguar SS100, dk. G, Thailand cast	4.00	10.00
Red Rider, R, England cast	2.00	5.00
Red Rider, R, Hong Kong cast	2.00	5.00
Red Rider, R, Macau cast	1.50	4.00
Red Rider, R, China cast	1.50	4.00
Midnight Magic, BLA	1.50	4.00
SIL sides, England cast		
Midnight Magic, BLA	1.50	4.00
SIL sides, Macau cast		
Midnight Magic, BLA	1.50	4.00
SIL sides, Hong Kong cast		
Flareside Pickup, met. BLU	2.00	5.00
326 BAJA BOUNCER tampo		
Flareside Pickup, OR	1.50	4.00
326 BAJA BOUNCER tampo		
Flareside Pickup, Y	40.00	100.00
WH interior, 8-spoke wheels		

'65 BRM RACING CAR

Flareside Pickup, Y	1.50	4.00
BLA interior, 8-spoke wheels		
Flareside Pickup, Y	1.50	4.00
BLA interior, racing slicks		
Flareside Pickup, khaki G	2.00	5.00
PUR/BLU design, racing slicks		
Flareside Pickup, WH	15.00	30.00
DEB tampo, racing slicks		
Flareside Pickup, R	15.00	30.00
326 BAJA BOUNCER tampo, 8-spoke wheels		
Flareside Pickup, LI	3.00	8.00
Flareside Pickup, R	3.00	8.00
BILL ELLIOTT 11 tampo, racing slicks		
Flareside Pickup, R	1.50	4.00
Y flames, racing slicks(1994)		
NASA Tracking Vehicle, WH	1.50	4.00
Peterbilt Tanker, BLU	1.50	4.00
WH tank, MILK tampos		
Peterbilt Tanker, BLU	1.50	4.00
WH tank, no markings		
Peterbilt Tanker, R	1.50	4.00
CHR tank, GETTY tampos		
Peterbilt Tanker, R	20.00	50.00
CHR tank, AMOCO on tank, GETTY on door		
Peterbilt Tanker, WH	1.50	4.00
GR tank, SHELL tampos		
Peterbilt Tanker, WH	3.00	8.00
GR tank, AMPOL tampos		
Peterbilt Tanker, WH	1.50	4.00
CHR tank, SHELL tampos		
Peterbilt Tanker, WH	3.00	8.00
CHR tank, SHELL, IC on doors		
Peterbilt Tanker, WH	5.00	12.00
Y tank, SUPERGAS tampos		
Peterbilt Tanker, WH	1.50	4.00
WH tank, AMOCO tampos		
Peterbilt Tanker, WH	15.00	40.00
WH tank, chrome pipes, no markings		
Peterbilt Tanker, WH	3.00	8.00
WH tank, GR pipes, Graffic Traffic		
Peterbilt Tanker, BLA	2.50	6.00
BLA tank, AMOCO tampos		
Peterbilt Tanker, BLA	6.00	15.00
BLA tank, INDY RACING FUEL		
Peterbilt Tanker, BLA	12.00	30.00
BLA tank, MATCHBOX, GETTY, Manaus cast		
Peterbilt Tanker, BLA	20.00	50.00
WH tank, AMOCO tampos		
Peterbilt Tanker, BLA	1.50	4.00
Y tank, SUPERGAS tampos		
Peterbilt Tanker, BLA	20.00	50.00
CHR tank, SUPERGAS tampos		
Peterbilt Tanker, OL, GAS tampos	2.00	5.00
Peterbilt Tanker, LI	3.00	8.00
R tank, Thailand cast		

'65 DODGE WRECK TRUCK

Carmichael Commando, WH (European model), POLICE RESCUE tampos	3.00	8.00
Carmichael Commando, R (European model), FIRE tampos	3.00	8.00
4x4 Mini Pickup, Mountain Man	1.50	4.00
Mustang Piston Popper(Rolamatic) Y, R interior, no markings	4.00	10.00
Mustang Piston Popper(Rolamatic) Y, R interior, 60 tampo	2.50	6.00
Mustang Piston Popper(Rolamatic) Y, WH interior, 60 tampo	5.00	12.00
Mustang Piston Popper(Rolamatic) OR, SUNKIST tampo	1.50	4.00
Peterbilt Wreck Truck, BLU BLA booms, no markings, Y windows	40.00	100.00
Peterbilt Wreck Truck, OR BLA booms, EDDIE'S WRECKER tampo	1.50	4.00
Peterbilt Wreck Truck, OR dk. G booms, BLA stripes	3.00	8.00
Peterbilt Wreck Truck, WH BLA booms, Macau cast	1.50	4.00
Peterbilt Wreck Truck, WH BLA booms, Manaus cast	12.00	30.00
Peterbilt Wreck Truck, WH BLU booms, 9 tampo	1.50	4.00
Peterbilt Wreck Truck, WH BLU booms, 911 tampo	1.50	4.00
Peterbilt Wreck Truck, WH OR booms, SFPD tampo	1.50	4.00
Peterbilt Wreck Truck, OL BLA booms	1.50	4.00
Peterbilt Wreck Truck, R BLA booms, POLICE tampo, Manaus cast	15.00	40.00
Snorkel Fire Engine, R open cab, LOS ANGELES tampos, England cast	3.00	8.00
Snorkel Fire Engine, R open cab, METRO FIRE tampos, Macau cast	1.50	4.00
Snorkel Fire Engine, R open cab, METRO FIRE tampos, China cast	1.50	4.00
Snorkel Fire Engine, R open cab, FIRE DEPT/shield tampos, China cast	1.50	4.00
Snorkel Fire Engine, R open cab, Japanese lettering, China cast	4.00	10.00
Snorkel Fire Engine, fluorescent LI/Y open cab, FIRE DEPT/shield, China cast	1.50	4.00
Snorkel Fire Engine, fluorescent OR open cab, RESCUE UNIT FIRE 1 & checked bars, China cast	1.50	4.00
Snorkel Fire Engine, fluorescent OR open cab, RESCUE UNIT FIRE 1/IC logo	4.00	10.00

'65 FERRARI BERLINETTA

Snorkel Fire Engine, R open cab, RESCUE UNIT FIRE I/checked bars, China cast	2.00	5.00
Snorkel Fire Engine, WH open cab, no markings, Graffic Traffic (stickers included in set)	3.00	8.00
Snorkel Fire Engine, R open cab, 12th RESCUE SQUAD, GOL trim(1995)	1.50	4.00
Snorkel Fire Engine, open cab R lower, WH upper, GOL/BLA trim (1996 5-Pack)	1.50	4.00
Tyrone Malone Bandag Bandit BLA, England cast	1.50	4.00
Tyrone Malone Bandag Bandit BLA, Macau cast	1.50	4.00
Tyrone Malone Bandag Bandit BLA, China cast	2.00	5.00
Tyrone Malone Super Boss, WH G windows, England cast	1.50	4.00
Tyrone Malone Super Boss, WH R windows, England cast	4.00	10.00
Tyrone Malone Super Boss, WH Macau cast	1.50	4.00
Tyrone Malone Super Boss, WH China cast	1.50	4.00
Tyrone Malone Super Boss, T GR armament replaces spoiler, Macau cast	3.00	8.00
1933 Willys Street Rod, WH flame tampos	1.50	4.00
1933 Willys Street Rod, BLU flame tampos, 313 on roof, Hong Kong cast	1.50	4.00
1933 Willys Street Rod, BLU flame tampos, 313 on roof, Macau cast	1.50	4.00
1933 Willys Street Rod, BLA flame tampos, 313 on roof, China cast	3.00	8.00
1933 Willys Street Rod, WH BLU/PI/Y tampos(1993)	1.50	4.00
1962 Corvette, BLU, WH accents	2.00	5.00
1962 Corvette WH WH base, R acc., BLU int.	4.00	10.00
1962 Corvette, WH WH base, R acc., SIL int.	2.00	5.00
1962 Corvette WH BLU base, R acc., SIL int.	4.00	10.00
1962 Corvette WH WH base, R flames, Macau	2.00	5.00
1962 Corvette WH WH base, OR flames, Macau	2.00	5.00
1962 Corvette WH WH base, R flames, Hong Kong	2.00	5.00
1962 Corvette, BLU FIRESTONE tampo, Macau	4.00	10.00
1962 Corvette, OR II/WH stripe tampo, Macau	2.00	5.00
1962 Corvette R 454 RAT tampo, Macau	2.00	5.00

'65 FIAT 1500

1962 Corvette OR 11/WH stripes	2.00	5.00
1962 Corvette G 11/WH stripes	2.00	5.00
1962 Corvette R HEINZ 57 tampo, Macau	12.00	30.00
1962 Corvette, BLU/G WH roof, CHR wind.	2.00	5.00
1962 Corvette WH, GT	3.00	8.00
1962 Corvette OR/BLA, 4	2.00	5.00
1962 Corvette BLU MAG/WH accents, CHR int.	1.50	4.00
Dodge Delivery Truck, R (European model), WH container, PEPSI labels	2.00	5.00
Dodge Delivery Truck, R (European model), WH container, SMITH'S labels	2.00	5.00
Dodge Delivery Truck, R (European model), WH container, KELLOGG'S labels	2.00	5.00
Dodge Delivery Truck, WH (European model), WH container, STREET'S ICE CREAM tampos	3.00	8.00
Dodge Delivery Truck, R (European model), WH container KELLOGG'S/MILCH-LAITE-LATTE	15.00	40.00
Dodge Delivery Truck, WH (European model), WH container JETSPRESS ROAD EXPRESS	3.00	8.00
Dodge Delivery Truck, G (European model), WH container MINTIES tampos	3.00	8.00
Dodge Delivery Truck, OR/Y (European model), Y container, RISI tampos	12.00	30.00
Dodge Delivery Truck, BLU (European model), BLU container MITRE 10 tampos	3.00	8.00
Dodge Delivery Truck, R (European model), R container NESTLES CHOKITO tampos	3.00	8.00
Dodge Delivery Truck, R (European model), R container, KIT KAT tampos	3.00	8.00
Dodge Delivery Truck, BLU (European model), BLU container, YORKIE	3.00	8.00
Dodge Delivery Truck, WH (European model), WH container PIRELLI GRIPPING STUFF	2.00	5.00
Dodge Delivery Truck, R (European model), WH container MATCHBOX USA SHERATON INN 1989	6.00	15.00
Dodge Delivery Truck, WH (European model), WH container XPRESS PARCELS LSYSTEMS	2.00	5.00

	LOOSE	IN PKG.
Dodge Delivery Truck, dk. G (European model), OR container C PLUS ORANGE	4.00	10.00
Dodge Delivery Truck, lt. GR/dk. BLU (European model), BRITISH AIRWAYS CARGO	2.00	5.00
Dodge Delivery Truck, WH (European model), WH container, WIGWAM	5.00	12.00
Dodge Delivery Truck, R (European model), WH container BIG TOP CIRCUS	1.50	4.00
Helicopter WH, pilot/large windows OR base, MBTV NEWS	1.50	4.00
Helicopter, WH, pilot/large windows BLA base, MBTV NEWS	2.00	5.00
Helicopter, WH, pilot/large windows BLA base, POLICE 36	2.00	5.00
Helicopter, WH, pilot/large windows BLA base, RESCUE	1.50	4.00
Helicopter, WH, pilot/large windows BLA base, Japanese lettering	4.00	10.00
Helicopter, WH, pilot/large windows R base, FIRE DEPT	1.50	4.00
Helicopter, WH, pilot/large windows R base, NASA	1.50	4.00
Helicopter, WH, pilot/large windows R base VIRGIN ATLANTIC	1.50	4.00
Helicopter, WH, pilot/large windows Y base, JCB	2.00	5.00
Helicopter, WH, pilot/large windows Y base, FIRE DEPT	1.50	4.00
Helicopter, WH, pilot/large windows OR base, RESCUE	1.50	4.00
Helicopter, BLA, pilot/large windows BLA base, AIR CAB	1.50	4.00
Helicopter, R, pilot/large windows WH base, RED REBELS	1.50	4.00
Helicopter, R, pilot/large windows WH base, FIRE DEPT	1.50	4.00
Helicopter, met. GR, pilot/large windows OR base, 600 tampo	2.00	5.00

1983 Matchbox

	LOOSE	IN PKG.
Dodge Challenger Hot Rod Y BLA roof, TOYMAN	1.50	4.00
Dodge Challenger Hot Rod Y BLA roof, TOYMAN, Macau	1.50	4.00
Dodge Challenger Hot Rod Y BLA roof, TOYMAN, China	1.50	4.00
Dodge Challenger Hot Rod Y BLA roof, China cast	1.50	4.00
Dodge Challenger Hot Rod WH WH roof, GT	2.00	5.00
Dodge Challenger Hot Rod LB BLA roof, CHALLENGER	1.50	4.00
Dodge Challenger Hot Rod WH BLA roof, TOYMAN, China	2.00	5.00

Dodge Challenger Hot Rod BLU	1.50	4.00
WH roof, HEMI, CHALLENGER		
Dodge Challenger Hot Rod Y	1.25	3.00
BLA accents/roof, HP interior		
Dodge Challenger Hot Rod WH	1.25	3.00
PUR splatter, BLA roof, PUR interior		
IMSA Mazda BLU	1.50	4.00
WH/OR tampos, Macau		
Volkswagen Ruff Rabbit 4x4	1.50	4.00
Greased Lightning Pantera R	1.50	4.00
Caterpillar Bulldozer	1.50	4.00
IMSA Mustang BLA, R/WH str.	1.50	4.00
FORD MUSTANG tampo		
IMSA Mustang BLA, Y/G flames	1.50	4.00
IMSA Mustang BLA, Y/G stripes	1.50	4.00
IMSA Mustang Y, BLA/R str.	1.50	4.00
47 tampos		
IMSA Mustang R	4.00	10.00
IMSA Mustang OR/Y	1.50	4.00
IMSA Mustang R	1.50	4.00
4x4 Mini-Pickup	1.50	4.00
1983 Corvette Conv. SIL/R int.	1.50	4.00
1983 Corvette Convertible R/GR	1.50	4.00
1983 Corvette Convertible R	1.50	4.00
350 CID tampo		
1983 Corvette Convertible R/WH upper	4.00	10.00
R lower, CHEF BOYARDEE		
1983 Corvette Convertible R/WH	1.50	4.00
R lower, 350 CID tampos		
1983 Corvett Convertible GR	2.00	5.00
PUR lower		
1983 Corvette Convertible, MAR	1.50	4.00
Y/PI graphics, Y interior		
Ford Sierra XR4Ti	1.50	4.00
AMX Pro Stocker SIL	1.50	4.00
R/BLA stripes, AMX tampo		
AMX Pro Stocker MAR	2.00	5.00
Dr. Pepper tampo		
Jeep Laredo/Eagle/Wrangler 4x4	1.50	4.00
Corvette Pace Car GR	2.00	5.00
BLU accents, PACE CAR on sides		
Corvette Pace Car WH	1.50	4.00
R accent/CORVETTE tampos, Thailand		
Toyota Mini Camper Bigfoot	1.50	4.00
Datsun 280ZX 2+2 BLA	1.50	4.00
GOL pin stripes		
Datsun 280ZX 2+2 BLA	1.50	4.00
TURBO ZX tampos, SIL wheels		
Datsun 280ZX 2+2 BLA	4.00	10.00
TURBO ZX tampos, GOL wheels		
Datsun 280ZX 2+2 WH	3.00	8.00
R/BLU TURBO 33 tampo		
Datsun 280ZX 2+2 BLA	1.50	4.00
OR/Y/WH TURBO tampo		
Datsun 280ZX 2+2 GR	3.00	8.00
OR/Y/WH accents, Laser Wheels		
Datsun 280ZX 2+2 R	2.00	5.00
BLA/OR tampos		

'65 TAXI

'65 TRAILER CARAVAN

Chevrolet Ambulance WH PACIFIC AMBULANCE	1.50	4.00
Chevrolet Ambulance WH OR accents, PARAMEDICS E11	1.50	4.00
Chevrolet Ambulance WH EMT AMBULANCE	1.50	4.00
Chevrolet Ambulance WH, GT	3.00	8.00
Chevrolet Ambulance Y PARAMEDICS E11	3.00	8.00
Chevrolet Ambulance OR AMBULANCE 7/INTERCOM CITY	5.00	12.00
Chevrolet Ambulance R WH/GOL/BLA acc, BLU wind.	1.50	4.00
Chevrolet Ambulance WH BLU/OR accents, AMBULANCE/DIAL 911	1.50	4.00
Citroen 15CV BLA, CHR base	1.50	4.00
Citroen 15CV BLA, GR base	1.50	4.00
Big Blue Volkswagen Beetle	2.50	6.00
Sand Digger VW Beetle GR SAND DIGGER	2.00	5.00
Sand Digger VW Beetle R DUNE MAN	2.00	5.00
BMW M1 WH, BMW M1	1.50	4.00
BMW M1 BLA, Pirelli 59	1.50	4.00
BMW M1 Y, 11/stripes	1.50	4.00
BMW M1 R, 1/stripes	1.50	4.00
BMW M1 Y, CHR wind.	2.00	5.00
BMW M1 CHR	8.00	20.00
Porsche 935 BLU ELF 71 SACHS tampo, SILW	2.00	5.00
Porsche 935 LB ELF 71 SACHS tampo, GOLW	15.00	40.00
Porsche 935 WH CADBURY BUTTONS tampo	5.00	12.00
Porsche 935 R, AUTOTECH 35	2.00	5.00
Porsche 935 met. R AUTOTECH 35 tampo	2.00	5.00
Porsche 935 WH PORSCHE 10 tampo, GOLW	2.00	5.00
Porsche 935 WH PORSCHE 10 tampo, SILW	2.00	5.00
Porsche 935 BLA 11 OX RACING TEAM tampo	5.00	12.00
Porsche 935 R 41 PORSCHE tampo	5.00	12.00
Porsche 935 R, PORSCHE	2.00	5.00
Porsche 935 Y, CHR win.	2.00	5.00
Porsche 935 CRE, CHR win.	2.00	5.00
Porsche 935 WH/OR BLU 935 tampo, CHR/BLA windows	2.00	5.00
Porsche 935 BLA, CHR/BLA win.	2.00	5.00
Porsche 935 Y, PORSCHE 10	2.00	5.00
Porsche 935 LB FAR PORSCHE 71 SACHS, Manaus	20.00	35.00
Ford Sierra XR4i WH	30.00	80.00
Ford Sierra XR4i WH/R int.	1.50	4.00
Ford Sierra XR4i GR/dk. GR	1.50	4.00

Ford Sierra XR4i BLA	1.50	4.00
GR lower body, WH/G stripes		
Ford Sierra XR4i Y/ BLA	1.50	4.00
Ford Sierra XR4i, Y/GR	10.00	25.00
Ford Sierra XR4i CRE/GR	4.00	10.00
Ford Sierra XR4i G/GR	1.50	4.00
Ford Sierra XR4i BLU	2.00	5.00
BLA lower body, DUCKHAMS RACE TEAM		
Ford Sierra XR4i WH	2.00	5.00
R lower body, VIRGIN ATLANTIC		
Ford Sierra XR4i BLA	1.50	4.00
TEXACO, PIRELLI tampos		
Ford Sierra XR4i R	2.00	5.00
TIZER THE APPETIZER tampo		
Ford Sierra XR4i R	5.00	12.00
FIRE DEPT		
Ford Sierra XR4i, Y/OR	8.00	20.00
AIRPORT SECURITY, R roof lights		
Ford Sierra XR4i, Y/OR	5.00	12.00
AIRPORT SECURITY, G roof lights		
Ford Sierra XR4i WH	5.00	12.00
SHERIFF		
Ford Sierra XR4i R upper	6.00	15.00
Y lower, BLU roof tampo		
Ford Sierra XR4i WH/BLA	1.50	4.00
GEMINI/N COOPER/1		
Ruff Trek Holden Pickup T	1.50	4.00
RUFF TREK tampo		
Ruff Trek Holden Pickup WH	1.50	4.00
RUFF TREK tampo		
Ruff Trek Holden Pickup WH, 217	1.50	4.00
Ruff Trek Holden Pickup WH/BLA	1.50	4.00
BRUT/FABERGE tampo		
Ruff Trek Holden Pickup WH/R	15.00	40.00
BRUT/FABERGE tampo		
Ruff Trek Holden Pickup BLU	15.00	40.00
STP/GOODYEAR tampo		
Ruff Trek Holden Pickup WH	2.00	5.00
tires in back, 7-UP tampo		
Ruff Trek Holden Pickup BR	3.00	8.00
tires in back, R/Y/BLU tampos		
Ruff Trek Holden Pickup WH	5.00	12.00
tires in back, flame tampos		
Ruff Trek Holden Pickup Y	1.50	4.00
tires in back, MATCHBOX RESCUE..		
Corvette Hardtop	3.00	8.00
Flame Out WH, R/OR flames	2.00	5.00

1984 Matchbox

	LOOSE	IN PKG.
1984 Corvette Convertible	2.50	6.00
Formula Racer R	1.50	4.00
BLA PIRELLI, FIAT 3		
Formula Racer WH/OR/G	12.00	30.00
Y WATSON'S on foil, MR. JUICY/SUNKIST		

'65 FIAT 1500

Formula Racer Y	1.50	4.00
R GOODYEAR, MATCHBOX RACING..		
Formula Race WH	1.50	4.00
BLU SHELL, MATCHBOX..		
Extending Ladder Fire Engine R	1.25	3.00
WH ladder		
Extending Ladder Fire Engine R	1.25	3.00
WH ladder, FIRE DEPT 7		
Extending Ladder Fire Engine R	3.00	8.00
WH ladder, Japanese lettering		
Extending Ladder Fire Engine R	1.50	4.00
WH ladder, 3/crest tampo		
Extending Ladder Fire Engine R	3.00	8.00
WH ladder, FIRE DEPT, no origin cast		
Extending Ladder Fire Engine R	2.50	6.00
Y ladder, Live'N'Learn/Preschool		
Extending Ladder Fire Engine Y	1.50	4.00
WH ladder		
Extending Ladder Fire Engine OR	1.25	3.00
4/checkered bar accents(1994)		
Extending Ladder Fire Engine OR	3.00	8.00
5/INTERCOM CITY tampo		
Extending Ladder Fire Engine OR/WH	1.25	3.00
Extending Ladder Fire Engine R	1.50	4.00
WH upper, GOL/BLA accents, #1		
Extending Ladder Fire Engine R	1.25	3.00
WH 12th, GOL RESCUE SQUAD		
Extending Ladder Fire Engine, R	1.25	3.00
WH 12th RESCUE SQUAD, WH trim		
Extending Ladder Fire Engine, WH	1.25	3.00
OR ladder		
Jaguar XK120 G/R int.	2.00	5.00
Jaguar XK120 CRE/R int., 414	1.50	4.00
Jaguar XK120 WH	2.00	5.00
MAR interior, CHR windshield		
Jaguar XK120 WH	1.50	4.00
BLU/OR flames		
Volvo Covered Tilt Truck BLU	12.00	30.00
Y canopy, England		
Volvo Covered Tilt Truck BLU	1.50	4.00
Y canopy, FRESH FRUIT CO., Macau		
Volvo Covered Tilt Truck Y	1.50	4.00
Y canopy, FERRYMASTERS		
Volvo Covered Tilt Truck WH	1.50	4.00
WH canopy, FEDERAL EXPRESS		
Volvo Covered Tilt Truck BLU	1.50	4.00
Y canopy, MICHELIN		
Volvo Covered Tilt Truck OL	6.00	15.00
T canopy, LS2020		
Volvo Covered Tilt Truck BLA	6.00	15.00
GR canopy, LS1506		
Volvo Covered Tilt Truck BLU	5.00	12.00
BLU canopy, HENNEIZ		
Volvo Covered Tilt Truck R	3.00	8.00
G canopy, Y wheels, Live'N'Lea..		
Volvo Covered Tilt Truck R	3.00	8.00
no canopy, 123 tampo		

'66 DODGE DUMP TRUCK

Volvo Covered Tilt Truck WH	1.50	4.00
PIRELLI GRIPPING STUFF		
Volvo Cable Truck Y	6.00	15.00
2 GR cable spools		
1984 Dodge Daytona Z R	2.00	5.00
GR lower body, England		
1984 Dodge Daytona Z R	12.00	30.00
GR lower body, Macau		
1984 Dodge Daytona Z SIL	2.00	5.00
BLA lower body, R/BLA stripes		
1984 Dodge Daytona Z, WH	2.00	5.00
BLU lower body, R/BLU stripes		
1984 Dodge Daytona Z R	3.00	8.00
GOL lower body, plastic arm.		
1984 Dodge Daytona Z BLU	4.00	10.00
BLA low. body, 5 GOAT RACING		
TEAM		
1984 Dodge Daytona Z R	2.00	5.00
Y/BLU TURBO Z tampos, SILW		
1984 Dodge Daytona Z R	2.00	5.00
Y BLU TURBO Z tampos, SFW		
Mercedes 280GE G-Wagon R	1.50	4.00
WH roof, RESCUE UNIT/check.		
Pattern		
Mercedes 280GE G-Wagon OR	1.50	4.00
WH roof, LUFTHANSA tampo		
Mercedes 280GE G-Wagon WH	2.00	5.00
WH roof, POLIZEI/check.pattern		
Mercedes 280GE G-Wagon OL	2.00	5.00
T roof, LS 2014		
Mercedes 280GE G-Wagon WH	1.50	4.00
OR roof, AMBULANCE/check. Pattern		
Mercedes 280GE G-Wagon WH	1.50	4.00
WH roof AUTO RESCUE..		
Mercedes 280GE G-Wagon R	3.00	8.00
R roof FIRE METRO AIRPORT		
Mercedes 280GE G-Wagon BLU	3.00	8.00
BLU roof, SWAT UNIT.		
Mercedes 280GE G-Wagon WH	2.50	6.00
G roof/doors, POLIZEI		
Mercedes 280GE G-Wagon WH	2.50	6.00
WH roof, LUFTHANSA		
Mercedes 280GE G-Wagon OR	1.50	4.00
WH roof, AUTO RESCUE..		
Jeep 4x4 w/roll cage/winch	1.25	3.00
Mercedes Benz 500SEC BLA	1.50	4.00
5400SEC tampos		
Mercedes Benz 500SEC BLA	6.00	15.00
R EXON/500SEC tampos		
Mercedes Benz 500SEC BLA	4.00	10.00
PACE CAR HEUE, RESCUE 911		
Mercedes Benz 500SEC BLA	3.00	8.00
PACE CAR HEUER tampo		
Mercedes Benz 500SEC CRE	3.00	8.00
EMERGENCY DOC.., RESCUE 911		
Mercedes Benz 500SEC CRE	3.00	8.00
EMERGENCY DOCTOR		
Mercedes Benz 500SEC R	1.50	4.00
AMG tampo, Macau		

Mercedes Benz 500SEC R	4.00	10.00
G/Y stripes		
Mercedes Benz 500SEC R	1.50	4.00
AMG tampos/stripes		
Mercedes Benz 500SEC WH	1.50	4.00
AMG tampo, BLU interior		
Mercedes Benz 500SEC WH	3.00	8.00
AMG tampo, BLA interior		
Mercedes Benz 500SEC WH	1.50	4.00
R/BLU 7 tampos, w/o SFW		
Mercedes Benz 500SEC WH	15.00	40.00
R/BLU 7 tampos, w/SFW		
Mercedes Benz 500SEC WH	4.00	10.00
1 PIG RACING TEAM		
Mercedes Benz 500SEC WH	2.50	6.00
CHR windows		
Mercedes Benz 500SEC WH	4.00	10.00
R/BLU stripes, POLICE, RESCUE 911		
Mercedes Benz 500SEC WH	3.00	8.00
R/BLU stripes, POLICE		
Mercedes Benz Unimog Y	1.50	4.00
snowplow, RESCUE tampo		
Mercedes Benz Unimog R	1.50	4.00
snowplow, UR83 tampo		
Mercedes Benz Unimog WH	2.50	6.00
snowplow, R/BLU tampos, plast.arm.		
Mercedes Benz Unimog WH	1.50	4.00
snowplow, C&S tampos		
Dune Man Volkswagen Beetle	2.50	6.00
Leyland Titan London Bus	1.50	4.00
Pontiac Firebird S/E Y	2.50	6.00
SON OF A GUN 55		
Pontiac Firebird S/E Y	2.50	6.00
PIRELLI 56		
Pontiac Firebird S/E Y	8.00	20.00
10 R/WH tampos, plastic base		
Pontiac Firebird S/E LB	1.50	4.00
10 BLU/Y tampos, metal base		
Pontiac Firebird S/E LB	4.00	10.00
10 BLU/Y tampos, plastic base		
Pontiac Firebird S/E BLU	3.00	8.00
10, BLU/Y tam., met. base, LW		
Pontiac Firebird S/E WH	1.50	4.00
FAST EDDIES 15, metal base		
Pontiac Firebird S/E WH	2.50	6.00
FAST EDDIES 15, plastic base		
Pontiac Firebird S/E WH	6.00	15.00
6 HORSE RACING TEAM		
Pontiac Firebird S/E BR	5.00	12.00
FAST EDDIES 15		
Pontiac Firebird S/E LG	5.00	12.00
FAST EDDIES 15		
Toyota Celica Supra	1.50	4.00
Dunes Racer 4x4 Pickup	2.50	6.00
Indy Racer BLU	2.50	6.00
R GOODYEAR foi, STP BOSCH 20		
Indy Racer Y	1.50	4.00
R GOODYEAR foil, MATCHBOX RACING..		

Indy Racer PI	1.50	4.00
R GOODYEAR foil, MATCHBOX RACING..		
Indy Racer LG	1.50	4.00
R GOODYEAR foil, MATCHBOX RACING..		
Indy Racer OR	1.50	4.00
R GOODYEAR foil, MATCHBOX RACING..		
Indy Racer R	1.50	4.00
R GOODYEAR foil, MATCHBOX RACING..		
Indy Racer peach	1.50	4.00
R GOODYEAR foil, MATCHBOX RACING..		
Indy Racer WH	3.00	8.00
R foil, BLU wheels, 123456		
Indy Racer WH/HP/BLU	1.50	4.00
PI RAIN-X airfoil, AMWAY..		
Indy Racer BLU/WH	1.50	4.00
BLU VALVOLINE foil, VALVOLINE 5		
Indy Racer OR/Y/BLU	1.50	4.00
Y KRACO foil, DRACO/OTTER..		
Indy Racer Y/BLA	1.50	4.00
Y GOODYEAR foil, INDY 11		
Indy Racer BLA	1.50	4.00
BLA HAVOLINE foil, HAVOLINE 86		
Indy Racer CHR	10.00	25.00
R GOODYEAR foil		
Indy Racer BLU/WH	2.50	6.00
BLU MITRE 10 foil MITRE 10		
Indy Racer WH	1.50	4.00
fuschia HYFLO EX. Foil, HYFLOW		
Dodge Caravan R	10.00	25.00
BLA stripes, England		
Dodge Caravan SIL	2.50	6.00
BLA stripes, England		
Dodge Caravan BLA	2.50	6.00
Dodge Caravan BLA	1.50	4.00
SIL stripes, England		
Dodge Caravan BLA	1.50	4.00
SIL stripes, Macau		
Dodge Caravan BLA	1.50	4.00
SIL/GOL stripes, China		
Dodge Caravan BLA	12.00	30.00
SIL/GOL stripes, Manaus		
Dodge Caravan WH	1.50	4.00
PAN AM, Macau		
Dodge Caravan WH	1.50	4.00
CARAVAN/stripes, Macau		
Dodge Caravan WH	1.50	4.00
FLY VIRGIN ATLANTIC, Macau		
Dodge Caravan BLA	80.00	200.00
SIL stripes, ADIDAS, England		
Dodge Caravan BLA	6.00	15.00
G/Y stripes, Macau		
Dodge Caravan WH	1.50	4.00
NASA SHUTTLE PERS.., Macau		

'66 JEEP CJ5

	LOOSE	IN PKG.
Dodge Caravan GR/BLU	1.50	4.00
BRITISH AIRWAYS, Thailand		
Dodge Caravan R	1.50	4.00
RED ARROWS/RAF, Thailand		
Sand Racer WH	10.00	25.00
GOODYEAR/UNION 211		
Fiat Abarth	2.00	5.00

1985 Matchbox

	LOOSE	IN PKG.
Pontiac Fiero, WH/BLU	1.50	4.00
GOLOLDYEAR, SIL wheels		
Pontiac Fiero, WH/BLU	2.50	6.00
GOODYEAR, GOL wheels		
Pontiac Fiero, WH/R, GT FIERO	1.50	4.00
Pontiac Fiero, Y/OR	1.50	4.00
PROTECH, SFW		
Pontiac Fiero, Y/OR	8.00	20.00
PROLTECH, SIL wheels		
Pontiac Fiero, Y/GOL	1.50	4.00
PROTECH, Laser wheels		
Pontiac Fiero, BLA/R	4.00	10.00
2 DOG RACING TEAM		
Peterbilt Petrol Tanker	7.50	15.00
F1 Racing Car	7.50	15.00
Ford Supervan II, WH	1.50	4.00
FORD SUPERVAN tampos		
Ford Supervan II, WH	1.50	4.00
STARFIRE tampos		
Ford Supervan II, WH	1.50	4.00
FUJI RACING TEAM tampos		
Ford Supervan II, WH	7.50	15.00
roof lights, AMBULANCE, Siren Force		
Ford Supervan II, WH	7.50	15.00
roof lights, AMBULANCE/RESCUE 911		
Ford Supervan II, WH	1.50	4.00
no markings, Graffic Traffic		
Ford Supervan II, R	7.50	15.00
roof lights FIRE OBSERVER, Siren Force		
Ford Supervan II, R	7.50	15.00
roof lights, FIRE OBSERVER/RESCUE 911		
Ford Supervan II, R	1.50	4.00
TIZER FLAVOURED SOFT DRANK tampos		
Ford Supervan II, dk. BLU	1.50	4.00
DUCKHAMS QXR ENGINE OILS tampos		
Ford Supervan II, dk. BLU	7.50	15.00
lights, POLICE CONTROL UNIT, Siren Force		
Ford Supervan II, dk. BLU	7.50	15.00
lights, POLICE CONTROL UNIT/RESCUE 911		
Ford Supervan II, dk. GR	1.50	4.00
DANGER HIGH EXPLOSIVE/HEAVY LOAD weapons, Roadblasters		

Ford Supervan II, lt. GR	7.50	15.00
DANGER HIGH EXPLOSIVE/HEAVY LOAD, weapons		
Ford Supervan II, Y	1.50	4.00
SERVICE CAR BP OIL tampos		
Ford Supervan II, Y	1.50	4.00
GOODYEAR PIT STOP tampos		
Peugeot 205 Turbo 16, WH	1.50	4.00
205/stripes, Macau cast		
Peugeot 205 Turbo 16, WH	1.50	4.00
205/stripes, China cast		
Peugeot 205 Turbo 16, WH	10.00	25.00
205 tampos, Manaus cast		
Peugeot 205 Turbo 16, OR-R	1.50	4.00
MIICHELIN/BILSTEIN/48		
Peugeot 205 Turbo 16, G	4.00	10.00
no markings		
Peugeot 205 Turbo 16, Y	1.50	4.00
PEUGEOT 205/BILSTEIN/48 tampos		
Pontiac Trans Am T-Roof	1.50	4.00
Ford Escort XR3 Cabriolet, WH	1.50	4.00
XR3i tampos, SIL wheels, Macau cast		
Ford Escort XR3 Cabriolet, WH	2.00	5.00
XR3i tampos, gold wheels, Macau cast		
Ford Escort XR3 Cabriolet, WH	1.50	4.00
XR3i tampos, Thailand cast		
Ford Escort XR3 Cabriolet, WH	1.50	4.00
3/stripes, SFW		
Ford Escort XR3 Cabriolet, R	4.00	10.00
XR3i/FORD tampos		
Ford Escort XR3 Cabriolet, met. BLU	1.50	4.00
3/stripes, Laser wheels		
Ford Escort XR3 Cabriolet, met. BLU	1.50	4.00
WH/OR spatter tampos		
Ford Escort XR3 Cabriolet, dk. BLU	1.50	4.00
XR3i tampos, Macau cast		
Ford Escort XR3 Cabriolet, dk. BLU	1.50	4.00
XR3i tampos, Thailand cast		
Volvo Container Truck, BLU	1.50	4.00
WH container, COLDFRESH labels		
Volvo Container Truck, WH	4.00	10.00
WH container, SCOTCH CORNER labels		
Volvo Container Truck, GR	5.00	12.00
GR container, SUPERSAVER DRUGSTORES		
Volvo Container Truck, BLU	15.00	40.00
WH container, MB1-75 #1 IN VOLUME SALES		
Volvo Container Truck, WH	1.50	4.00
WH container, FEDERAL EXPRESS		
Volvo Container Truck, WH	3.00	8.00
WH container, UNIC		
Volvo Container Truck, BLU	3.00	8.00
WH container, UNIC		
Volvo Container Truck, BLU	3.00	8.00
BLU container, CROOKE'S HEALTHCARD		

'66 DAIMLER BUS

'66 GRIT SPREAD TRUCK

Volvo Container Truck, WH	12.00	30.00
WH container, KELLOGGS/MILCH-LAIT-LATTE		
Volvo Container Truck, BLU	15.00	40.00
WH container, KELLOGGS/MILCH-LAIT-LATTE		
Volvo Container Truck, WH	1.50	4.00
WH container, TNT IPEC		
Volvo Container Truck, G	5.00	12.00
GR container, HIKKOSHI SEMMON CENTER		
Volvo Container Truck, BLU	3.00	8.00
BLU container, ALLDERS		
Volvo Container Truck, WH	3.00	8.00
WH container, XP PARCELS		
Volvo Container Truck, BLU	5.00	12.00
BLU container, COMMA PERFORMANCE MOTOR OILS		
Volvo Container Truck, R	5.00	12.00
BR container, MERKUR KAFFEE labels		
Volvo Container Truck, G	4.00	10.00
WH container, M/G stripes		
Volvo Container Truck, R	4.00	10.00
WH container, DENNER		
Volvo Container Truck, WH	3.00	8.00
WH container, FAMILY TRUST		
Volvo Container Truck, BLU	3.00	8.00
R container, CHRISTIANSEN		
Volvo Container Truck, WH	12.00	30.00
WH container, KIT KAT		
Volvo Container Truck, WH	12.00	30.00
WH container, YORKIE		
Volvo Container Truck, R	1.50	4.00
WH container, BIG TOP CIRCUS		
Volvo Container Truck, BLU	2.00	5.00
WH container, BIG TOP CIRCUS		
Volvo Container Truck, WH	4.00	10.00
LB container, CO-OP PEOPLE WHO CARE		
Volvo Container Truck, WH	3.00	8.00
LB container, 99 TEA		
Volvo Container Truck, BLA	1.50	4.00
BLA container, COOL PAINT CO. (1993)		
Volvo Container Truck, OR	1.50	4.00
MATCHBOX logo on doors GET IN THE FAST LANE		
Volvo Container Truck, OR	1.50	4.00
no logo on doors GET IN THE FAST LANE		
Volvo Container Truck, OR	3.00	8.00
Y container, NORTH AMERICAN DIECAST TOY COLLECTORS ASSOCIATION 2ND ANNIVERSARY NOVEMBER 1995		
Peugeot Quasar, WH	1.50	4.00
QUASAR trampos		
Peugeot Quasar, dk. BLU	1.50	4.00
SFW, 9/PI stripes		

Peugeot Quasar, met. BLU Laser wheels, 9/Pl stripes	1.50	4.00
Peugeot Quasar, BLA G/OR stripes, Roadblasters	1.50	4.00
Peugeot Quasar, PUR QUASAR tampos	1.50	4.00
Peugeot Quasar, Y 3 tampos, stripes/flames, Preschool	2.50	6.00
Peugeot Quasar, MAR Y accents	1.25	3.00
BMW 323i Cabriolet, met. SIL BLU 323i tampos	1.50	4.00
BMW 323i Cabriolet, R 323i tampos	1.50	4.00
BMW 323i Cabriolet, WH BMW/323i tampos	4.00	10.00
BMW 323i Cabriolet, R GLIDING CLUB tampos	1.50	4.00
BMW 323i Cabriolet, WH ALPINA tampos	1.50	4.00
BMW 323i Cabriolet, dk. BLU 323i/BP tampos	4.00	10.00
BMW 323i Cabriolet, WH PUR/OR/BLU tampos	1.50	4.00
NASA Rocket Transporter, WH NASA logo, U.S. flag	1.25	3.00
NASA Rocket Transporter, WH NASA logo/heckerboard tampos	1.25	3.00
NASA Rocket Transporter, BLA GR camouflage, Commando	15.00	40.00
NASA Rocket Transporter OL camouflage, OL missile(1996 5-Pack)	1.50	4.00
NASA Rocket Transporter, OL OL missile	1.50	4.00
Faun Mobile Crane, Y REYNOLDS CRANE HIRE, England cast	1.50	4.00
Faun Mobile Crane, Y REYNOLDS CRANE HIRE, Macau cast	1.50	4.00
Faun Mobile Crane, Y REYNOLDS CRANE HIRE, China cast	1.50	4.00
Faun Mobile Crane, Y no markings, Y plastic crane cab	1.50	4.00
Faun Mobile Crane, Y road/bridge design, R plastic crane cab	1.50	4.00
Faun Mobile Crane, Y OR crane cab, IC/checkerboard pattern	3.00	8.00
Faun Mobile Crane, OR BLA crane, lt. GR boom(1996)	1.50	4.00
Mission Chopper w/retractable tail dk. BLU, met. GR base/skids, OR tampos	1.50	4.00
Mission Chopper w/retractable tail dk. BLU, met. GR base/skids, bullseye tampos	1.50	4.00

Mission Chopper w/retractable tail R, WH base/skids, SHERIFF/AIR 1 tampos	1.50	4.00
Mission Chopper w/retractable tail OL, T base/skids, Skybusters	1.50	4.00
Mission Chopper w/retractable tail OL, BLA base/skids, AC15, Commando	1.50	4.00
Mission Chopper w/retractable tail BLA, GR base/skids, AC99 Commando	1.50	4.00
Mission Chopper w/retractable tail R, WH base/skids, REBELS/RESCUE/ AIR 1	1.50	4.00
Mission Chopper w/retractable tail WH, BLU base/skids, POLICE/crest	1.50	4.00
Mission Chopper w/retractable tail G, WH base/skids, POLIZEI tampos	1.50	4.00
Mission Chopper w/retractable tail BLA, WH base/skids, POLICE tampos	1.50	4.00
Mission Chopper w/retractable tail T, BR camouflage(1993)	1.50	4.00
Mission Chopper w/retractable tail G w/BR/BLA camouflage(1996 5-Pack)	1.50	4.00
Mission Chopper w/retractable tail OL, AT-7521(1996)	1.50	4.00
Mercedes Sauber Group C Racer, R, BLA airfoil, BASF CASSETTES tampo	2.00	5.00
Mercedes Sauber Group C Racer WH, BLA airfoil, JR. COLLECTORS CLUB	3.00	8.00
Mercedes Sauber Group C Racer WH, BLA airfoil, CASTROL SAUBER 61	1.50	4.00
Mercedes Sauber Group C Racer Y, BLU airfoil, OR/BLU accents	1.50	4.00
Mercedes Sauber Group C Racer BLA, BLA airfoil, CARGANTUA	3.00	8.00
Mercedes Sauber Group C Racer R, armaments, no airfoil, Roadblasters	1.50	4.00
Mercedes Sauber Group C Racer WH/OR, OR airfoil, BISOTHERM/ BAUSTEIN	4.00	10.00
Mercedes Sauber Group C Racer R, R foil, ROYAL MAIL SWIFTAIR	2.00	5.00
Mercedes Sauber Group C Racer LB, BLA foil, GRAND PRIX 46	2.00	5.00
Mercedes Sauber Group C Racer WH, BLA airfoil, GRAND PRIX 46	2.00	5.00
Mercedes Sauber Group C Racer CHR, BLA airfoil, no markings	10.00	25.00
Mercedes Sauber Group C Racer PI/BLU, BLU airfoil, Lightning	1.50	4.00
Mercedes Sauber Group C Racer OR/Y, Y airfoil, Lightning	1.50	4.00
Mercedes Sauber Group C Racer BLU/PI, BLU foil, Lightning	1.50	4.00
Mercedes Sauber Group C Racer MATCHBOX USA 11TH ANNUAL CONVENTION/TOY SHOW 1992	6.00	15.00

School Bus, Y, SCHOOL DISTRICT 2	1.50	4.00
School Bus, OL, GOVT PROPERTY	4.00	10.00
School Bus, Y, SCHOOL DISTRICT 2, CHEF BOYARDEE	3.00	8.00
School Bus, OR/Y, 1+2=3/abc, Preschool	3.00	8.00
School Bus, OR-Y, ST. PAUL PUBLIC SCHOOLS	20.00	50.00
School Bus, BLU, POLICE 88	1.50	4.00
School Bus, BLU, HOFSTRA UNIVERSITY	5.00	12.00
School Bus, Y, HARVEY WORLD TRAVEL	3.00	8.00
School Bus, OR, SCHOOL DISTRICT 2	2.00	5.00
School Bus, WH/dk. BLU, PENN STATE/ THE LOOP	3.00	8.00
School Bus, PI, 1994 Collectors Choice from White Rose Collectibles	3.00	8.00
Chevy Blazer 4x4 Police, WH SHERIFF 7 tampos, Macau cast	1.50	4.00
Chevy Blazer 4x4 Police, WH SHERIFF 7 tampos, Thailand cast	1.50	4.00
Chevy Blazer 4x4 Police, WH SHERIFF 7 tampos, Manaus cast	20.00	50.00
Chevy Blazer 4x4 Police, PUR OR/R/BLA tampos, Roadblasters	1.50	4.00
Chevy Blazer 4x4 Police, BLU BLA/WH accents, OR 50 on roof, BLU windows	1.50	4.00
Chevy Blazer 4x4 Police, BLU BLA/WH accents, OR 50 on roof, R windows	1.50	4.00
Camaro IROC Z, G, IROC Z	3.00	8.00
Camaro IROC Z, BLU, IROC Z on sides only	1.50	4.00
Camaro IROC Z, BLU, IROC Z on sides/hood	1.50	4.00
Camaro IROC Z, R CARTER/GOODYEAR	1.50	4.00
Camaro IROC Z, met. R CARTER/GOODYEAR	1.50	4.00
Camaro IROC Z, Y, IROC Z	1.50	4.00
Camaro IROC Z, met. OR CARTER/GOODYEAR	1.50	4.00
Camaro IROC Z, G BP STUNT TEAM/stripes	4.00	10.00
Camaro IROC Z, BLA Z28/R accents	1.50	4.00
Camaro IROC Z, BLA Z28, OR accents	1.50	4.00
Airport Foam Pumper, R WH roof, FOAM UNIT/checkerboard	4.00	10.00
Airport Foam Pumper, Y FOAM UNIT/METRO AIRPORT	1.50	4.00
Airport Foam Pumper, R FOAM UNIT/METRO AIRPORT	1.50	4.00
Rolls Royce Silver Cloud, met. SIL-GR	2.50	6.00
Rolls Royce Silver Cloud, CRE	1.50	4.00
Rolls Royce Silver Cloud, met. GOL CHR windows, World Class	1.50	4.00
Dodge Caravan	1.50	4.00

'67 REFRIGERATED TRUCK

'67 CLAAS COMBINE

	LOOSE	IN PKG.
Lamborghini Countach OP500S, R Lamborghini hood logo, SIL wheels	1.50	4.00
Lamborghini Countach OP500S, R Lamborghini hood logo, GOL wheels	4.00	10.00
Lamborghini Countach OP500S, BLA 5/stripes, SIL wheels	1.50	4.00
Lamborghini Countach OP500S, BLA 5/stripes, GOL wheels	1.50	4.00
Lamborghini Countach OP500S, WH LP500S/stripes, SFW	1.50	4.00
Lamborghini Countach OP500S, SIL Laser wheels	1.50	4.00
Lamborghini Countach OP500S, R G 15/BP tampos	4.00	10.00
Lamborghini Countach OP500S, Y 10 TIGER RACING TEAM tampos	4.00	10.00
Lamborghini Countach OP500S, Y LAMBORGHINI/COUNTACH tampos	1.50	4.00
Lamborghini Countach OP500S, Y LP500S, CHR windows, World Class	1.50	4.00
Lamborghini Countach OP500S, BLA LP500/stripes, SFW	6.00	15.00
Lamborghini Countach OP500S, CHR no markings	10.00	25.00
Lamborghini Countach OP500S, R COUNTACH, CHR windows, World Class	2.00	5.00
Lamborghini Countach OP500S, WH no markings, Graffic Traffic	2.00	5.00
Lamborghini Countach OP500S, CRE COUNTACH/logo	1.50	4.00
Lamborghini Countach OP500S, Y/BLU PI interior	1.25	3.00
Lamborghini Countach OP500S, R WH LAMBORGHINI/bull log on sides	1.50	4.00
Plane Transporter RESCUE, Y RESCUE/Checkerboard pattern	4.00	10.00
Plane Transporter RESCUE, OL BLA/T camouflage, Commando	15.00	40.00

1986 Matchbox

	LOOSE	IN PKG.
Scania T143 WH R/OR/Y stripes	1.50	4.00
Scania T143 BLU R/OR/Y stripes	1.50	4.00
Firebird Halley's Comet Comm.	1.50	4.00
Volvo Container Truck	1.50	4.00
VW Trans./Ambul. WH Ambulance markings/roof lights	1.50	4.00
VW Trans./Ambul. Vanagon BLA G markings	1.50	4.00
VW Trans./Ambul. Vanagon WH	1.50	4.00
Breakdown Van R WH boom, 24 HOUR SERVICE	1.50	4.00
Breakdown Van Y BLA boom, AUTO RELAY 24	1.50	4.00
Breakdown Van BLA GR boom, Y stripes	3.00	8.00

	LOOSE	IN PKG.
Breakdown Van R	3.00	8.00
G boom, BLU wheels		
Breakdown Van OR	1.50	4.00
OR boom, AUTO RELAY 24..		
Breakdown Van OR	1.50	4.00
BLA boom, AUTO RELAY 24..		
Breakdown Van WH, GT	1.50	4.00
Breakdown Van OR	4.00	10.00
INTERCOM CITY..		
VW Golf Gti R	2.00	5.00
VW Golf Gti WH	2.00	5.00
FEDERAL EXPRESS		
VW Golf Gti WH, QUANTUM	2.50	6.00
VW Golf Gti GR	2.00	5.00
VW Golf Gti Y, PTT	4.00	10.00
VW Golf Gti WH	2.00	5.00
ABSTRACT/graphics		
VW Golf Gti WH	10.00	25.00
LIPPISCHE LANDES-ZEITUNG		
Chevy Stocker Halley's Comet	2.00	5.00
4x4 Pickup Camper	1.50	4.00
Ford Escort XR3i Cabriolet	1.50	4.00
Mercury Parklane Halley's Comet	2.00	5.00
Plane Transporter RESCUE	4.00	10.00

1987 Matchbox

	LOOSE	IN PKG.
Austin FX4R London Taxi BLA	2.00	5.00
no markings		
Austin FX4R London Taxi BLA	2.00	5.00
GREAT TAXI RIDE..		
Austin FX4R London Taxi Y	1.50	4.00
ABC TAXI, preschool series		
Austin FX4R London Taxi BLA	1.50	4.00
LONDON TAXI/British flag on left		
side only		
Porsche 959 GR	1.50	4.00
PORSCHE tampos on doors		
Porsche 959 WH	1.50	4.00
PORSCHE tampos, WH wheels		
Porsche 959 WH	1.50	4.00
PORSCHE tampos, SIL wheels		
Porsche 959 GR	1.50	4.00
PORSCHE 959 tampos		
Porsche 959 WH	3.00	8.00
PORSCHE 959, R/Y/BLA stripes		
Porsche 959 PI	1.50	4.00
PORSCHE 959 tampos		
Porsche 959 PUR	1.50	4.00
PORSCHE 959 tampos		
Porsche 959 WH	12.00	30.00
REDOXON tampos		
Porsche 959 WH	1.50	4.00
PACE CAR/SHELL tampos		
Porsche 959 WH	1.50	4.00
PIRELLI GRIP. STUFF 313 tampos		
Porsche 959 BLA, PORSCHE	1.50	4.00
Porsche 959 CHR	8.00	20.00
Porsche 959 WH, LLOYDS	4.00	10.00

Porsche 959 MAG	1.50	4.00
RAGE tampo, BLA/Y accents		
Vauxhall Astra Police(Euro.)	1.50	4.00
Toyota MR2 WH	1.50	4.00
MR2 PACE CAR tampos		
Toyota MR2 BLU	1.50	4.00
MR2 tampos/PI stripes, SFW		
Toyota MR2 BLU	2.00	5.00
MR2 tampos/PI stripes, LW		
Toyota MR2 G	6.00	15.00
7 SNAKE RACING TEAM tampos		
Buick Stock Car BLA	1.50	4.00
WH base, 4/355 CID tampos		
Buick LeSabre Stock Car PUR/WH	2.50	6.00
KEN WELLS/QUICKSILVER, LW		
Buick LeSabre Stock Car LG	1.50	4.00
WH base, 4/355 CID tampos		
Buick LeSabre Stock Car BR	1.50	4.00
WH base, 4/355 CID tampos		
Buick LeSabre Stock Car OR	2.50	6.00
WH base, 4/355 CID tampos		
Buick LeSabre Stock Car R	2.50	6.00
WH base, 4/355 CID tampos		
Buick LeSabre Stock Car Y	1.50	4.00
R base, 10/SHELL/MARSHALL tampos		
Buick LeSabre Stock Car WH	1.50	4.00
R base, 10/SHELL/MARSHALL tampos		
Buick LeSabre Stock Car R	1.50	4.00
WH base, 07/TOTAL RACING tampos		
Jeep Eagle/Laredo	1.50	4.00
1987 Corvette Convertible Y	2.00	5.00
CORVETTE/logo		
1987 Corvette Convertible WH/R	2.00	5.00
350 CID, Laser wheels		
1987 Corvette Convertible WH/R	2.00	5.00
350 CID, SFW		
1987 Corvette Convertible R	2.00	5.00
CORVETTE/logo		
1987 Corvette Convertible OR	2.00	5.00
CORVETTE/logo		
1987 Corvette Convertible BLU	2.00	5.00
CHR windshield, World Class		
1987 Corvette Convertible R	2.50	6.00
1987 Corvette Convertible WH	2.00	5.00
1987 Corvette Convertible, LG	3.00	8.00
rubber tires, RALLY OFFICIAL		
1987 Corvette Convertible R	2.00	5.00
SIL CORVETTE, 40th Ann.		
1987 Corvette Convertible R	2.00	5.00
Y/MAG design, Y interior		
1987 Corvette Convertible WH	2.00	5.00
BLU/OR design, BLU interior		
GMC Wrecker WH	1.50	4.00
FRANK'S GETTY		
GMC Wrecker WH	1.50	4.00
FRANK'S GETTY", no origin cast		
GMC Wrecker WH	6.00	15.00
ACCESSORY WHOLES		

GMC Wrecker BLA, INDY 500	4.00	10.00
GMC Wrecker PUR	1.50	4.00
Y accents, PARKHILL TOWING		
Nissan 300 ZX Turbo GR	1.50	4.00
GOL stripes/TURBO tampos		
Nissan 300 ZX Turbo WH	1.50	4.00
hood opens, FUJICOLOR tampos		
Nissan 300 ZX Turbo R	1.50	4.00
hood opens, R/OR stripes		
Nissan 300 ZX Turbo R	1.50	4.00
hood opens, R/OR stripes		
Nissan 300 ZX Turbo WH	4.00	10.00
hood opens, 96/BP RACING TEAM		
Nissan 300 ZX Turbo Y	4.00	10.00
4 MONKEY RACING TEAM		
Jeep Cherokee WH	1.50	4.00
Jeep Cherokee T, HOLIDAY..	1.50	4.00
Jeep Cherokee Y	2.00	5.00
FOREST RANGER COUNTY PARK		
Jeep Cherokee Y	4.00	10.00
BP CHIEF, G/R stripes		
Jeep Cherokee Y, MR. FIXER	1.50	4.00
Jeep Cherokee LG, MR. FIXER	1.50	4.00
Jeep Cherokee BR, MR. FIXER	1.50	4.00
Jeep Cherokee WH	1.50	4.00
NATIONAL SKI PATROL		
Jeep Cherokee SIL	1.50	4.00
Jeep Cherokee PUR	1.50	4.00
OR/CRE flames		
Jeep Cherokee R	1.50	4.00
BLA lower body, GOL trim/shield		
Rolls Royce Silver Cloud	1.50	4.00
Ford RS200 WH, 7	1.50	4.00
Ford RS200 BLU, 2	1.50	4.00
Ford RS200 WH	2.50	6.00
Ford RS200 BLU	6.00	15.00
Jaguar XJ6 R	1.50	4.00
Jaguar XJ6 BLA	15.00	40.00
W/M/crest tampos		
Jaguar XJ6 G	6.00	15.00
REDOXON/JAGUAR tampos		
Jaguar XJ6 WH	3.00	8.00
Renault 11 Turbo Alliance BLA	1.50	4.00
Vauxhall Astra GTE R	1.50	4.00
GTE/stripes		
Vauxhall Astra GTE WH	1.50	4.00
AC DELCO 48, SIL wheels		
Vauxhall Astra GTE WH	1.50	4.00
AC DELCO 48, WH wheels		
Vauxhall Astra GTE WH	1.50	4.00
STP/SPHERE DRAKE tampos		
Vauxhall Astra GTE Y	1.50	4.00
MOBILE PHONE/TELECOM tampos		
Vauxhall Astra GTE Y	4.00	10.00
Vauxhall Astra GTE, BLA	4.00	10.00
BP52, 7, Y stripe		
Peugeot Quasar	1.50	4.00
Mercedes Benz 300E LB	1.50	4.00

'67 GREYHOUND BUS

Mercedes Benz 300E WH	1.50	4.00
G stripe, POLIZEI 5075		
New Ford Transit R	1.50	4.00
MOTORSPORT		
New Ford Transit R	15.00	40.00
New Ford Transit R	1.50	4.00
left hand drive, no markings		
New Ford Transit R	3.00	8.00
AUSTRALIA POST		
New Ford Transit R	3.00	8.00
ROYAL MAIL		
New Ford Transit R	3.00	8.00
right driver, AUSTRALIA POST - WE DELIVER		
New Ford Transit R, BLICK	5.00	12.00
New Ford Transit WH	1.50	4.00
FEDERAL EXPRESS		
New Ford Transit WH	3.00	8.00
right driver, ORMOND ST. APPEAL		
New Ford Transit WH, WELLA	3.00	8.00
New Ford Transit WH	3.00	8.00
AUSTRALIA TELECOM		
New Ford Transit WH	2.00	5.00
XP EXPRESS PARCELS		
New Ford Transit WH	2.00	5.00
right hand drive, FEDERAL EXPRESS		
New Ford Transit WH	4.00	10.00
PETER COX PRESERVATION		
New Ford Transit WH, KIOSK	4.00	10.00
New Ford Transit WH	30.00	75.00
left or right hand drive, KELLOGGS		
New Ford Transit WH, DCS	30.00	75.00
New Ford Transit WH GT	3.00	8.00
New Ford Transit WH	12.00	30.00
SUPERTOYS		
New Ford Transit WH	30.00	75.00
McKESSON		
New Ford Transit WH	3.00	8.00
GARDEN FESTIVAL WALES		
New Ford Transit WH	1.50	4.00
R cross/stripes		
New Ford Transit WH, UNICHEM	4.00	10.00
New Ford Transit WH	2.50	6.00
right hand drive, JCB JOB SITE		
New Ford Transit WH	2.50	6.00
right hand drive, XP EXPRESS PARCELS		
New Ford Transit WH, WIGWAM	4.00	10.00
New Ford Transit LI	6.00	15.00
New Ford Transit OR, OVAL	4.00	10.00
New Ford Transit SIL/GR	4.00	10.00
ISOTAR/PERFORM/POWERPLAY		
New Ford Transit Y	1.50	4.00
BRITISH TELECOM		
New Ford Transit Y, RYDER	1.50	4.00
New Ford Transit Y	1.50	4.00
CADBURY FLAKES		
New Ford Transit G	2.00	5.00
TARONGA ZOOMOBILE		

'67 HONDA CYCLE & TRAILER

	LOOSE	IN PKG.
Volvo 760 GR	1.50	4.00
Volvo 760 dk. GR	1.50	4.00
Volvo 760 PUR	1.50	4.00
Volvo 760 WH GT	1.50	4.00
Volvo 760 R	2.50	6.00
Icarus Bus WH	2.00	5.00
OR roof, VOYAGER		
Icarus Bus WH	1.50	4.00
R roof, GIBRALTAR		
Icarus Bus WH/G roof	1.50	4.00
CITY LINE TOURIST		
Icarus Bus WH/G	6.00	15.00
pictograms, 2384584		
Icarus Bus WH	3.00	8.00
CANARY ISLAND		
Icarus Bus WH	1.50	4.00
WH roof, ESPANA		
Icarus Bus WH/OR	2.50	6.00
WH roof, AIRPORT LIMOUSINE		
Icarus Bus WH GT	4.00	10.00
Icarus Bus CRE, IKARUS	1.50	4.00
Icarus Bus T/BR roof, MARTI	3.00	8.00
Camaro IROC Z	1.50	4.00
Ford Supervan II	1.50	4.00
Ford Utility Truck GR	1.50	4.00
OR front end, ENERGY INC		
Ford Utility Truck R	2.00	5.00
53, Y wheels, Preschool		
Ford Utility Truck Y	1.50	4.00
R front end, ENERGY INC.		
Ford Utility Truck Y	1.50	4.00
TELEPHONE CO		
Ford Utility Truck T	1.50	4.00
G base/boom TREE CARE		
Ford Utility Truck G	1.50	4.00
met. GR base, WH TREE CARE		
Ferrari Testarossa R	1.50	4.00
Ferrari Testarossa BLA/SIL	1.50	4.00
Ferrari Testarossa GR/GOL	1.50	4.00
Ferrari Testarossa Y	1.50	4.00
R/BLU/Y accents, Roadblasters		
Ferrari Testarossa Y	3.00	8.00
9 RABBIT RACING TEAM		
Ferrari Testarossa R/SIL acc.	1.50	4.00
Ferrari Testarossa WH GT	1.50	4.00
Ferrari Testarossa R	1.50	4.00
CHR windows, World Class		
Ferrari Testarossa WH	1.50	4.00
CHR windows, World Class		
Ferrari Testarossa Y	1.50	4.00
BLA accent stripes, HP flames		

1988 Matchbox

	LOOSE	IN PKG.
Diesel Road Roller G	3.00	8.00
comm. China 40th Ann. GP		
Diesel Road Roller BLU	1.50	4.00
Massey Harris Tractor R, 40th ann.	2.50	6.00

Massey Harris Tractor G, 40th ann.	1.50	4.00
London Bus 40th ann.	2.50	6.00
BUY MATCHBOX SERIES		
London Bus 40th ann.	1.50	4.00
MATCHBOX ORIGINALS		
Horse Drawn Milk Float OR	3.00	8.00
40th Ann.		
Horse Drawn Milk Float LB	3.00	8.00
Dennis Fire Escape 40th ann.	3.00	8.00
Dennis Fire Escape Y reels	1.50	4.00
1988 Corvette Convertible	2.50	6.00
Saab 9000 R	1.50	4.00
Saab 9000 BLU, Laser wh.	3.00	8.00
Saab 9000 WH	1.50	4.00
Saab 9000 GR	3.00	8.00
Rover Sterling R	1.50	4.00
Rover Sterling GR	1.50	4.00
R/WH/BLU stripes, Laser wheels		
Rover Sterling BLU	2.50	6.00
Y base, BLU wheels, no hood,		
Preschool		
Rover Sterling Y	3.00	8.00
Rover Sterling GR	1.50	4.00
ROVER STERLING tampos		
Rover Sterling WH GT	2.00	5.00
Skoda 130LR Rally WH	1.50	4.00
SKODA 44		
Ford LTD Police WH	1.50	4.00
BLA accents, POLICE PD-21		
Ford LTD Police WH	1.50	4.00
BLU accents, POLICE PD-21		
Ford LTD Police PUR	1.50	4.00
POLICE PD-21		
Ford LTD Police R	1.50	4.00
POLICE PD-21		
Ford LTD Police R	1.50	4.00
FIRE DEPT/FIRE CHIEF		
Ford LTD Police WH	2.50	6.00
policeman, Matchbox Preschool		
Ford LTD Police WH GT	1.50	4.00
Ford LTD Police BLU	1.50	4.00
POLICE R-25		
Ford LTD Police WH	3.00	8.00
POLICE PD-21, INTERCOM CITY		
Ford LTD Police BLU	1.50	4.00
Y accent stripe, STATE POLICE		
Ford LTD Police BLU	1.50	4.00
Y accent stripe, STATE POLICE		
Mercury Wagon WH/GR base	1.50	4.00
T-Bird Turbo Coupe PUR	1.50	4.00
TURBO COUPE		
T-Bird Turbo Coupe GOL	1.50	4.00
MOTORCRAFT, Laser wheels		
T-Bird Turbo Coupe LG	1.50	4.00
TURBO COUPE		
T-Bird Turbo Coupe BR	1.50	4.00
TURBO COUPE		
T-Bird Turbo Coupe PI	1.50	4.00
TURBO COUPE		

T-Bird Turbo Coupe R	1.50	4.00
T-Bird Turbo Coupe GR	1.50	4.00
R int., CHR win., WC		
T-Bird Turbo Coupe GR	1.50	4.00
BLA int., CHR win., WC		
T-Bird Turbo Coupe BLU	1.50	4.00
PUR/PI stripes		
Cadillac Allante SIL	1.50	4.00
Cadillac Allante BLA	1.50	4.00
R/SIL stripes, Laser wheels		
Cadillac Allante PI	1.50	4.00
GR interior, CADILLAC tampos		
Cadillac Allante PI	1.50	4.00
WH interior, G/BLU accents		
Cadillac Allante GR	1.50	4.00
CHR windshield, WC		
Rolls Royce Silver Spirit R	1.50	4.00
Rolls Royce Silver Spirit T	2.00	5.00
Rolls Royce Silver Spirit GR/GOL	2.00	5.00
Ford Skip Truck Y	1.50	4.00
GR metal skip		
Ford Skip Truck BLU	2.00	5.00
R metal skip, Preschool series		
Ford Skip Truck Y	1.50	4.00
GR plastic skip		
Ford Skip Truck Y	1.50	4.00
R plastic skip		
Porsche 944 Racer R	1.50	4.00
944 turbo on sides		
Porsche 944 Racer BLA	1.50	4.00
944 Turbo on sides, CHR windows, World Class		
Porsche 944 Racer R	3.00	8.00
944 Turbo/CREDIT CHARGE tampos		
Porsche 944 Racer WH	6.00	15.00
DUCKHAMS tampos		
Porsche 944 Racer G	1.50	4.00
Williams Honda F1	1.50	4.00
WH/LB, GOODYEAR/SHELL		
Williams Honda F1	1.50	4.00
R, FIAT/27, metal base		
Williams Honda F1	2.50	6.00
R, FIAT/27, plastic base		
Williams Honda F1	1.50	4.00
R, SCOTCH, TARGET		
Williams Honda F1	1.50	4.00
Y, PENNZOIL/2		
Williams Honda F1	5.00	12.00
Y, PENNZOIL/4		
Williams Honda F1	1.50	4.00
dk. OR/WH, INDY/4		
Williams Honda F1	1.50	4.00
CHR, no markings		
Williams Honda F1	1.50	4.00
BLU, PANASONIC/7		
Williams Honda F1	1.50	4.00
WH/BLU, INDY/76		
Williams Honda F1	1.50	4.00
WH/BLA, HAVOLINE/Kmart/6		

'67 VOLKSWAGEN 1600

	LOOSE	IN PKG.
Williams Honda F1	1.50	4.00
OR/lt. PUR/WH, INDY		
Williams Honda F1	1.50	4.00
WH/PI, BLU spots, 7		

'67 VW CAMPER

1989 Matchbox

	LOOSE	IN PKG.
Modified Racer OR	1.50	4.00
CHR exhaust pipes		
Modified Racer OR	1.50	4.00
BLA exhaust pipes		
Modified Racer PUR	2.00	5.00
Action Pack, w/accessories		
Modified Racer WH	1.50	4.00
no markings, Graffic Traffic		
Modified Racer CHR	6.00	15.00
Modified Racer OR/R	1.50	4.00
Super Color Changers		
Modified Racer R	2.00	5.00
MIKE 15		
Modified Racer R, 36	2.00	5.00
Modified Racer R, 12/stripes	2.00	5.00
Modified Racer BLU, 12	2.00	5.00
Modified Racer Y	2.00	5.00
(Nutmeg Coll.), REGGIE 44/MAGNUM OILS		
Modified Racer WH	2.00	5.00
(Nutmeg Coll), U2 JAMIE		
Modified Racer WH	2.00	5.00
(Nutmeg Coll.), TONY 1/UNI. JOINT SALES		
Modified Racer WH/BLU	2.00	5.00
(Nutmeg Coll.), ADAP 15		
Modified Racer WH, 41	2.00	5.00
(Nutmeg Coll.)		
Modified Racer R	2.00	5.00
(Nutmeg Coll.), JERRY COOK		
Modified Racer WH	2.00	5.00
(Nutmeg Coll.) MAYNARD TROYER		
Modified Racer dk. BLU	2.00	5.00
(Nutmeg Coll.) RON BOUCHARD		
Modified Racer OR/Y	2.00	5.00
(Nutmeg Coll.), 4 BUGS		
Modified Racer R	2.00	5.00
(Nutmeg Coll.), JAMIE TOMAINO		
Modified Racer OR/Y	2.00	5.00
(Nutmeg Coll.) SATCH WIRLEY		
Modified Racer dk. BLU	2.00	5.00
(Nutmeg Coll.), DOUG HEVERON		
Modified Racer BLA	2.00	5.00
(Nutmeg Coll.), GEORGE KENT		
Modified Racer BLU	2.00	5.00
(Nutmeg Coll.), MIKE McLAUGHLIN		
Grand Prix Racer	1.50	4.00
Saab 9000	1.50	4.00
Ferrari F40 R	1.50	4.00
clear windows, BLA interior		
Ferrari F40 R	1.50	4.00
CHR windows, World Class		

Ferrari F40 CHR, cl.windows	4.00	10.00
Ferrari F40 R	1.50	4.00
CHR/BLA windows, Lightning series		
Ferrari F40 Y	1.50	4.00
BLU CHR/BLA win. Lightning series		
Ferrari F40 WH	1.50	4.00
BLU CHR/BLA windows, Lightning series		
Ferrari F40 BLA	1.50	4.00
BLA/CHR windows, Lightning series		
Ferrari F40 R	2.00	5.00
BLA windows, Triple Heat series		
Ferrari F40 Y	2.00	5.00
WH CHR windows, World Class		
Ferrari F40 R	1.50	4.00
BLA spots, Y windows		
Ferrari F40 PUR/PI	1.50	4.00
BMW 5-Series 535i GR	1.50	4.00
BMW 5-Series 535i WH	1.50	4.00
FINA 31/BMW TEAM		
Ford Utility Truck	1.50	4.00
Ford Bronco II WH	1.50	4.00
BRONCO/stripes		
Ford Bronco II WH	1.50	4.00
COAST GUARD BEACH PATROL		
Ford Bronco II BLU	1.50	4.00
WH splash, OR BRONCO 4x4		
Ford Bronco II BR	1.50	4.00
BRONCO/stripes		
Ford Bronco II OR	1.50	4.00
BRONCO/stripes		
Ford Bronco II Y	2.00	5.00
R flames/4X4		
Ford Bronco II R	2.00	5.00
Y tires, Preschool series		
Ford Bronco II WH	1.50	4.00
POLICE PD-22		
Ford Bronco II BLA	1.50	4.00
OR piranha design, interior		
Ford Bronco II SIL	1.50	4.00
OR piranha design, BLU interior		
Lincoln Town Car WH	1.50	4.00
Lincoln Town Car WH, plas.base	1.50	4.00
Lincoln Town Car BLA	1.50	4.00
CHR windows		
Lincoln Town Car SIL	1.50	4.00
PI/Y accents		
Lincoln Town Car Y	3.00	8.00
BLU wheels, Preschool series		
Dodge Dakota Pickup R	1.50	4.00
BLA/WH stripes		
Dodge Dakota Pickup R	1.50	4.00
DAKOTA ST, BLA/WH stripes		
Dodge Dakota Pickup R	1.50	4.00
DAKOTA ST, BLA/WH stripes		
Dodge Dakota Pickup G	1.50	4.00
MB CONSTRUCTION		
Dodge Dakota Pickup WH GT	2.00	5.00

	LOOSE	IN PKG.
Dodge Dakota Pickup BLU	1.50	4.00
DAKOTA ST/stripes		
Dodge Dakota Pickup OR	1.50	4.00
FIRE CHIEF I/INTERCOM CITY		
Faun Dump Truck	1.50	4.00
Oldsmobile Aerotech SIL	1.50	4.00
Oldsmobile Aerotech OR	1.50	4.00
Oldmobile Aerotech PUR/WH	1.50	4.00
TV News Truck BLU	1.50	4.00
GR roof, 75 NEWS/MBTV MOBILE ONE		
TV News Truck WH GT	2.50	6.00
TV News Truck WH	1.50	4.00
BLU roof, SKY SATELLITE TELEVISION"		
TV News Truck BLU/WH	1.50	4.00
GR roof, ROCK TV		
Volvo 480ES GR/G stripes	2.00	5.00
Volvo 480ES WH, Macau	2.00	5.00
Volvo 480ES WH, China	2.00	5.00
GMC Wrecker	1.50	4.00

1990 Matchbox

	LOOSE	IN PKG.
Corvette Grand Sport BLU	1.50	4.00
15 on doors		
Corvette Grand Sport BLU	1.50	4.00
CORVETTE on doors		
Corvette Grand Sport BLU	6.00	15.00
HEINZ 57		
Corvette Grand Sport BLU	1.50	4.00
2/doors, from 40th Ann.Corvette Coll.		
Corvette Grand Sport R	4.00	10.00
CHR windows, BLA base, World Class		
Corvette Grand Sport R	1.50	4.00
CHR win., CHR base, WC		
Corvette Grand Sport WH/BLU	2.50	6.00
9/R stripes, Goodyear tires		
Corvette Grand Sport WH	1.50	4.00
R accent stripe, CORVETTE		
Corvette Grand Sport OR	1.50	4.00
Corvette Grand Sport, WH	1.50	4.00
BLA widow tampo		
Corvette Grand Sport BLA	1.50	4.00
BLA widow tampo		
Mack CH600 WH, BLA/R stripes	1.50	4.00
Mercedes Benz 500SL Convertible, met. GR	1.50	4.00
Mercedes Benz 500SL Convertible, BLA	1.50	4.00
CHR windows, World Class		
Mercedes Benz 500SL Convertible, WH	1.50	4.00
GR accents		
Ford LTD Police	1.50	4.00
Dodge Dakota Pickup	1.50	4.00
Opel Vectra/Chevrolet Cavalier GS, met. R	1.50	4.00
Opel Vectra/Chevrolet Cavalier GS, G	3.00	8.00
Lincoln Town Car	1.50	4.00
Leyland Titan London Bus	1.50	4.00
Corvette Convertible	1.50	4.00

BMW 5-Series 535i	1.50	4.00
Modified Racer	1.50	4.00
Sprint Racer R ROLLIN THUNDER 2	2.00	5.00
Sprint Racer BLU ROLLIN THUNDER 2	2.00	5.00
Sprint Racer BLU LUCKY 7, Action Pack	2.00	5.00
Sprint Racer R, LUCKY 7	2.00	5.00
Sprint Racer R (Nutmeg Coll), WILLIAMS 5M BLU	2.00	5.00
Sprint Racer R (Nutmeg Coll.), WILLIAMS 5M WH	2.00	5.00
Sprint Racer BLA (Nutmeg Coll.), TMC 1	2.00	5.00
Sprint Racer WH (Nutmeg Coll.), MAXIM 11	2.00	5.00
Sprint Racer, WH (Nutmeg Coll.), SCHNEE 8D	2.00	5.00
Sprint Racer Y (Nutmeg Coll.), BEN COOK/SONS 33X	2.00	5.00
Sprint Racer BLU (Nutmeg Coll.), BEN ALLEN 1A	2.00	5.00
Sprint Racer, R (Nutmeg Coll.), JOE GAERTE 7	2.00	5.00
Sprint Racer R (Nutmeg Coll.), GAMBLER 4	2.00	5.00
Sprint Racer Y (Nutmeg Coll.), F&G CLASSICS EAST 17	2.00	5.00
Sprint Racer Y (Nutmeg Coll.), D.BLANEY/VIVARIN 7C	2.00	5.00
Sprint Racer LB (Nutmeg Coll.), SCHNEE-D. KRIETZ 69	2.00	5.00
Sprint Racer BLA (Nutmeg Coll.), DOUG WOLFGANG 49	2.00	5.00
Land Rover Ninety BLU WH roof, Y/OR stripes	1.50	4.00
Land Rover Ninety Y WH roof, PARK RANGER	1.50	4.00
Land Rover Ninety G WH roof, Y/OR stripes	1.50	4.00
Land Rover Ninety R WH roof, BLU/GR stripes, COUNTRY	1.50	4.00
Land Rover Ninety WH WH roof, BLA/R stripes, COUNTRY	1.50	4.00
Land Rover Ninety WH WH roof, no mark., GRAFFIC TRAFFIC	1.50	4.00
Land Rover Ninety BLU WH roof, ROYAL NAVY	2.00	5.00
Land Rover Ninety BLA GR roof, GR/Y camo., Commando ser.	1.50	4.00
Land Rover Ninety GR/BLU GR roof, R stripes	1.50	4.00

'67 HAY TRAILER

Land Rover Ninety WH	1.50	4.00
BLU roof, KLM		
Land Rover Ninety WH	1.50	4.00
BLU roof, SAS		
Land Rover Ninety WH	1.50	4.00
BLU roof, ALITALIA		
Land Rover Ninety WH	4.00	10.00
WH roof, BACARDI RUM		
Land Rover Ninety R	1.50	4.00
WH roof, RED ARROWS/RAF		
Land Rover Ninety WH	1.50	4.00
WH roof, RESCUE POLICE		
Land Rover Ninety WH	1.50	4.00
WH roof, CIRCUS CIRCUS		
Land Rover Ninety WH	3.00	8.00
GR roof, GARDEN FESTIVAL WALES		
Ford Bronco II 4x4	1.50	4.00
1921 Ford Model T Van Y	2.00	5.00
R roof, BLU base, BIRD'S CUSTARD POWDER		
1921 Ford Model T Van LB	2.00	5.00
BLA roof, BLU base, GOODYEAR		
1921 Ford Model T Van R	3.00	8.00
BLA hood/roof, ROYAL MAIL GR		
1921 Ford Model T Van CRE	6.00	15.00
BLU roof/base, 3RD MICA..		
1921 Ford Model T Van CRE	6.00	15.00
BLU roof/base, 5TH MICA CONVENTION 1990		
1921 Ford Model T Van BLA	6.00	15.00
MICA NA CON..		
1921 Ford Model T Van WH	6.00	15.00
LB roof/base, MICA 7..		
1921 Ford Model T Van CRE	6.00	15.00
BLU roof, GREETINGS..		
1921 Ford Model T Van WH	3.00	8.00
LB roof/base, PARA 90		
1921 Ford Model T Van WH	3.00	8.00
LB roof, CHESTER DOLL		
1921 Ford Model T Van G	8.00	20.00
BLA roof, GR base, SWARFEGA		
Ford Model T Van BLA, MARS	3.00	8.00
1921 Ford Model T Van R	3.00	8.00
R roof, BLA base, MARS		
1921 Ford Model T Van CRE	3.00	8.00
R roof, G base, PG TIPS		
1921 Ford Model T Van WH	3.00	8.00
R roof, BLU base, LLOYDS		
1921 Ford Model T Van BLA	3.00	8.00
WILLIAMS LUSTY		
Chevrolet Highway Maint. Truck Y	1.50	4.00
Y dumper/plow, INT. AIRPORT AUTHORITY 45		
Chevrolet Highway Maint. Truck Y	1.50	4.00
R dumper/plow, INT. AIRPORT AUTHORITY 45		
Chevrolet Highway Maint. Truck R	1.50	4.00
GR dumper/plow, ASPEN SNOW REMOVAL		

'68 ISO GRIFO

	LOOSE	IN PKG.
Chevrolet Highway Maint. Truck OR R dump/plow, INT. AIRPORT AUTHORITY 45	1.50	4.00
Chevrolet Highway Maint. Truck WH BLU dumper/plow, R HIGHWAY DEPT tampos(1995)	1.50	4.00
Rolls Royce Silver Spirit	1.50	4.00
New Ford Transit Van	1.50	4.00
NASA Rocket Transporter	1.50	4.00
Nissan 300ZX Y, no open parts 300ZX on doors	1.50	4.00
Nissan 300ZX Y, no open parts NADTCA 1ST ANN., NOVEMBER 1994	1.50	4.00
Nissan 300ZX BLU no open parts, Y acc., HP interior	1.50	4.00
Nissan 300ZX BLU no open parts, SIL/BLA design/hood, PI interior	1.50	4.00
Nissan 300ZX BLA, no open parts OR/R/WH graffiti, OR/R interior	1.50	4.00
Oldsmobile Aerotech	1.50	4.00
Mercedes Benz Farm Tractor LG, no markings, G interior	1.50	4.00
Mercedes Benz Farm Tractor LG, no markings, Y interior	1.50	4.00
Mercedes Benz Farm Tractor LG, MB Trac tampos	1.50	4.00
TV News Truck	2.00	5.00

1991 Matchbox

	LOOSE	IN PKG.
Jaguar XJ6 Police WH POLICE tampos, BLU/Y stripes	1.50	4.00
Jaguar XJ6 Police WH POLICE tampos, checkerboard pattern/stripes	1.50	4.00
Alfa Romeo R, BLA roof no markings, China cast	1.50	4.00
Alfa Romeo R, R roof no markings, China cast	3.00	8.00
Alfa Romeo R, BLA roof ALFA ROMEO, China cast	1.50	4.00
Alfa Romeo R, R roof ALFA ROMEO, China cast	1.50	4.00
Alfa Romeo LI, LI roof ALFA ROMEO, China cast	1.50	4.00
Mercedes Benz Farm Tractor	1.50	4.00
Fork Lift Truck	3.00	8.00
Nissan Prairie BLU SIL tampos	1.50	4.00
Nissan Prairie SIL NISSAN tampos	1.50	4.00
Nissan Prairie WH no markings, Graffic Traffic	2.00	5.00
Nissan Prairie R, NISSAN tampos	1.50	4.00
Nissan 300ZX	1.50	4.00
Mercedes Benz 600SEL SIL	1.50	4.00

	LOOSE	IN PKG.
Road Roller	1.50	4.00
Opel Vectra/Chevrolet Cavalier	1.50	4.00
Isuzu Amigo BLU	1.50	4.00
ISUZU AMIGO tampos		
Isuzu Amigo Y/PI stripes	1.50	4.00
Isuzu Amigo R AMIGO SIL/OR	1.50	4.00
Mack Floodlight Heavy Rescue	1.50	4.00
Auxiliary Power Truck Y		
Mack Floodlight Heavy Rescue	1.50	4.00
Auxiliary Power Truck, OR FIRE RES		
Mack Floodlight Heavy Rescue	2.00	5.00
Auxiliary Power Truck, WH		
Mack Floodlight Heavy Rescue	1.50	4.00
Auxiliary Power Truck R, FIRE RES		
Mack Floodlight Heavy Rescue	1.50	4.00
Auxiliary Power Truck R, WH/GOL acc.		
Porsche 944	2.00	5.00

1992 Matchbox

	LOOSE	IN PKG.
Atlas Excavator	1.50	4.00
Airport Fire Tender OR/R	1.50	4.00
BLU/WH pattern		
Dodge Cattle Truck G	2.00	5.00
Y stake, 2 BLA steers		
Sunburner Y, sun/fla. Tampo	1.50	4.00
Sunburner WH, sun/fla. Tampo	1.50	4.00
Sunburner BLU, WH stripes	1.50	4.00
Sunburner Y	1.50	4.00
Lamborghini Diablo Y	1.50	4.00
Lamborghini Diablo R	1.50	4.00
CHR windows, rubber tires, WC		
Lamborghini Diablo BLU	1.50	4.00
PI/WH accents		
Lamborghini Diablo Y	1.50	4.00
BLA spots, PI int.		
Lamborghini Diablo R	1.50	4.00
BLA spots, Y interior		
Ford Courier Delivery Van PUR	3.00	8.00
MILKA tampos		
Ford Courier Delivery Van WH	6.00	15.00
COURIER tampos		
Ford Courier Delivery Van BLU	4.00	10.00
MATCHBOX-THE IDEAL PREMIUM		
Ford Courier Delivery Van R	1.50	4.00
Mercedes Benz 600SL SIL	1.50	4.00
Ford LTD Taxi Y	1.50	4.00
RADIO XYZ CAB		
Fork Lift Truck	1.50	4.00
Road Roller	1.50	4.00

1993 Matchbox

	LOOSE	IN PKG.
Quarry Truck	1.50	4.00
T-Bird Stock Car WH, MAUI 17	1.50	4.00
T-Bird Stock Ca BLU, RACE..	1.50	4.00
T-Bird Stock Car PI	1.50	4.00
10/checkered flag		

	LOOSE	IN PKG.
T-Bird Stock Car	1.50	4.00
Kyle Wieder 11		
Bedford Wreck Truck	1.50	4.00
MG Midget Sports Car	1.50	4.00
READY MIX Concrete Truck	1.50	4.00
Chevy Van	1.50	4.00
Jaguar XJ220 SIL	1.50	4.00
Jaguar XJ220 BLU	1.50	4.00
Jaguar XJ220 Y/OR	1.50	4.00
BLU accents		
Jaguar XJ220 PUR	1.50	4.00
CHR win., Goodyear tires, WC		
Jaguar XJ220 OR, BLA acc.	1.50	4.00
Jaguar XK140 Coupe	1.50	4.00
Pontiac Stock Car Y, SEA..	1.50	4.00
Pontiac Stock Car Y, PRO..	1.50	4.00
Pontiac Stock Car BLA/BLU	1.50	4.00
LB int., 7 OUTLAW		
Cosmic Blues	1.50	4.00
Pontiac Firebird S/E BLA	1.50	4.00
HP/BLU accents		
Pontiac Firebird S/E, HP	1.50	4.00
Y sides/hood		
Pontiac Firebird S/E, HP	1.50	4.00
Y accents on sides, not hood		
BMW 850i SIL	1.50	4.00
BMW 850i WH	1.50	4.00
BMW 850i MAR, PI/Y tampos	1.50	4.00
BMW 850i SIL, CHR win.	1.50	4.00
BMW 850i R, RIPPER	1.50	4.00
skull/crossbones on hood		
BMW 850i R, RIPPER sides	1.50	4.00
Ford Model A Hot Rod	1.50	4.00
Military Tank T	1.50	4.00
Military Tank OL	1.50	4.00

1994 Matchbox

	LOOSE	IN PKG.
Hummer T, OR cross	1.50	4.00
Hummer T, OR bar	1.00	3.00
Hummer OL, WH star	1.00	3.00
Hummer OL, BR/BLA camo	1.50	4.00
Mazda RX-7 Y, BLA/R acc.	1.00	3.00
Mazda RX-7 R, Y acc.	1.00	3.00
Mazda RX-7 GOL/R	1.00	3.00
Dodge Viper R, GOL wh.	1.50	4.00
Dodge Viper R, SIL wh.	1.50	4.00
Mustang Convertible R	1.50	4.00
Mustang Convertible BLA	1.50	4.00
Ferrari 456 GT BLU	1.00	3.00
456 GT in Y on sides		
Ferrari 456 GT PUR, WH tam.	1.00	3.00
Ferrari 456 GT PUR	1.00	3.00
WH tampo on sides only		
Ferrari 456 GT R	1.00	3.00
Tailgator G	1.00	3.00
Tailgator dk. G	1.00	3.00
'62 Corvette BLU	1.50	4.00
WH/MAG accents on sides/hood		

'69 ISO GRIFO

'62 Corvette BLU	1.50	4.00
WH/MAG accents on sides only		
Corvette Stingray PUR	1.00	3.00
WH/MAG accents		
Corvette Stingray WH	1.00	3.00
R/Y accents(1996)		
Camaro Z-28 BLA	1.00	3.00
WH/MAG/G-BLU side/hood stripes		
Camaro Z-28 BLA	1.00	3.00
WH/MAG/G-BLU side stripes only		
Camaro Z-28 GR	1.00	3.00
WH/MAG/G-BLU side stripes, not on		
hood(1996)		
Ford Probe GT R, OR/Y acc.	1.00	3.00
Ford Probe GT BLA, BLU/PI acc.	1.00	3.00
Ford Probe PUR, G/WH acc.	1.00	3.00
Porsche 959 HP	1.00	3.00
RAGE on doors		
Escort Cosworth WH	1.00	3.00
rally acc., MOBIL 1		
Rhino Rod GR	1.00	3.00
Flareside Pickup R	1.00	3.00
Y/OR flames on hood		
Flareside Pickup OR	1.00	3.00
Aston Martin G, DB-7	1.00	3.00
Aston Martin G	1.00	3.00
Jeep Cherokee	1.50	4.00

'70 FORD GT

1995 Matchbox

	LOOSE	IN PKG.
Audi Avus, CHR	1.00	3.00
Mitsubishi Spyder BLU	1.00	3.00
LG interior, accents		
Mitsubishi Spyder BLU, LG int	1.00	3.00
Mitsubishi Spyder BLU, WH int.	1.00	3.00
Toyota Supra WH	1.00	3.00
R/Y flames on sides/hood		
Toyota Supra WH	1.00	3.00
R/Y flames on sides		
Toyota Supra R	1.00	3.00
WH/OR flames on sides		
Plymouth Prowler PUR, GR int.	1.50	4.00
Ford Mondeo BLU	1.00	3.00
WH accents, MONDEO		
Abrams M1 Tank T	1.00	3.00
Abrams M1 Tank OL	1.00	3.00
Abrams M1 Tank OL	1.50	4.00
BR/BLA camo		
Isuzu Rodeo BLA, PI mud	1.00	3.00
Isuzu Rodeo WH, PI mud	1.00	3.00
Camaro Police Pursuit BLA	1.50	4.00
Ford F-150 4x4 R	1.50	4.00
Ford F-150 4x4 BLU	1.00	3.00
Stinger Y/BLA	1.00	3.00
Mustang Cobra R	1.00	3.00
Mustang Cobra BLA	1.00	3.00
Rotwheeler BR	1.50	4.00

1996 Matchbox

	LOOSE	IN PKG.
The Buster BLU/Y/HP	1.00	3.00
Mercedes GTC BLU	1.00	3.00
VW Concept Car R/BLA	5.00	10.00
Street Streak PUR/WH	1.00	3.00
Street Streak OR/BLA	1.00	3.00
Ponitac GTO OR	1.00	3.00
Chevrolet K-1500 BLA	1.00	3.00
Formula Racer WH	1.00	3.00
R spoiler, MB RACING 1		
Ferrari F50 R	1.00	3.00
Dunes Racer	1.00	3.00
Weasel Tank	1.00	3.00
Ferrari Testarossa	1.00	3.00

1997 Matchbox

	LOOSE	IN PKG.
Dodge Viper GTS Coupe	1.50	4.00
Alfa Romeo 155	.75	2.00
'97 Corvette	1.50	4.00
Chrysler Atlantic	.75	2.00
'97 Firebird Formula	.75	2.00
BMW Z-3	.75	2.00
'69 Camaro SS 396	1.00	3.00
'56 Ford Pickup	.75	2.00
Ford Ambulance	.75	2.00
Crown Victoria Police Car	.75	2.00
Opel Calibra DTM	.75	2.00
'68 Mustang Cobra Jet	1.00	3.00
Ferrari F50 Coupe	.75	2.00
Corvette Grand Sport	1.00	3.00
Jeep Wrangler	.75	2.00
Escavator	.75	2.00
T-Bird Stock Car	1.00	3.00
Mazda RX-7	.75	2.00
Earth Mover	.75	2.00
Dodge Viper RT/10	1.00	3.00
Audi Avus	.75	2.00
The Buster	.75	2.00
'87 Corvette	.75	2.00
Mustang Mach III	.75	2.00
Ford LTD Police	.75	2.00
Ferrari 456 GT	.75	2.00
Extending Ladder Truck	.75	2.00
Cement Truck	.75	2.00
GMC Wrecker	.75	2.00
Lamborghini Diablo	.75	2.00
Volvo Container Truck	.75	2.00
Ferrari F-40	.75	2.00
Chevy Van	.75	2.00
Tailgator	.75	2.00
Mitsubishi Spyder	.75	2.00
Shovel Nose Tractor	.75	2.00
Toyota Supra	.75	2.00
Jaguar XJ-220	.75	2.00
'62 Corvette	1.00	3.00

	LOOSE	IN PKG.
Utility Truck	.75	2.00
Plymouth Prowler	1.00	3.00
Mercedes GTC	.75	2.00
Garbage Truck	.75	2.00
Jeep 4x4	.75	2.00
Corvette Stingray III	1.00	3.00
Ford Bronco II	.75	2.00
Cosmic Blues	.75	2.00
Mobile Crane	.75	2.00
Camaro Z-28	.75	2.00
Probe GT	.75	2.00
Maintenance Truck	.75	2.00
Military Chopper	.75	2.00
School Bus	.75	2.00
VW Concept Car	2.00	5.00
Chevy Blazer	.75	2.00
Escort Cosworth	.75	2.00
Rhino Rod	.75	2.00
Ford Flareside	.75	2.00
Isuzu Rodeo	.75	2.00
Auxiliary Power Truck	.75	2.00
Corvette T-Top	1.00	3.00
Camaro Z28 Police	.75	2.00
Helicopter	.75	2.00
Nissan 300-ZX	.75	2.00
Street Streak	.75	2.00
Snorkel Fire Truck	.75	2.00
Bulldozer	.75	2.00
Ford F-150 Pickup	.75	2.00
Lamborghini Countach	.75	2.00
Stinger	.75	2.00
Pontiac GTO Judge	.75	2.00
Mustang Cobra	.75	2.00
Chevy 1500 Pickup	.75	2.00
Rotwheeler	.75	2.00
Formula Racer	.75	2.00

1998 Matchbox

	LOOSE	IN PKG.
Dodge Viper GTS Coupe	1.00	3.00
Corvette Stingray III	.75	2.00
Corvette Grand Sport	1.00	3.00
Mustang Mach III	.75	2.00
BMW Z3	.75	2.00
Excavator	.50	1.50
Refuse Truck	.50	1.50
Cement Truck	.50	1.50
Utility Truck	.50	1.50
Quarry Truck	.50	1.50
Maintenance Truck	.50	1.50
School Bus	.50	1.50
Shovel Nose Tractor	.50	1.50
Bulldozer	.50	1.50
Mobile Crane	.50	1.50
Street Streak	.75	2.00
VW Concept 1	1.50	4.00
Plymouth Prowler	1.00	3.00
Chrysler Atlantic	.50	1.50

The Buster	.50	1.50
Auxiliary Power Truck	.50	1.50
4X4 Chevy Blazer	.75	2.00
Ladder Fire Truck	.75	1.50
LTD Police Car	.75	2.00
Ford Ambulance	.75	2.00
Snorkel Fire Engine	.75	2.00
Camaro Police	.75	2.00
Crown Victoria Police	.75	2.00
Helicopter	.50	1.50
Chevy Tahoe Police	.75	2.00
'57 Chevy Bel-Air	.75	2.00
'70 El Camino	.50	1.50
'69 Camaro SS 396	.75	2.00
'33 Ford Street Rod	.50	1.50
'56 Ford Pick-Up	.50	1.50
'57 Chevy Convertible	.75	2.00
'70 Boss Mustang	.75	2.00
Pontiac GTO	.75	2.00
'71 Camaro	.75	2.00
'68 Mustang Cobra Jet	.75	2.00
Stinger	.75	2.00
Rotwheeler	.50	1.50
Rhino Rod	.50	1.50
Volvo Container	.50	1.50
Alligator	.50	1.50
'97 Chevy Tahoe	.50	1.50
M2 Bradley Tank	.50	1.50
Hummer	.75	2.00
Mission Chopper	.50	1.50
'97 Ford F-150	.50	1.50
Ford Bronco II	.50	1.50
Jeep 4X4	.75	2.00
Ford F-150 4X4	.50	1.50
Chevy K-1500 4X4	.50	1.50
Flareside Pick-Up	.50	1.50
Dodge Viper	.75	2.00
Ferrari F40	.50	1.50
'97 Corvette	.75	2.00
Ferrari F-50	.50	1.50
Lamborghini Countach	.50	1.50
Formula Racer	.50	1.50
Alfa Romeo 155	.50	1.50
GMC Wrecker	.50	1.50
T-Bird Stock Car	.75	2.00
Opel Calibra DTM	.50	1.50
'97 MGF	.50	1.50
Mazda RX-7	.50	1.50
Porsche GT-1	.50	1.50
Mitsubishi Spyder	.50	1.50
'97 Mercedes E Class	.50	1.50
'97 Jaguar XK-8	.50	1.50
'97 Firebird Ram Air	.50	1.50
Mustang Cobra	.50	1.50
Corvette T-Top	.50	1.50
'94 Camaro Z-28	.50	1.50

'70 FORD GT

Johnny Lightning

'69 Mako Shark

Despite producing some nice cars, Johnny Lightning stopped production in 1971 and is just now making a comeback

When it comes to die-cast cars, imitation is the sincerest form of flattery.

Just as Hot Wheels was introduced as a way to grab a portion of a dominant market share from Matchbox, other brands such as Aurora soon sprung up to ride the wake of Mattel's almost instant success. Perhaps the best known brand among these imitators was Johnny Lightning.

Johnny Lightning cars were made by Topper, a company that was owned by Henry Orenstein. He made no secret of the fact that he was imitating Hot Wheels, and boasted that his company could build a better car. Orenstein had Topper engineers create cars with opening hoods and doors, plus low-friction wheels mounted on plastic bushings that were lubricated with whale oil.

The engineers prepared castings for 15 cars to be released, but just 11 made it to production in 1969. Prototypes of the other four are known to exist. Topper didn't last long, but the company made a practice of planning for models that ultimately weren't produced. Topper published three annual catalogs for toy buyers, but of the 81 models promised less than 50 made it to production.

Topper only produced Johnny Lightnings from 1969 to 1971, and the company was never on solid financial ground. The company was always making money-saving changes, so many car variations were never produced. Paint jobs, a switch to blackwall tires, doors and hoods that no longer opened — all fell victim to cost-cutting measures.

The company did produce several sets and accessories each year. In 1970, some of the cars were "Jet Powered." These cars could be filled with compressed air, which would send the cars flying upon release.

With or without the jet boost, Topper cars were generally considered to be much faster than Hot Wheels. Unfortunately for Orenstein, sales weren't any where close to Mattel's. Orenstein, knowing that he needed to boost the popularity of Johnny Lightning, had the brand sponsor cars that raced in the Indianapolis 500 race, striking deals with legends such as A.J. Foyt and Parnelli Jones. The gamble paid off when Al Unser Sr. carried the Johnny Lightning brand to the winner's circle at the 1970 Indy 500. Sales increased 10-fold by the end of the year.

1999 Johnny Lightning

1999 Johnny Lightning

The success, however, was short lived. Orenstein tried to take the company public to raise money, but couldn't save it. The company closed its doors for good in December of 1971.

Thomas E. Lowe was one of those young boys who played with the Topper-released Johnny Lightnings. Lowe grew up to be a successful entrepreneur, inventing Kitty Litter and Tidy Cat brand cat litter and building a successful company in Safe Care Products.

Lowe, believing that sales of nostalgia-related products were booming, discovered that the trademark for his favorite die-cast cars, Johnny Lightning, had been abandoned in the early 1970s. He applied for and was granted the Johnny Lightning trademark in 1993.

Lowe has since brought the brand back to life as part of his Playing Mantis toy company. The first production of these later-day Johnny Lightnings hit the shelves in 1994. The line has been expanded each year, and now includes a wide variety of releases ranging from die-cast replicas from your favorite movie or television series to show cars, hot rods and race cars of the past.

1969–71 Topper Johnny Lightning

	LOOSE	IN PKG.
A.J. Foyt Indy Car	35.00	60.00
Al Unser Indy Racer	35.00	60.00
Baja	35.00	60.00
Big Rig	70.00	125.00
Bubble	35.00	60.00
Bug Bomb	60.00	110.00
Condor	60.00	110.00
Custom '32 Ford Hot Rod	40.00	80.00
Custom Dragster	30.00	50.00
Custom El Camino	100.00	200.00
Custom Ferrari	30.00	50.00
Custom GTO	150.00	250.00
Custom Mako Shark 'Vette	50.00	100.00
Custom Spoiler	25.00	45.00
Custom T-Bird	100.00	200.00
Custom Turbine	25.00	45.00
Custom XKE	30.00	50.00
Double Trouble	35.00	60.00
Eldorado	125.00	225.00
Flameout	50.00	90.00
Flying Needle	30.00	50.00
Frantic Ferrari	40.00	75.00
Glasser	35.00	60.00

CUSTOM DRAGSTER

CUSTOM EL CAMINO

ELDORADO

CUSTOM GTO

MAKO SHARK

MAD MAVERICK

TNT

CUSTOM TURBINE

	LOOSE	IN PKG.
Hairy Hauler	50.00	90.00
Jumpin Jag	25.00	40.00
Leapin Limo	40.00	75.00
Mad Maverick	40.00	75.00
Monster	35.00	70.00
Movin Van	35.00	60.00
Nucleon	45.00	80.00
Parnelli Jones Indy Car	35.00	70.00
Pipe Dream	50.00	100.00
Sand Stormer	30.00	50.00
Slingshot	30.00	50.00
Screamer	30.00	50.00
Smuggler	35.00	60.00
Stilletto	25.00	45.00
TNT	35.00	60.00
Toronado	125.00	225.00
Triple Threat	35.00	60.00
Twin Blaster	60.00	110.00
Vicious 'Vette	30.00	50.00
Vulture	75.00	125.00
Wasp	30.00	50.00
Wedge	25.00	40.00
Whistler	75.00	150.00
Wild Winner	35.00	60.00

WHISTLER

1968 Aurora

	LOOSE	IN PKG.
Corvette Stingray	30.00	60.00
Ferrari Berlinetta	20.00	35.00
Mako Shark	25.00	40.00
Ford J-Car	15.00	30.00
Ford GT	25.00	40.00
Lola GT	15.00	30.00
Ford XL-500	20.00	35.00
Buick Riviera	20.00	35.00
Thunderbird	30.00	50.00
Dino Ferrari	20.00	35.00
Porsche 904	15.00	30.00
Cobra GT	20.00	35.00
Camaro	40.00	75.00
Cougar	30.00	50.00
Mustang Convertible	35.00	60.00
Magusta	25.00	40.00
XKE Jaguar	20.00	35.00
Mustang Hardtop	40.00	75.00
AC Cobra	40.00	70.00
Firebird	30.00	50.00
Willy's Gasser	40.00	70.00
Cheetah	30.00	50.00
Volkswagen	40.00	70.00

CHEETAH

AC COBRA

MUSTANG CONVERTIBLE

TORINO

WILLY'S GASSER

CONTRIBUTORS

Mark Winkelman, whose collection is featured in the photographs of this book, is one of the world's most renowned collectors of toy cars. He helped Mattel put together its Toy Fair and Hot Wheels Convention displays for the company's 30th anniversary celebration, and in his spare time he works for Ford Motor Co. A collector of toy cars since the mid-1960s, Winkelman still has in his possession many of the cars he purchased as a child. He also has a collection of real Cobra cars.

Photos from the Richardson, Texas, toy cars convention by Doug Hopfer.

Book design: David Timmons Graphic Design